Chieftain

CHIEFTAIN

Rob Griffin

The Crowood Press

First published in 2001 by
The Crowood Press Ltd
Ramsbury, Marlborough
Wiltshire SN8 2HR

© Rob Griffin 2001

All rights reserved. No part of this publication may be reproduced or
transmitted in any form or by any means, electronic or mechanical, including
photocopy, recording, or any information storage and retrieval system,
without permission in writing from the publishers.

British Library Cataloguing-in-Publication Data
A catalogue record for this book is available from the British Library.

ISBN 1 86126 438 0

Designed and typeset by Focus Publishing, The Courtyard, 26 London Road,
Sevenoaks, Kent TN13 1AP

Printed and bound in Great Britain by Antony Rowe, Chippenham

Contents

Acknowledgements

I could not have put this book together without the help of many individuals and organizations, so I would like to say thank you to you all. I would also like to thank all the private owners who helped me but wish to remain private. And finally, if I have missed you out, I am sorry.

Bob Fleming, Bob Grundy, Dennis Lunn, BUDGE, Capt (retd) Dave Clegg MBE RE, Capt Andy Vick QRH, Capt Kevin Griffin QRL, Charles Lemons, Charles Perkins, Chris Trigg, Clement Laforce, Colin Brown, Dave Powell, David Fletcher, Derek Hanson, DERA, Equipment Support (Land) Census Team, Geoff Stobbart, Ian Young RDG, Jackson's, Lt Col Everard OBE QRL, Jean Santry DEREA, Lawson Kent, Len Wallis, Maj Geoff Orcheston-Finlay RTR, Mark Hazzard, Mark Wagstaff, Maj Graham Thomas RE, Maj Mick Burgess Gunnery School, Merlin Robinson, Michael Duplessis, MoD, Neil Hamilton, Nigel Montgomery, Ossie Orsgood, Paul Briggs, Paul Sykes, Peter Kirkbride, Public Record Office, Ralph Bagnall-Wilde, RCMS Shrivenham, Robert Rector, Stan Serr (Five Star), Steve Olsfield, Tim Royall and Witham Vehicle Specialists.

Rob Griffin, Quedgeley, Glos

1 Prototypes and Trials

It is usual procedure in the development of armoured fighting vehicles (AFVs) that when a vehicle is introduced into service, its replacement is already being planned. For instance, at the time of writing we have seen much on the media heralding the new Challenger 2 and its deployment into Kosovo – but already plans are under consideration for its replacement in around twenty to twenty-five years. Another example is the series of Clansman radios fitted to the current fleet of British military vehicles: these were introduced in the early seventies, but at the same time plans for the next model were already being drawn up – although for various reasons the new radios will not be seen in service for at least another year or two.

This gives an idea of how long it takes for a new piece of military equipment to see the light of service: it encounters all sorts of problems, from the Treasury (usually itself the biggest problem), from new technology, and because of design requirements stipulated by the user which are difficult to meet. Compare this to the car industry, where it is more usual for the designers to tell us, the user, what we need.

A TANK FOR THE POST-WAR YEARS

In 1953 Britain was at last emerging from the austere years of World War II, and in the Centurion had finally produced a world-beating tank design. It had been developed to meet criteria first mooted by Field Marshal Montgomery, amongst others, who had been appalled at the sacrifices made by British tank crews. These crews had been obliged to fight better armed and armoured German tanks in vehicles that were obsolescent before they even reached France. This was the unfortunate and costly legacy of Treasury interference in funding, and a blinkered view of the type of vehicle that was required, to the extent of dallying with two-man tankettes because they were cheaper and easier to produce.

In 1953 the Fighting Vehicles Research and Development Establishment (FVRDE) prepared a report for the Ministry of Supply. In its foreword it stated that for some time now it was the considered opinion of tank designers in the UK and in other countries that the tank in its traditional form – of a tracked vehicle mounting a turret – had now reached a limiting stage. New avenues should therefore be explored.

This desire for a new initiative was partly due to the introduction of the FV 214 Conqueror to support Centurion against primarily the Soviet JS3. Conqueror was a large, heavy vehicle and quite full of new ideas that did not always work, such as an automatic ejector for the spent brass cases ejected from the gun. It was also prone to breakdowns. Nevertheless it was still liked by most of the people who served on it, not the least because it gave them a certain sense of elitism, since there were on average only nine Conquerors issued to any one regiment. Conqueror's most significant advantage perhaps lay in the fact that it was issued with a 120mm gun: this enabled the Royal Armoured Corps to dominate the battlefield, since it well outranged the twenty-pounder (9kg) that Centurion currently carried, and meant that Conqueror certainly outgunned and outranged its opponents.

Problems Encountered

On the down side, the FVRDE report stated that any further increase in the length of gun fitted would in all probability hamper vehicle mobility, and would also place undue strain on the suspension, and in particular the front assemblies. Larger guns would mean larger turrets, and this would push weight levels up to over 70 tons; and clearly, fielding vehicles of this weight would also upset traditional ideas of mobility. Furthermore, the loading of ammunition for a larger gun would cease to be a feasible task for one man: the whole operation would have to become mechanical, and this would inevitably lead to more complications and cost. It also might mean having to introduce further crew members (the Americans found this out when they introduced the M103: it required two loaders to serve the same gun as Conqueror's, that was served by just one loader, and was also a lot faster).

Nor was it a sound idea to have two front-line vehicles with no common parts, as this created a strain on the supply of replacements: far better to have one standard vehicle, thus cutting the problems in half at one go. It was considered that at some stage a way would have to be found to merge the Conqueror and the Centurion into a single new vehicle – but this concept in itself almost acted as a sheet-anchor against forward thinking and design.

Ideas and Suggestions

Many ideas were suggested for a replacement vehicle; these included some form of turretless vehicle, such as was eventually produced by Sweden, in the S tank. This concept had been around for a long time, but had never found support with British designers. Nevertheless, it was one of those ideas that would not go away, and even in the mid-seventies the author's Regiment A Squadron of the 4th/7th Royal Dragoon Guards – whilst stationed in Tidworth, had their Chieftain modified so that they had only limited traverse.

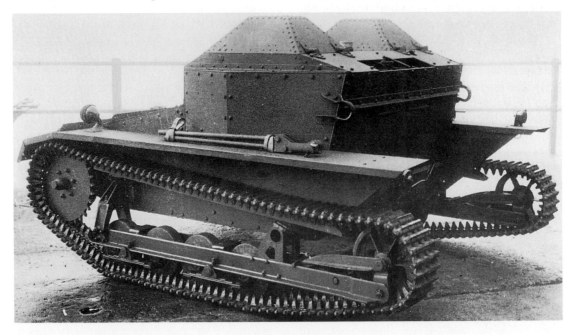

Carden-Lloyd tankette from the between-the-wars period. This was the type of vehicle that was to be the inspiration for Project Prodigal. (Tank Museum)

Contentious, this has the characteristic to be part of the Project Prodigal scheme, as it is built from Comet/Cromwell parts and was laid by hydraulic power. (Tank Museum)

This was one of the concepts being investigated in the plan for Chieftain replacement: it meant that the vehicle height could be significantly reduced by having the top of the limited traverse turret at the same height as the engine. However, when the squadron was tasked to fight the remainder of the regiment using normal tactics, the limited traverse turret proved a major obstacle in fighting the vehicle, and many times left it defenceless.

Other suggestions included an armoured version something like the Swedish Sno-Cat, or trailers towed into battle and armed with Malkara guided missiles. On the face of it, all these ideas had their good points, but most were impractical; however, one that surfaced like a blast from the 1920s was the one-man tank – although the revamped model was rather more aggressive in nature than the little Carden-Lloyd vehicles of thirty years previously. This concept was particularly popular with some, since logistically, if a normal tank regiment were converted to a regiment of one-man tanks, obviously far more tanks could be fielded than when using the conventional type. (The fact that the Russians – as our potential enemy at the time – would still be able to field more conventional tanks anyway was overlooked, or at worst discounted.)

PROJECT PRODIGAL: THE FV4401

The report also proposed that using a one-man tank destroyer in conjunction with the main armour had the advantage of not giving any one method the monopoly. On the down side, whatever the merits of the one-man tank, to have it operating in conjunction with the main armour still meant there would be two types of vehicle on the battlefield to supply. But the project did gain ground, and development under the auspices of Project Prodigal took place: the vehicle became known as FV4401.

It is still not clear today whether those in power planned to use this vehicle as a direct replacement for Centurion and Conqueror. The vehicle as described was built in at least one version other than a wooden mock-up: we know this because there is considerable correspondence about it, also test reports relating to the vehicle, and information passed on to our allies. One such War Office (WO) letter states that 'we must be very circumspect in any account of Prodigal that is sent out of the country. We do not want to attract visitors to Chobham who will inevitably ask to see what we are doing.'

Other memos describe showing the vehicle on open days, and the debate as to how close visitors would be allowed. Yet others describe the vehicle in very broad terms, and it will be seen from this how the design changed over the years. The concept of Prodigal 3, as it was then known, was that of a small, air-portable, heavily armoured vehicle with good cross-country performance and a given range of 500 miles (800km), with a crew of one or two, the weapons being loaded by auto-loader. The armament was to be a 160mm low-pressure gun firing a high explosive squash head (HESH)-type projectile weighing 60lb (27kg), at a muzzle velocity of 1,900ft (600m) per second. Liquid propellant might be used, as the propelling charge and the mounting would be recoil-less. A great deal still remained to be achieved, however, as it was then stated that elevation would be by a 'hitherto untried system'.

Research Vehicle

As the memos continued to flow, it became apparent that a number of vehicles were built, although what they looked like is not clear: an authority to build a research vehicle at FVRDE states that they had to be built using only existing components from other vehicles. The vehicles were to be used for the following tests: to decide whether the vehicle should be tracked or wheeled; to test particular armour arrays; and to investigate gun-laying problems. It was also to be used to examine the trunnion stresses that would be placed on such a light vehicle by such a large calibre weapon. (A similar problem would haunt the USA in later years with Sheridan and the gun/launcher system.)

General Requirements
The final specification for FV 4401 is for the vehicle that can be seen in pictures, and by means of the available drawings. It was built to meet the following criteria, to provide a one-man vehicle having the following properties:

• tank-destroying capabilities;
• good armour protection;
• low weight to utilize the power from the Rolls-

Royce series B engine to be fitted;
• low cost of production: estimated at one fourth that of Conqueror;
• low silhouette compared to Conqueror.

Armament
It was to be armed with two recoil-less rifles of 120mm, based on the current infantry weapon,

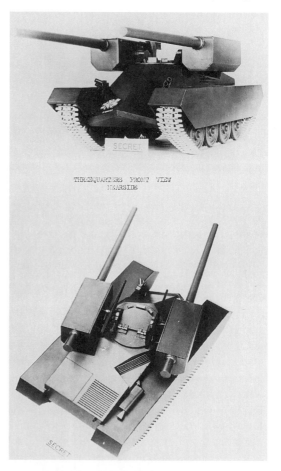

Above: *Prodigal FV 4401 The one man tank concept that was seriously considered for production before it was decided to manufacture on a conventional tank that eventually become Chieftain.*

Right: *Drawing showing the layout of the proposed one–man tank.*
Copyright Public Record Office.

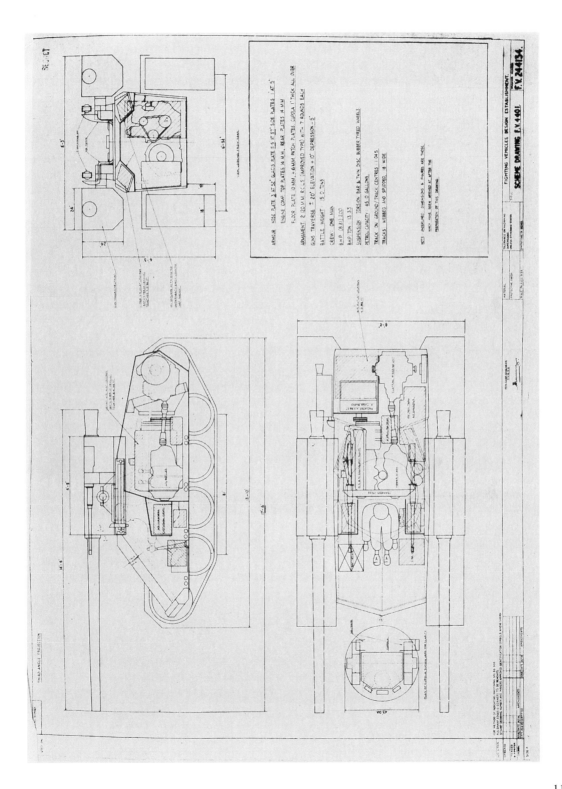

the BAT. The guns were to be fed by rotary magazines, each holding seven rounds; a co-axial machine gun was to be fitted, and also a spotting rifle in order to aid range-finding. A Centurion gunner's sight would be fitted, and two vision scopes, the whole cupola rotating with the weapons; the weapons had a elevation of 10 degrees, and a depression of 7 degrees, the same

M551 Sheridan int the Gulf. Showing its small size and its 152mm gun/launcher. (Chris Johnson)

as Conqueror. The standard radios of the day were to be fitted, and the vehicle was to be powered by a modified version of the current Rolls-Royce engine, the B80; renamed the B81, they were basically identical except for the power output. The method of elevation was still being investigated, but would probably have ended up with some form of hydraulic elevating system.

The Project is Cancelled

Trials of FV 4401 continued for some time, but eventually it was realized that this was not the answer, and the project was cancelled. What happened to the trial vehicles? No one knows or is prepared to admit what happened to them: the nearest that we have surviving to this day is a vehicle called 'Contentious', housed at the Tank Museum in Bovington. David Fletcher, Bovington's librarian and a noted author on armour, says that the museum is unsure of Contentious' pedigree, since at the time of writing there is very little documentation on it.

The so-called 40-ton Centurion, built from Centurion parts to prove Chieftain concepts such as the prone driving position and no mantlet. Three were built; one survives at the tank museum, and one at REME Bordon.

The vehicle currently resides in the museum's reserve collection – although looking at it, I do believe it may well be a survivor or descendant of the FV 4401 Project Prodigal.

THE MEDIUM GUN TANK NO. 2: THE FV 429

The first real step forward in replacing Centurion came in a memorandum from the WO, which resulted in the authorization for the development and production of the medium gun tank no. 2. The motivation for this was evidently the realization that Centurion was outmatched by T54 – and since it was accepted that in any future war we would always be outnumbered, it was essential that we had a clear superiority of performance. It is believed that the successor to the T54 is already being built, and presumably it will be a superior vehicle, thus placing Centurion at even more of a disadvantage. The Army council therefore approved the introduction of medium gun tank no. 2 as part of the family of weapons for the future equipment of the Army as the replacement for Centurion (Army council minutes April 1956).

Various other requirements were stipulated at that time, such as the calibre of gun and bagged charges for the propellant system. It was also stated that the current Russian heavy tank, the JS3 – the advent of which had been the main reason for the introduction of Conqueror – was itself being replaced by T10. Conqueror was in service in small numbers, and there were no plans to build more than 150 of this vehicle; rather, authority was given to build a guided anti-tank missile to counter the T10, a project that became known as the Orange William project.

Nevertheless, for several reasons it was felt that the destruction of enemy armour could not be left to the long-range anti-tank missile, and must be entrusted to a tank: at that time the weapon was costly to operate, it was not reliable, there was no suitable transport to carry enough of them to be a viable fighting unit, it was vulnerable

whilst the missile was in flight, it was unable to engage when it was caught in the open, and the missile itself had a dangerously long time of flight. Indeed, some of these problems are only today being resolved.

In 1957 the Fourth Tripartite conference with America, Britain and Canada was held in Quebec, and it made the recommendation that medium and heavy gun tanks should be embodied in one class of vehicle, to be known as the 'main battle tank'. It is of interest that the terms 'medium' and 'heavy' tank were used at this conference, having been abandoned some years previously during FV 200 development, on the

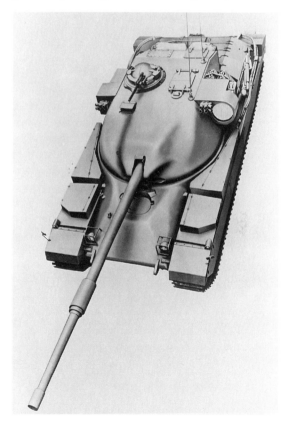

The concept drawing for the Chieftain: most of the main features of the prototype are there. The searchlight is not yet fitted into its armoured barbette and so is shown fitted to the cup; the decision to use it came later. (Tank Museum)

grounds that any such categorizing title restricted designers.

As far as the UK was concerned, the concept was already embodied in the proposed medium gun tank no. 2 (no. 1 being 'Caernarvon', part of FV 214 development). Eventually the vehicle would be known as 'Chieftain', although for the present it would be known as FV 4201. Its design would be a radical departure from anything British, and incorporated several innovative ideas; amongst these was the aim to keep the weight down, thus producing a more agile vehicle – however, it would seem that, somewhere along the line, this ideal was lost.

Medium No. 2 Experimental Vehicle FV 4202

To help in the development of the new features that were to be incorporated in the new vehicle, Leyland motors developed and built medium no. 2 experimental vehicle FV 4202. It was also known as the 40 ton Centurion, as it was built from readily available Centurion parts (in fact it weighed out at more like 42 tons). It featured the reclining seat for the driver, and the turret was built without a mantlet. In 1956 three vehicles were built, with five road wheels per side. One of these survives at the Tank Museum at Bovington, another is working as a recovery aid at the REME base at Bordon, and the fate of the third has become rather shrouded in mystery and legend. It was supposed to have been shipped to Israel by mistake along with Centurions and their spares, but on arriving in Israel no one apparently knew what to do with it, and it seems to have disappeared.

Design Ideas for the Medium Tank

Authority for the new tank was not issued until the late fifties; however, design work on various other projects was already taking place. The original designs for the new medium tank were started in 1951 using concept designs based around the standard American 105mm gun that could fire the following ammunition: HVAP, HEAT and AP. But the size of the American gun precluded its adoption, and this led to FVRDE and ARDE investigating the possibility of employing a liquid propellant gun. This had always been an attractive idea to designers, as the requirement for higher MV meant larger charges, which in their turn took up more valuable space in which to stow it and for the loader to manoeuvre it within the turret confines.

Experimenting with Liquid Propellant

All this resulted in the trunnions for the gun having to be moved forwards, and this, coupled with the increased weight of the gun breech and armour, made it very difficult to provide a finely

Above: *T95 showing off its ability to raise and lower itself on hydro-pneumatic suspension. (Mike Duplessis)*

Right: *Probably the only surviving late T95 hull. The glacis bears a resemblance to that of the Chieftain. (Mike Duplessis)*

balanced turret – and this was required to ensure that any stabilisation system worked to its best advantage. However, if liquid propellant were used it could be piped in exact measured quantities to the gun chamber space, and the loader would only be required to manoeuvre the projectile and allow for recoil. Propellant tanks could be made to fit into areas that were unsuitable for conventional stowage, and it was also hoped that an auto-loader could be included in the system.

The downfall of the system was that, unlike a conventional charge that could be ignited whenever it was required, liquid propellant had to be injected into the chamber in a constant spray and ignited immediately to allow a build-up of pressure. Significantly, the pump required to match the pressure in the chamber became so large that its on-board mass made the concept unfeasible. A working gun had been built and tested, and had proved the theory that the system could work, but not as a viable alternative to the high velocity gun – yet even to this day, experiments with liquid propellants continue.

Experimenting with a Bagged Charge Gun
Because the experiments with liquid propellant had not proved as successful as had been hoped,

in 1954 a design by FVRDE was submitted for consideration. This showed a vehicle mounting a bagged charge gun of 105mm, which as we have seen would be the perceived maximum calibre for a medium tank (although the WO requirement had merely been for a gun of sufficient calibre). The design sought to show that there were advantages to using a bagged system, both in operation and in the installation of the system. The sad part of the requirement was that mobility was only asked to be 'about the same as Centurion': and in this the WO took about ten strides backwards in their forward thinking. While other countries were taking a hard look at mobility and its importance, the UK conceived the millstone that was to compromise Chieftain's capabilities all its life.

Considering the pressing need to field a new tank, the effort expended was relatively small, with time in effect being squandered on trying to make the liquid propellant gun feasible. Furthermore the team working on designs at FVRDE was very small. Nevertheless it was then decided that a 'full and thorough assessment' should be made of the 1954 proposal, also to determine if 105mm was the right calibre. Here again we can see the designers moving at the speed of light in response to new ideas.

Proposed Armament

Meanwhile the tripartite members whom we met earlier had decided that any future weapon must be capable of defeating 120mm of armour sloped at 60 degrees at a range of 2,000yd (1,800m). The team from FVRDE and ARDE took this set of figures as their baseline to work from, and in April 1956 came to the conclusion that the ideal calibre would be 120mm. What the pundits who had advocated 105mm as the maximum size thought of this decision is not recorded anywhere, but it must have been a heated meeting. The good news was that the gun envisaged could be fitted into the current design of vehicle: this was originally to have been armed with a 105mm bagged gun, it featured a reclining driver's position, and

The American T95 with its gun barrelled at 90mm. It was planned that the turret could be interchangeable with that of the Chieftain. (Mike Duplessis)

was to have been powered by a meteor engine. But the use of the 120mm system meant an unacceptable increase in weight.

In June 1956, however, a new design concept was produced, which made use of the 120mm bagged gun system and the reclining the driver's position, but adopted a 90-degree V8 engine and automatic gearbox. This brought the vehicle weight to around 47 tons, and it was hoped that this could be reduced still further to the target weight of 45 tons.

Standardizing the Design Vehicle

The main contractor at this time was Leyland Motors, and they could now start a limited design study based on the suspension units; the rest of the vehicle design was still not sufficiently confirmed to allow design work to proceed.

The UK and the US then came to a period of indecision as to what extent the two countries should and could standardize. The first sugges-tion was that both the UK 120mm and the US 90mm smooth bore must be interchangeable within the FV4201 and the American T95. In this exchange the British would be getting the worse deal, since the projected figures for the 120mm showed it to be superior to the 90mm. In an effort to make the task of standardization easier, it was then decided to make the turrets interchangeable, a project that involved a great deal of redesign.

Fortunately this plan never came to fruition: if it had, it would have caused terrible training problems, since it would have required crews to have been proficient in both systems. There is evidence to suggest that trials were carried out in turret changing, but the results are not known.

All the while more tripartite agreements kept the designers busy with changes, the latest of which called for frontal armour to be made thicker. During this period the WO also mooted for the first time a requirement for infrared night-fighting capabilities to be included in the vehicle.

THE MULTI-FUEL ENGINE

In the later stages of 1957 a decision was taken that was to adversely affect Chieftain until its final days: it involved a change from the projected V8 that it was hoped Rolls-Royce would produce, to a multi-fuel engine. In January 1958 Chieftain effectively said goodbye to reliability when the government adopted a European requirement for all future MBTs to have an engine that worked on the multi-fuel capability.

In theory this was an excellent idea, because it meant that in times of conflict vehicles could refuel from a variety of fuels including petrol, kerosene, diesel and aviation spirit. However, it also meant that the engines would be more complicated, and in many cases would need modifying by fitters before they could run on a different fuel. The idea of being able to draw up and fill up without any modifications to the engine was just not practical – in Chieftain's case, eight hours was quoted by REME as the length of time needed to convert from diesel to petrol.

But as so often happens, the UK did as it was requested, and plodded on with this mission impossible while the rest of Europe and the US designed practical diesel engines for their next vehicles. Adopting the multi-fuel concept meant that the engine compartment had to be completely redesigned, which added a further ton to the weight of the vehicle: at this stage in its design and development this was approximately 50 tons. In turn this necessitated a whole reassessment of the armour distribution and vehicle components, until eventually a design was produced that reduced the weight to 48 tons. If the user requested a further reduction to 45 tons, it was felt that this could be achieved by developing a lightened version of the same engine, making it a four-cylinder one. This was never proceeded with, due to insufficient development time and not enough designers who could be spared to work on it.

Unusually for the period, this prototype poses for the camera with no canvas cover on the turret or bin over the glacis plate.
(Tank Museum)

Vickers-Armstrong Joins the Field

In 1958 it became evident that although the work being carried out at the parent designers Leyland Motors was progressing well, it was still not moving fast enough, and the project was starting to fall behind schedule. In August 1958 it was therefore decided to bring in a second main contractor in the shape of Vickers-Armstrong, one of the most famous names in the British armaments industry: they were given the task of designing the turret. By splitting the work in this fashion, work on the design advanced at a greater pace than before, and it was even possible to hold a mock acceptance meeting during March 1959. As a result of this meeting a great many modifications were requested by the user, involving a number of structural alterations to both the turret and the hull.

Testing the L60

Meanwhile development of the L60 – as the multi-fuel engine was now known – had proceeded to the stage where a single-cylinder test bed was running by the end of 1958. The company was also successfully producing the TN12 semi-automatic transmission, based on the design that was to have been used in the defunct FV300 light

AFV series. In March 1959 the first TN12 gear-box had been tested on a dynamometer, and this had revealed a number of defects in the design. These were rectified over the summer months, and the gearbox passed its type tests towards the latter part of September 1959.

Also around this date the first low-powered version of the L60 was completed and running, so both units could be fitted into the first prototype FV4210 P1. Once the assemblies were success-fully installed, the vehicle was subjected to a lim-ited amount of running on Leyland's test track; however, the suspicion is that it was not driven too hard, as it was due to be shown at the DRAC conference in December. The vehicle was viewed in an unfinished state and was not fitted with a turret; instead a weighted superstructure known as a Windsor turret was fitted (someone had allegedly once remarked on its similarity to one of the towers in Windsor castle).

Whatever the truth of the story, the main pur-pose of the turret was to simulate the all-up weight of a completed vehicle, and the system is still used today. After the DRAC conference, the vehicle was sent back to the FVRDE in January 1960, whence it was followed by P2 in April 1960; both these vehicles were built purely as automotive test beds.

In June 1959, six additional Chieftains had been ordered for use in troop trials, and the con-struction of these was to be split between the two big tank companies in the UK: Vickers, and the Royal Ordnance Factory at Leeds. Delivery of these vehicles commenced in July 1961, and was completed in April 1962. A further two vehicles were ordered by the Federal Republic of Germany; these were to be used for comparison in their tests with the new Standardkampfpanzer, eventually to see the light of day as the Leopard 1.

Coping with Design Failures

In the early part of 1960 the two prototypes P1 and P2 both carried out a limited amount of road run-ning, with the L60 speed governed to a maximum of 1,800rpm; by the end of May of that year, P1 had

An all too familiar sight for Chieftain crews. The 260 pack being replaced. (Mark Wagstaff)

completed a total of about 660 miles (1,000km). During this running period many failures occurred; these were caused by vibration of the engine, and its tendency for torsional oscillation, amongst others. Perhaps the most serious was a failure in the gear train connecting the top and bottom crankshafts; as a result of this, design changes were requested by FVRDE into the method of mounting the gears, and to the teeth. Fitting dampers to the crankshafts eventually stopped the vibration and so solved the problem, and this in its turn stopped the gear teeth from fracturing.

While all this was taking place, the designers took the opportunity to alter the ratio of the gear train so that it would permit a maximum crankshaft speed of 2,100rpm. This was lower than the original intended crankshaft speed of 2,400rpm, and it was instigated so as to take full advantage of the engine combustion characteristics as shown by the single-cylinder version running at Rootes. The reduction in the crankshaft speeds actually saved about two years in development time, since it would have taken that long to design a fuel injection system to cope with the higher crankshaft speed. Unfortunately these things do not happen overnight, and the engines embodying all these modifications were not available until late August 1961.

Further Problems

Having solved one problem, the modifications now caused a problem of their own, because quite apart from the serious interruption of the trials that were meant to be taking place, there was a knock-on effect on all the other components that were also meant to be on trial. And it resulted in a great deal of time and manpower being wasted at workshops because of having to modify both prototype and trials vehicles: this involved substantial structural changes before the modified engines could be accepted, due in part to the fact that the engine was now longer, because of the fitting of the dampers to the crankshafts.

Another area that caused problems was the hydraulic fan drives that had been fitted in an effort to reduce the time taken to change the fan belts, amongst other considerations. The problem was only solved by the design and introduction of belt-driven fans. The incidence of hydraulic and coolant leaks was greatly improved by the fitting of dampers, as mentioned already.

Work was still going on at both Rootes and Leyland to try and solve one of the major problems with the engine: it was still considered underpowered at 500bhp. Many modifications were made, to the fuel injection system as well as to the lubrication and cooling systems, and this all resulted in a uprated engine of 550bhp, the first of these available in October and November; they were fitted with the dampers, and had belt-driven fans.

GEARBOX TRIALS

The amount of time lost due to these problems and because of other component failures meant that very limited running time had been accumulated on the gearbox, especially cross-country. In fact it had reached the stage that by the end of October 1960, only three gearboxes had completed more than 500 miles (800km) – although to be positive about this, only minor problems had been experienced. However, this was running on the early low-powered engines, with the speed restricted to 1,800rpm as opposed to 2,100rpm.

By June 1961 the gearbox in P1 had completed 660 miles (1,060km) when it developed clutch slip; it was found that this was due to the duplex bearing seizing – and on further investigation it was discovered that the wrong type of bearing had been fitted in the first place! P2's gearbox failed at 948 miles (1,525km) during the cross-country trials; once again this was due to a bearing failure, but this time it was because it was misaligned.

By March 1962, two gearboxes had accumulated 1,500 miles (2,400km) between them with no major faults coming to the surface, and the remaining boxes had totalled 600miles (965km);

all hoped that this was a good sign, considering the problems that had been encountered to date with the engine. But towards the end of 1961 and early 1962 during the early user trials, problems started to occur with the electrical solenoids that controlled the gear selection on the gearbox. These were overheating, partly because they were affected by hot gases escaping from the exhaust system, and partly because the box itself was inadequately cooled by the flow of air over it. The combined effect of this produced gear selection failure and mechanical breakdown.

To rectify this problem, the oil flow inside the gearbox was improved, a gearbox heat exchanger was added, and the exhaust system was modified: this included placing the silencers outside the vehicle on the rear hull wall. The production vehicles were to benefit from these problems in that two larger radiators were fitted, an improvement made possible by the lengthening of the hull to take the modified engine. The opportunity was also taken to increase the louvered decks to allow a much better airflow within the engine compartment.

RUNNING GEAR PROBLEMS

One knock-on effect of all the modifications that had been carried out was the increase in weight: the vehicle now weighed in the region of 49.5 tons, and it is easy to guess where the next problems were going to occur: in the running gear. This had been designed for a tank with an all-up weight of 45 tons, and now problems arose that were a direct result of its having to contend with a heavier loading; for instance the suspension brackets distorted under certain running conditions, and the road wheels were not lasting as long as they should. For the time being, strengthening brackets were fitted to the suspension units of the prototype and user trials vehicles; on full production models, however, a revised running gear would be used (such as the fitting of only three top rollers, one to each suspension unit, instead of the type used on the Centurion).

The suspension units were also fitted with rudimentary shock absorbers (see photographs). These were fitted to the front and rear stations, with the provision that they could be fitted to the centre station as well if required. The new units would dispense with the coil spring-type shock absorber, and would have a hydraulic unit fitted to the front unit only.

It was decided to fit Centurion-type road wheels, and to reposition the final drives and idler wheels: this gave an increase in ground clearance from 17in (43cm) to 22in (56cm), and was achieved at the cost of only 1in (2.5cm) increase in overall height. This was a good move, as the trials crews had been complaining that the vehicle tended to belly easily because its ground clearance was too low.

THE FIRST PROTOTYPES

By the beginning of 1961 the trials had been confined to limited automotive running with P1 and P2, and to the development of the gun control equipment on P3. These were the only vehicles that had been delivered so far, but they had all had various faults, which in itself was informative: many were only minor, but ways of solving them still had to be investigated, and what was learned could be passed on, to the benefit of the next build. While some of the modifications were considered essential and were embodied both on the prototypes and the trials vehicles, others were classed as merely desirable, and were only incorporated on the production-build vehicles.

The vehicles were modified at FVRDE workshops (P1, 2 and 3), the rest partly during build at the factory and then completed at FVRDE workshops. This in fact placed a considerable strain on the workshops, as there were other projects to be administered as well as the FV 4201.

The delivery dates of the prototype vehicles are shown below; these indicate the pattern for the later trials and troop trials.

P5 going through its paces at Bovington. Unusually, note the high mounting for the commander's .30 mg, and still sporting the canvas cover over the turret front and sheet-metal box glacis plate. (Tank Museum)

TESTING THE ARMAMENT

During the same period as the automotive trials, the first main armament firing took place at the Kirkudbright ranges in May 1961, using War Office prototype vehicle W3. The main aim of this trial was to assess the vehicle's suitability for user trials. A team from Lulworth was there to observe and to glean some first-hand experience of the fighting arrangements inside the turret, since as of yet no training manuals had been written for gun drill.

Inevitably criticisms were made, and some defects came to light. One of the most serious concerned the contra-rotation of the commander's cupola, which could only be operated by hand; also there were concerns that the commander's mg mount did not allow accurate aiming of the weapon. W3 was then returned to FVRDE in the early part of June for further modifications, and to rectify some of those defects discovered on the range. Once these had been completed, it was intended that the vehicle be passed over to the user.

In 1961 a number of proof firings of the gun and the cradle mounting were conducted from fire

stands. These are concrete bases with a framework to accept weapons and their cradles, so that trials on the weapon can carry on without the vehicle being present. Although it will not replicate the effects on a particular weapon on the vehicle, it does allow the gathering of data on the weapon in a safe, controlled environment.

In July, the first FVRDE vehicle to take part in firing trials (P4) was delivered to FVRDE; after outstanding modifications had been completed, it was sent to Kirkudbright. Once there it took part in obturation trials: this involves the sealing of the breech against escaping gases, traditionally carried out by the expanding shell case; in FV4201, however, there is no metal case, so this was achieved by metal plates in the breech block and ring: see Chapter 5 for more detail.

Once this was satisfactorily concluded in January 1962, the testing moved to accuracy and 'jump' trials: when a round leaves a barrel it does not follow the centre line of the barrel, but 'jumps'; once the jump is known, then it can be included in the calculations when ballistic graticules are designed.

A Ranging Gun: the .50 Browning

It had always been part of the design of FV 4201 to be fitted with a ranging gun: this establishes the range to a target to maximize the chance of a first-round hit. Prior to this, all British AFVs, apart from Conqueror, relied either on the human eye, or on wasting a round in ranging; but almost inevitably, these methods were either unreliable or not tactical.

The weapon chosen was the American M85 – and even before the weapons had fired a round, problems were being encountered with the deliveries from America. Once the firing trials started they highlighted problems with the ejector system, and finally the gun was pronounced unsafe due to the chamber pressures generated by the current British ranging round. The aftermath of this trial resulted in the cancellation of the M85, and a .50 Browning was chosen as the replacement.

This was a modification of the standard .50 Browning machine gun, fitted with a special barrel and a solenoid on the body that would permit only three rounds at a time to be fired. These were used as the ranging burst, and the number of rounds that hit enabled the commander to issue a fairly accurate range in his fire order to the gunner.

The .50 Browning proved to be a very good choice as an RMG: it was an excellent weapon and easy to maintain. It did, however, take a bit of adjusting when boresighting it to the main armament, and many is the time that a turret crew will have boresighted 100 per cent accurately, only to find that in locking up all the adjusting nuts on the mounting cradle they had distorted the body. In fact this was easily done; it did not cause damage, but it meant that the whole boresighting procedure would have to start again.

Once the decision had been taken to adopt the Browning, steps were taken to modify the production turrets to take the new weapon.

Night-Fighting Equipment

Trials using P3 were also carried out on the infrared night-fighting equipment; this had already been subject to trials on Centurion in March/April 1960, and had been accepted into service at that time. The major difference

Prototype Status

P1	Delivered January 1960	Reworked at various stages
P2	Delivered April 1960	Ditto
P3	Delivered August 1960	Ditto
P4	Delivered July 1961	
P5	Delivered April 1962	
P6	Delivered November 1962	
W1	Delivered March 1961	To user 8.1.62 at Bovington
W2	Delivered April 1961	To user 8.1.63 for BAOR trials; fitted with Windsor turret, then returned to Leeds for rework to near production standard
W3	Delivered April 1961	To user 24.4.61 sent to Kirkcudbright for user experience then returned to FVRDE for essential mods 6.6.61; then to Lulworth for firing trials 20.9.61; then to BAOR for troop trials 22.12.62
W4	Delivered December 1961	To user 2.11.62 for joint user/FVRDE 1,000 mile (1,600km) trials at Bovington
W6	Delivered February 1962	
G1	Delivered January 1962	To user 15.2.62 to Lulworth for gunnery trials
G2	Delivered November 1962	

P5 and 00 DA 05 – an early prototype – can be seen, albeit in a battered state, on the range at Kirkcudbright in Scotland; remarkably they are both fitted with the original power pack, before major changes were made to it.

between the two systems was that in Centurion, not only did the crew have to change their day sights for the IR night sights, they also had to mount the 22in (56cm) searchlight if it had been stowed in its carrier on the rear basket. FV4201 had its searchlight mounted on the left of the turret in originally an armoured barbette with doors that opened towards the centre of the light. This was changed on the production model to an unarmoured barbette with a single door.

The searchlight was capable of producing 2kw of power, and could either be used in the IR role or as white light. The author can remember that at one time, one of the techniques used for night firing was for one tank in the troop to engage the target with white light while the remainder would use main armament. This was never a popular technique, especially if you were the illuminating tank; it was also hard to control. The commander and gunner

	Vehicles Compared			
	Centurion Mk3	**FV4201**	**T10**	**T95 (90mm)**
Height	9ft 75in	9.5ft (2.895m)	8ft (2.4m)	9ft 33in
Weight	111,966lb (50,788kg)	121,275lb (55,000kg)	114,640lb (52,000kg)	84,300lb (38,238kg)
Length	32ft 3in (9.8m) gun front	35,418ft (10,795m) gun front	34ft 9in (10.6m) gun forward	32ft 4in (9.8m) gun front
Width	11ft 11in (3.6M)	12ft (3.657m)	11ft 8in (3.55m)	10ft 3in (3.12m)
Speed	20mph (32kmph)	30 mph (48kmph) road	26mph (42kmph)	35mph (56kmph)
Range	62.5 miles (100km) road 32.5 miles (52km) cross–country	250–300 miles (400–500km) road 124–190 miles (200–300km) cross–country	115 miles (185km)	145 miles (233km)
Crew	4	4	4	4
Main Gun	20pdr	120mm	122mm	90mm T208
Co–ax	7.92 Besa	.30 Browning	14.5mm	.30 Browning
Engine	Rolls-Royce Meteor	Leyland L60 compression ignition	V–2IS 12 cyl V diesel	Continental AOI 1195–5 8cyl horizontaly opposed
Cmdrs MG	.30 Browning	.30 Browning	14.5mm	
Armour	17–152mm		20–250mm	

Right: *Prototype Chieftain showing revised production engine decks, but still with the early mark no. 11 cupola. Of note is the Conqueror gun crutch still attached to the barrel. (Bob Grundy)*

Below: *Rear view of gate guard at DERA, Chertsey, the modern equal to FVRDE. From this shot it is plain that there is a lot to do on the rear design of the hull. (Author)*

Bottom: *Prototype serving as gate guard. By now the shape of the hull and turret becomes more recognizable as a Chieftain.*

had IR sights that were interchangeable with their conventional day sights, but this also took up a lot of time and adjustment before they were boresighted.

The driver was issued with a pair of IR goggles to be worn over a helmet, but these proved very unpopular: drivers complained about the weight, and also the smell associated with them; this came from the type of rubber in the stowage box, and it was quite disgusting. Needless to say, most CUBS – their official title – tended to remain in the troop stores. It took a great deal of time and effort to set up the IR equipment, but once it was up and working, it was hugely impressive to watch a tank suddenly fire its main armament and almost simultaneously to see a flash down-range as the round struck its target.

The main disadvantage with IR was that it could be detected, and it did not give a clear enough image to allow identification. This would lead to the development of other systems that would be used in the future.

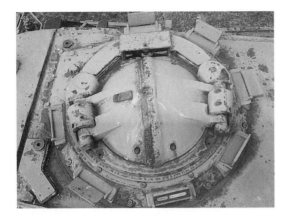

Above: *Close-up of vehicles at Aberdeen proving ground, USA. Note the layout, the split hatches and cupola sights on this no. 11 cupola.*

Right: *Level view of the no. 11 cupola. Note also the cover for the gunner's sight in front of the cupola. This has no armoured cover that can be raised/winched to protect the sight, and was replaced on production. (Author)*

Just about there! A fine shot of a Mk 1. This was almost the layout that was adopted for the Mk 2. Notice the location of the small gut exhaust. This would be moved to the right side above the right main exhaust. (Tank Museum)

The Contra-Rotation Equipment

A further outcome of the above trials was that the commander's contra-rotation gear was found to be unsatisfactory; a modification kit was therefore supplied towards the end of 1961, which improved it – though this was not considered the final answer. The first vehicles were equipped with a Mk1 cupola (cupola AFV no 11): this had the split hatches like the later marks of Centurion. Subsequent vehicles had the Mk2 cupola (cupola AFV no. 15 Mk1), with a single-piece hatch. A development of this cupola was fitted to later marks of the vehicle, and remained with it throughout the rest of its service life.

The purpose of the contra-rotation equipment was to allow the commander to traverse his cupola off the line of the main gun to search for targets. When he found a target he could – depending on the vehicle – select contra-rotation, and the main turret would be driven to line up with the cupola, when the gunner could hopefully pick up the target in his field of view. Conqueror took this a stage further by laying the gun on for elevation as well and injecting the range from the commander's fire control turret into the gunner's sight. Even today, with Challenger 2, the same sort of system operates, except that instead of a cupola it is a independently mounted, panoramic

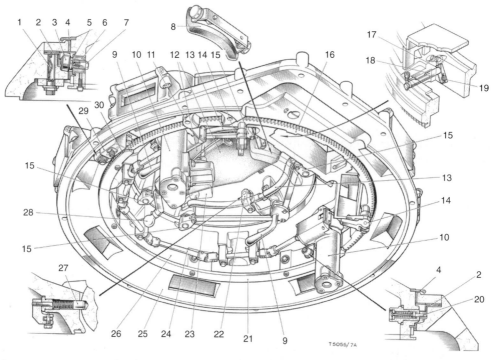

1 Lead wire	9 Cupola door locking handle	17 Catch locking pin	25 Cupola fixed ring
2 Slip ring	10 Elevating gear	18 Periscope sight locking pin	26 Cupola rotating ring
3 Roller	11 Rotating gear bracket	19 Catch spring	27 Locking pin
4 Dust cover	12 Cupola doors	20 Earthing brush	28 Elevating gear handle
5 Roller Shaft	13 Door closing handles	21 Rack guard	29 Direction sensing switch
6 Metalastic brush	14 Periscope retaining catch	22 Door locking catch	30 Nylon roller
7 Screw	15 Locking lever	23 Wiper motor	
8 Brow pad	16 Contra–rotating gear rack	24 Elevating gear drive shaft	

User handbook drawing of the no. 11 cupola showing the controls and mounting points for the sights.

A good shot taken during trial of W4 at Bovington. Of note is the early deck layout; also visible on the right side is the top roller layout, similar to the Centurion, and the Centurion-type front idler wheel. Both were changed on production vehicles. (Tank Museum)

sight with 360 degrees of traverse that is used, and hi tech electronics have taken the place of micro switches to line everything up.

WHY TRIALS ARE IMPORTANT

It may seem to the reader that all these problems made the gestation period unacceptably long. Certainly the time-scale was long, but it was preferred to give the crews a vehicle that had been well designed, and to discover as many of its problems as possible before it entered service. Lasting memories of some of the vehicles rushed into service in World War II still remain; these often let their crews down, but it is the crew that is the most important commodity, and current feeling was that the vehicle given to them had to be the best that could be provided.

An example of how the trials have helped the user can be seen in just one component of the weapon system. We have already seen that the gun uses split ammunition, and because of that, sealing of the breech had to be obtained in some other way, as traditionally it was the expanding brass case that sealed the chamber. For FV4201, a system using inserts in the breech block and one in the rear of the chamber was used. During the firing trials the obturators were missing, so when the gun was fired, a flashback occurred in the turret causing two of the crew to be killed and the other seriously injured.

As a result of this incident, interlocks were designed and fitted that ensured that the breech could not be closed unless both obturators were in place, thus preventing any similar accident in the future. Thankfully incidents like this are rare, but they show only too clearly why it is important for these long design and trial periods to take place.

PRELIMINARY AND USER TRIALS

A great deal of time and effort is put into preliminary trials even before a vehicle is sent for user trials. This is so the user has the best chance of evaluating it without needing to report minor faults that should have been solved before it was issued.

I am very grateful for the information provided by Major (retd) Ralph Bagnall-Wilde ex-RTR; this has helped explain a lot of the trial problems. As we have seen, the vehicle had already been subjected to many modifications before the user trail was contemplated; it could be said that the only trouble with finding faults is often the difficulty of making someone take notice of what you are saying, and more important, doing something about it. At worst, someone will be killed: as we have seen, that is what happened to the Chieftain turret on the Conqueror hull, which fired without the obturators fitted.

INITIAL USER TRIALS

The two regiments chosen to carry out the user trial were the 1st RTR and 5th RTR in BAOR. On collecting his tank and giving it a quick glance over, Maj Bagnall-Wilde immediately opined that it was not ready for the trial: he found the sight-mounting loose, with a gap of _in (2cm) between it and the turret roof. This was bodged up in the traditional manner of making things work. On complaining to the OC at Chertsy and getting no useful response, the matter was then referred to the brigadier – who bluntly told him that his job was to take the tank to Germany and say how good it was, so that the RAC would then be allocated one of them. Luckily for the RAC the Royal Tank Regiment does not operate like that, as events were to prove that the tank was indeed not ready.

The tanks arrived in BAOR in the winter of 1962, and it was noticed straightaway how well they managed on the ice and snow compared to Centurion; so that was as good a start as any. These trials are particularly useful for the 'hands on' experience of the men testing the vehicle: their practical approach and criticism can often prevent the most awful pieces of equipment being issued to service vehicles. For example, if the designers had had their way with Chieftain, the method of checking the firing circuit would have involved more circuits and voltmeters to measure a drop in voltage. However, thanks to 5RTR gunnery expert Brian Hayward-Cripps, this unnecessary complication was avoided: instead, he drilled a hole in the base of a used vent tube, and fitted a small bulb known as a pea bulb: this was then located in the breech block in the same way

Prototype Chieftain undergoing trials. Notice the no. 11 cupola in the umbrella position; also the second Chieftain in the background. (Tank Museum)

as a normal tube. If the circuit was all right, the bulb lit up; if not, it didn't, indicating that there was a circuit problem: all very simple, and the idea stayed with Chieftain until the end.

Gunnery Problems

One of the more exotic features in the turret of the new tank was a powered rammer to assist the loader in his drills – but unfortunately, even though the designer might have had the loader's best intentions at heart, the system was totally unworkable. In theory the rammer would hinge up from its location, ram the rounds, and then return to its stowed location; the trouble was, it had a habit of ramming anything in sight – and it also had the habit of starting a ramming sequence when it felt like it, thus making it very dangerous. All in all, it was felt by the trial team in both regiments that ramming the projectile using a bag charge would be safer and quicker. But this solution was dismissed by the designers as dangerous, on the grounds that it might damage the bag charge. Radical action was therefore needed to make them change their minds, so it was arranged to drop a bag charge from one of the high wooden towers on Hohne ranges: this was done, and amazingly no damage was done to it! That proved the theory, and eventually the rammer was removed, much to everyone's delight.

Also issued to the vehicle in case of rammer failure was a wooden handle, to be used to carry out ramming drills. This proved to be totally ineffective and clumsy, and was also discarded.

When it was first issued for trial, Chieftain was equipped with two machine guns of American manufacture: the M85, that was to be the RMG; and the M73 for co-ax, and possibly for the commander's cupola. The M83 had many problems, and was subjected to an ordnance board examination where it failed a test known as 'oily proof': this meant that if the rounds were slightly oily when they were fed into the gun, problems would be caused, such as increased chamber pressure. It also suffered from feed mechanism problems.

The 4/7 DG crew poses in front of their Mk 4 Chieftain during trials in the USA. (Chris Trigg)

Security

The crews on the trial were also subject to tight security, as Cpl Barry Cobley from 5 RTR recalls:

Accommodation for the other ranks involved in the Chieftain trial – there were about six of us in a crew – was in a separate block, which tended to keep us away from the mainstream regiment for three months. When we were actually working on the vehicles we were not allowed to take any photographs at all for souvenirs, because the security people were worried that they might be copied by enemy agents whilst they were being processed; so a lot of what happened was never recorded, which is a great shame. I found that some of the tasks were definitely a lot easier than on Centurion: one was the track bashing, also there was no problem in changing spark plugs, thanks to the diesel engine. That could take nearly all day on a Centurion if you were unlucky.

In view of these problems, the gun was required to be stripped and thoroughly inspected by a REME armourer every twenty-five rounds – but obviously this made it very difficult to complete the firing trials and produce sensible figures. One result of this was the replacement of both weapons with the L21 .50 Browning – adopted as the RMG – and the tried and proven .30 Browning as co-ax and commander's mg. In a bid for commonality of equipment within NATO, the .30 was then replaced by the Belgian 7.62 GPMG, leaving the .50 to soldier on until replaced by the TLS. In fact the removal of the RMG was seen by many as an act of pure stupidity, as it was an ideal weapon for taking out soft-skin vehicles and light armour such the Russian BMP and BRDM, thus saving main and co-ax ammunition for better targets.

TRIALS AND TRIBULATIONS

Sgt Bob Harriman (as he was then; he was later commissioned) 5 RTR ran the driving side, and his observations were no different to those expressed by others many years later: the biggest problem was the main engine and gearbox, which failed far more quickly than those in Centurion. This was very frustrating for the crews, particularly as nothing could really be done about it.

Bob also recounted the story of being in the turret when a flashback occurred. Not realizing what had happened, he was fairly cool about it – although the loader is recorded as achieving a very fast evacuation time from the turret. Evidently Bob was considerably taken aback on being told the reason by Ralph Bagnall-Wilde.

One very positive conclusion that came from the trial was that Chieftain was a cold tank compared to Centurion that had a heater. Unfortunately the authorities never saw the need for a crew heater – but then, they were not the ones stuck in the turret at 3am with the condensation running down the walls.

One of the trials was a seventy-two-hour closed-down exercise, when the crews were not allowed out of the turret at all. Most regiments in the early days conducted such an exercise, some for seventy-two hours, others for as little as twenty-four, and it certainly brought home the problems of doing everything within the confines of the turret. Although it all generally started off as a bit of fun, keeping patience and remaining level-headed whilst still carrying on with the job in hand, soon became hard work.

CONCLUSIONS

After three months the trial was concluded, and both regiments were required to produce their trial reports. These were written up separately, but in fact they came to very much the same conclusion: that the tank had great potential, but was not ready to be issued to the troops yet. This was not what the 'top brass' had wanted to hear, and the Brigadier tried to reject the report, but it was supported at General level. A meeting was held at the MoD where the reports were discussed, and the outcome was that the 'in service' date for Chieftain was moved back.

From this point on, some of the recommendations from the reports were instigated into the production vehicles, while others, for various reasons, were not; some even surfaced years later and were then introduced.

Chieftain was also subjected to trials in the hot sandy climate of Aden: these were conducted in 1966 by 1st RTR. They found that the vehicle performed very well as long as reasonable care was taken, though one major problem early on was that the first prototype air cleaners were not capable of filtering out the fine desert sand; this was rectified in later versions, however. Thus when the 4/7RDG and 13/18 H took Chieftain to the USA in the seventies it had no problems with sand blocking filters, and in fact ran very well.

A great deal more could be said on the process of trials, but a lot more information has yet to be released. Suffice it to say that trials and experiments are always being carried on throughout the vehicle's life, and this is essential in order to ensure that the equipment utilized is of the best, for both the safety and the efficiency of the crew.

2 Appearance and Layout

Although Chieftain broke new ground in some aspects of its design, in layout it was no more advanced in some respects than Cromwell or Centurion. But before considering this topic more closely, it is worth taking a look at how the various marks of Chieftain evolved, a subject that suffers from a certain confusion, with some sources quoting vehicle marks that in fact never got further than the drawing board.

To simplify matters somewhat we shall discount the Mk 1 vehicles, since they were generally only used for training (although some Mk 1/4s were converted into AVLBs, and still serve at the time of writing). We shall also leave out the Mk 4, of which only two were built.

MODIFICATION PROGRAMMES

The production vehicles from Mk 2–3/3 were put through a programme called Exercise Totem Pole, a series of modification programmes designed to make all current in-service vehicles compatible with the new-build Mk 5, and as reliable. The programme was divided into three, designated X, Y and Z. The X programme involved modifications to the sighting system for computability with the extended-range ammunition

used with the RMG. The Y programme was mainly automotive, with modifications including a low-loss air cleaner, and a 12:1 parking brake; it included a facility for the commander to fire the main armament and to stop the main engine in an emergency; and the sight mounting for a TLS was also installed. The Z programme involved modifications to the powerpack and gearbox, and to the hull and exhaust systems. The no. 6 Mk 2 NBC pack was also fitted at this stage.

The next phase was the fire control retrofit programme, its purpose to improve the fire control facilities in Chieftain Mk 5–8 (as listed). This introduced the tank laser sight (TLS), a muzzle reference system (MRS), and an improved fire control system (IFCS). Certain modifications were also carried out to the cupola at the same time. This programme was split into two phases, with each phase itself split into two stages. Stage one of phase one involved the fitting of a TLS, and mountings for the MRS light source; on completion of this phase, vehicle numbers were given the suffix '/1', as can be seen in the table. Stage two involved completion of the installation of MRS, and removal of the RMG and its associated equipment; on completion, stowage vehicles then received the suffix '/2'.

Stage one of phase two involved the installation of the IFCS system and fittings for SIMFICS

Exercise *Totem Pole* Up–grading Programme

Production Mark	X	Y	Z	X&Y	X&Z	Y&Z	Final Mark
2	2(X)	2(Y)	2(Z)	2(XY)	2(XZ)	2(YZ)	6
3	3(X)	3(Y)	3(Z)	3(XY)	3(XZ)	3(YZ)	7
3/G	3/G(X)	3/G(Y)	3/G(Z)	3/G(XY)	3/G(XZ)	3/G(YZ)	7
3/2	3/2(X)	3/2(Y)	3/2(Z)	3/2(XY)	3/2(XZ)	3/2(YZ)	7
3/S	3/S(X)	3/S(Y)	3/S(Z)	3/S(XY)	3/S(XZ)	3/S(YZ)	7
3/3	3/3(X)	3/3(Y)	3/3(Z)	3/3(XY)	3/3(XZ)	3/3(YZ)	8

Specification – Chieftain

This data is based on the Mk5 there are varying small differences for each mark.

Weight
Estimated laden weight without crew 64.9 tonne (54 ton)

Bridge classification
Laden 60
Unladen 60

Nominal ground pressure
Laden 90kNm2 (13lbf/in2)

Dimensions
Length hull 7.59m (24ft 11in)
Length overall (gun front) 10.87m (35ft 8in)
Length overall (gun rear) 9.75m (32ft 0in)
Height to top of commanders MG 2.89m (9ft 6in)
Height to top of turret 2.51 (8ft 3in)
Width overall including search light 3.66m (12ft 0in)
Width over tracks 3.33m (10.11in)
Ground clearance 0.508m (1ft 8in)

Performance
Maximum road speed 43.5km/h (27mph)
Vertical obstacle 0.90m (2ft 11½in)
Maximum gradient 70% (35 degrees)
Trench crossing 3.15m (10ft 4in)
Shallow fording 1.07m (3ft 6in)

Armament
Main gun Ordnance Breech Loading 120mm Tk L11A5
Co–axial MG 7.62mm MG Tk L8A2
Commanders MG 7.62 MG L37A2
Smoke protection Two 6 barrel smoke dischargers

Sighting and vision
Commander One periscope AV 37 Mk 1–5
Nine periscopes AV No 40 Mk2
Two periscopes AV No 41 Mk1
Projector reticule image No 22 Mk1 or 24 Mk1
One periscope AV L5A1 (non Togs vehicles)
Gunner One sight laser rangefinder AV No 2 Mk1 or 2
(IFCS vehicles only)
One sight laser rangefinder AV No 6 Mk1
(II sight vehicles only)
One sight laser rangefinder AV No 11 Mk1
(TOGS vehicles only)
Loader One periscope AFV No 30 Mk1
Driver One periscope AFV No 36 Mk1
One periscope AF II L4A1 or
One periscope AV II L112A1

Gun control system	F/VGun control equipment No 10 Mk1
Power pack weight (with coolant)	2743kg (6048lb)
Engine	
Type	Leyland L60 no4 Mk 13A, 6 vertical cylinders opposed pistons, two stroke compression ignition
Idling speed	335–355 rev/min
Governed speed	2250 rev/min (crankshaft) 2812 rev/min (output shaft)
Starting	Cold starting by hydraulic drive from generating engine, subsequentlyby electric starter motor
Generating unit engine	
Engine type	Coventry climax H30, No 4 Mk7A or Mk10A. 3 cylinders, opposed pistons two stroke compression ignition
Governed speed	
Idling	800–850 rev/min
Charging (normal running)	1900–2100 rev/min
Cold starting (Mk 10A only)	3100 rev/min
Starting	Electric starting motor
Gearbox	
Type	Tn12 Mk4 electro–hydraulic gear selection (foot pedal operated)
Clutch	Centrifugal
Take up speed	400=480 rev/min
Fuel engagement	1100 rev/min
Steering brakes	Disc, hydraulically operated
Main brakes	Disc, hydraulic power operated
Parking	Band, mechanically operated by multi pull hand brake lever
Accelerator	Mechanical, foot pedal operated

Gear Speeds and turning radii

Gear	Max Speeds		Turning Radii	
	Km/h	mph	Metres	Feet
1	4.41	2.74	3.18	10.4
2	7.61	4.74	5.51	18.1
3	12.35	7.68	8.92	29.3
4	19.35	12.03	13.97	45.8
5	28.80	17.88	20.77	68.2
6	42.70	26.46	30.74	100.9
Low reverse	6.58	4.09	4.75	15.6
High reverse	9.83	6.11	7.10	23.3
Emergency reverse	3.93	2.11	2.37	7.6

The above speeds are based on a government engine speed; vehicles may well vary by up to as much as 10 per cent.

Specification – Chieftain *continued*	
Suspension	
Type	Horizontal helical spring
Number fitted	Three each side
Shock absorbers	Hydraulic on front units only
Wheel deflection	Bump 159mm (62.5in) one wheel rising
	Rebound 82.5mm (3.25in)
Tracks	
Type	Dry pin removable rubber pads
Width	610mm (24in)
Pitch	157MM (6.18in)
Links per track (new)	96
Weight	4763kg (10,500lb)
Ventilation/NBC system	NBC pack No 6 Mk2. A four stage filtration unit. Air is ducted to each crew station. Or No 16 Mk1 with NBC pack No 11 Mk1

(a training aid), and conversion of the TLS no.1 Mk 2 and no. 3 Mk 1 to no. 2 Mk 2. The FVGCE was changed from no. 7 Mk 4 or Mk 5 to FVGCE no. 10 Mk 1. Stage two involved improvements to the no. 15 cupola, and vehicles thus modified received the suffix '/3'.

When Clansman radios were fitted, the letter 'C' was added to the suffix. Another up-grade was the operational emergency round installation: this was carried out so that ready racks could be installed to carry APFSDS, to allow conversion of the sights with new graticules, and changes to the computer software; vehicles were then marked '/4'. The second stage involved completing the fitting of the racking to accommodate APFSDS, together with an increase in ammunition carrying capacity: vehicles were then marked '/4/1'.

Following on were two more improvement programmes, the first being the crew protection package: this involved replacing the NBC system with the no. 11 Mk 1 and a new control panel. There was also improved armour protection, which altered the turret shape quite drastically (Stillbrew). The final programme was the fitting of the thermal observation gunnery system (TOGS) as used by Challenger 1; this was fully integrated with the current computerized sighting system (CSS).

Another improvement for the future would be the fitting of electric heaters (…at last, and twenty years too late…). And if Chieftain had remained in service, other improvements would have included hydraulic track adjusters, a new computer sighting system (ICSS), and finally the fitting of the high-

Up markings

On Completion of:

Veh Basic Mark	FC Phase 1 Stage 1	Stage 2	FC Phase 2	OE Round Installation	Increased Ammo Stowage	Installation of II Sight
5	5/1	5/2	5/3	5/4	5/4/1	5/5/1
6	6/1	6/2	6/3	6/4	6/4/1	6/5/1
7	7/1	7/2	7/3	7/4	7/4/1	7/5/1
8	8/1	8/2	8/3	8/4	8/4/1	8/5/1

The result of the decision not to fit heaters: crews try to keep warm in the middle of a Canadian winter. (Author)

pressure gun (HP) that finally came to see the light of day in Challenger 2 as the L30. If these modifications had been allowed to take place, the vehicle marks would have been as indicated in the table. Notice that although Marks 12 and 13 are mentioned, they never actually saw service, so that the Mark 11 was the last mark of gun tank to be completed. There is also a Mark 15, but this is a builder's specification and it was not used by the British Army; this vehicle was in fact built for Oman.

CHIEFTAIN LAYOUT

As can be seen, Chieftain went through many changes during its life, and to complicate the matter even more, not all vehicles received the modifications, and some received none at all. So trying to describe its layout is no easy task. Reference will be made to the variations that can be found, depending on the mark of vehicle.

One very good reason why heaters were needed: yet another blizzard in Canada! The depth of snow was the result of one night's snowfall. (Author)

35

Mark 9	**Mark 10**	**Mark 11**	**Mark 12**	**Mark 13**
Basic up–date built standard Mk 5/4–8/4	Mark 9 with CSS	Mark 10 with TOGS	Mark 10 with HP gun and ICSS (no TOGS)	Mark 11 with HP gun and ICSS

As already stated, Chieftain was not innovative in its layout, having the driver in the front of the vehicle, the rest of the crew in the turret, and the power train in the rear. We shall start our tour inside Chieftain with the driver's station: the driver is quite often the most maligned member of the crew – inevitably he will get really dirty, and his position is isolated, situated as it is away from the rest of the crew. But I can assure the reader that a good driver is more than worth his weight in gold: it is the difference of being stuck in a bog due to bad driving, to arriving at the leaguer first and the food is still hot; perhaps this oversimplifies the case, but nonetheless it is very true.

THE OUTSIDE APPEARANCE AND LAYOUT

The Chieftain hull is a fabrication of cast and welded plates, unlike its predecessors Centurion and Conqueror. The hull floor is welded in a V-shape, and the hull sides are sloped to help minimize the effects of anti-tank mines. The forward part of the upper hull is a casting that includes the driver's hatch area; this casting extends to roughly halfway along the vehicle, where it joins the welded portion of the rear hull. Again, the layout is conventional, with the driver in the front of the vehicle, the fighting compartment in the centre, and the engine and transmission filling the rear of the hull.

A Mark 2 Chieftain showing the original layout of single headlights and full-width splash guard.

Low angle of view showing the headlight and splash-guard arrangement on later marks.
This vehicle is waiting to be used as a hard target. (Tim Babb)

At the very front of the vehicle is a splash plate, and depending on the mark of tank, it will be either full width covering either headlights, or a plate situated between both groups of twin headlights. Its official purpose is to prevent debris riding up the glacis plate when fording and with the driver travelling 'opened up', when it would be quite easy for a sheet of ice to decapitate him. Unofficially the plate provides a suitable stowage for the driver's web kit: this must be at hand at all times, and this is why the driver's webbing is usually the most soiled.

Due to a very large turret ring, it was necessary to build hull panniers that extended over the tracks. The drive is at the rear of the hull, with the track-adjusting idler wheel at the front; the vehicle rode on a six-suspension unit bolted to the side of the hull. To protect the suspension and the lower hull, skirting plates or 'bazooka' plates are fitted: there are six of these, and they are simply bolted onto brackets on the hull; in earlier vehicles they were steel plate, and in later marks aluminium.

Each unit carries two sets of twin road wheels, and the spring is of the Horstman type, similar to that used on Centurion and Conqueror.

The turret carries the other three members of the crew: the commander, the gunner and the loader/operator. It also contains the main 120mm armament and the 7.62mm co-axial machine gun, and the commander's cupola with another 7.62mm machine gun.

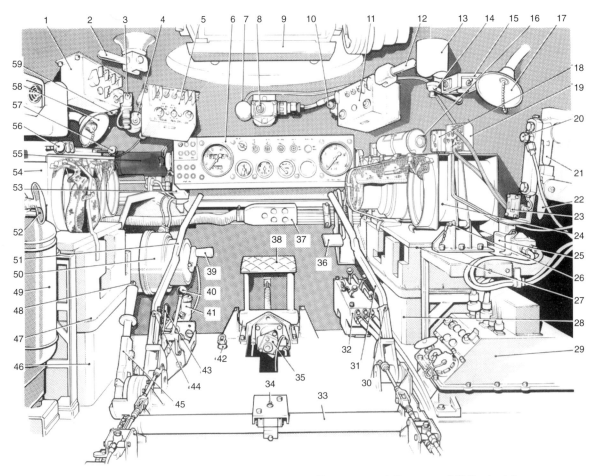

1 Lighting switchboard	16 Portable fire extinguisher	29 Battery master switchbox	47 Battery insulation
2 Access hatch cover locking handle	17 Driver's periscope washer tank filler	30 Steering lever locating pawl	48 Parking brake lever release button
3 Reverse button	18 Engine oil low level alarm control box	31 Steering lever	49 Fixed fire extinguisher
4 Fire alarm warning light	19 Crew heater controls (hull and driver's)	32 Auxiliary control box	50 Gearbox controller
5 Generating unit engine switchboard	20 Brake pressure line manifold	33 Steering lever interlock	51 Steering lever
6 Instrument panel	21 Brake pressure warning light switch	34 Interlock lubrication nipple	52 Fixed fire extinguisher operating handles (2 off)
7 Engine oil low level alarm warning light	22 Governor override pressure switch	35 Main brake	53 Negative line junction box
8 Driver's safety switch	23 Battery thermal switch junction box	36 Accelerator pedal	54 Projectile rack
9 Driver's periscope	24 Prijectile rack	37 Driver's ventilation duct	55 Crew heater (driver's)
10 Horn button	25 Dozer harness plug (stowed)	38 Main brake pedal	56 Generator cooling duct valve lever
11 Main engine switchboard	26 Projectile rack retaining pin	39 Gearbox controller pedal	57 Main engine air cleaner duct valve lever
12 Access hatch cover spring tube	27 Battery insulation	40 Hydraulic starter control lever	58 Drinking water tank filler
14 Access hatch cover catch release arm	28 Battery box	41 Hydraulic starter master cylinder and reservoir	59 Main engine air cleaner restriction indicator
15 Radio distribution box		42 Hull drain plug	
		43 Hydraulic pump clutch lever	
		44 Steering lever location pawl	
		45 Parking brake lever	
		46 Battery box	

Layout of a late mark driver's compartment. Note the heater highlighted – at last fitted.
(Crown Copyright)

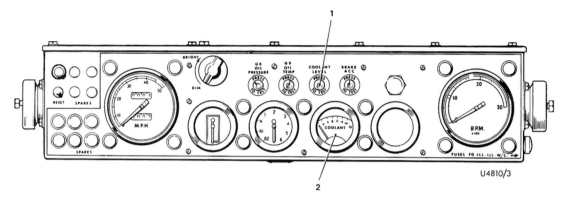

1 Coolant level warning light   2 Coolant temperature gauge

User handbook drawing of the driver's instrument panel with all its main gauges. (Crown Copyright)

THE DRIVER'S COMPARTMENT

As we have seen, the driver is located in the front of the hull in a central location; to his right is the driver's hatch, which in Chieftain is not like the Centurion's, but rather in the Conqueror's style of 'lift and swing'. This type of hatch gives the driver a far better chance of survival than the sort that lifts and opens back – although getting through it for the first time seems to be a task for a contortionist! This is how the driver normally enters the vehicle, although vehicle crews are trained to evacuate him through the turret if required; however, this would have to be in the event of a real emergency, as it is not an easy task to carry out.

Once settled in the driver's seat, the first impression is of a mass of cables and switches, and very little space. Nevertheless, if the reader studies the drawing of the driver's cab it becomes apparent after a while that although it is crowded, the designers have done a good job of fitting everything into the space allowed.

The Driver's Seat

The most obvious feature is the driver's seat. This has to be the best seat on the tank, with an adjustable back and headrest. It is extremely

> ### A Chieftain in Ireland
>
> When the author was a few years younger and stationed in Omagh, Northern Ireland, the 4/7 DG were due to move to Germany and take on the role of an armoured regiment. A Chieftain was sent to Omagh to help in the conversion courses, making it the first tank to have been in the province since the war, and conversation around the NAAFI tables at break-time always centred on comparisons between the Chieftain and the Centurion. However, without the chance to actually drive it – there really was nowhere in Northern Ireland to drive a tank – some of the remarks were very unfair, and in fact most people did change their minds on reaching Germany (at least for a while).

comfortable, and is undoubtedly the best place to be on those nights when the crew has to sleep in the vehicle.

The main reason for its being better than any of the others is because it tips back when the tank is closed down: in effect the driver is therefore driving in a reclined position. On previous vehicles if a driver closed down to drive, he simply lowered his seat and closed the hatches above him; this meant that in the design, there had to be enough space for a driver sitting upright, which of course raised the vehicle's silhouette. In

Above: *Another view of the L60 and auxiliary generators pictured as looking to the rear of the vehicle. The L60 top is painted to show it has been through the Sundance programme. (Author)*

Above right: *Showing the general layout of the L60: notice the twin fans and the large amount of cables and pipes. (Crown Copyright)*

Opposite right: *Two views of the early auxiliary generator and two of the later model. (Crown Copyright)*

Chieftain, the only way to obtain that long, low, sloping glacis plate was to place the driver in the reclined position.

For those used to driving Centurion closed down it was a strange experience, but one that was soon mastered. In order to navigate in daylight hours when closed down, the Chieftain driver is equipped with a single wide-angle periscope; for night driving this can be changed for one of two types of image-intensified sights.

Before the advent of TOGS it was not unknown for the vehicle commander to borrow the II sight for observation from his cupola, using it like a pair of binoculars; needless to say this was not officially sanctioned, but it worked. The driver's sight mounting also provided a heater for the sight eyepieces, and a washer-wipe system.

We will now take a closer look at the bewildering array of switches, cables and levers that confronts the driver. Most are explained in the drawing and photographs, but we will consider some of them in more detail to give a better idea of how all this equipment is used.

Starting the Engines

Chieftain is equipped with two engines, though only one is used to actually propel the vehicle: the Leyland L60 No. 4 Mk 13A – six vertical cylinders, opposed pistons, two-stroke, compression ignition. The 13A was the last in a long line of the L60, and to a certain extent solved a lot of the problems of the earlier engines.

The smaller engine works in conjunction with the main engine generator when this is running, and provides the electrical power required for all the various systems on the vehicle, and to maintain the vehicle batteries on a constant charge. It also provides a means of starting the main engine by hydraulic power; and it can be used to provide power to all services on the vehicle independent of the main engine when the vehicle is to be stationary for long periods. This is both tactically and environmentally useful as it lessens the heat and smoke signature, and cuts down the fuel used. This is a significant benefit, and one that, even after all these years, other countries are only just starting to appreciate; a good example was the bolt-on APU (auxiliary power unit) that the Americans had to provide for the MI Abrams in the Gulf War. The turbine had to be running at all times in order for it to provide power – and turbines are thirsty engines.

The Engines in Service

In service the smaller engine is officially known as the 'generating unit engine' (GUE), though colloquially to the crews as the 'genny' or 'aux gen'. The current model fitted is the Coventry Climax H30, NO4 Mk 7A or Mk 10A: vertical cylinders, opposed pistons, two-stroke, compression ignition. Unsuspecting new recruits were often told that because it was so much quieter than the L60, it would be used to creep up on the enemy!

To control these two engines the driver has two switchboards: apart from the writing on them, which is different, they are identical in

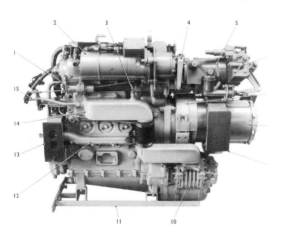

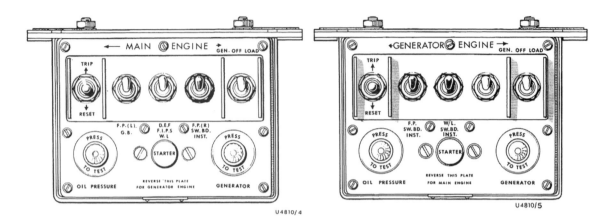

As referred to in the text, these are the panels for starting both the main and the auxiliary generator engines. (Crown Copyright)

layout (items 5 and 11 in the drawing). Instead of an ignition key, most military armoured vehicles have a switch for cutting off the battery power when it is not required: this is known as the 'battery master switch' (item 29 in the drawing).

First of all the driver will carry out what is known as the 'first parade', when he will check all the fluid levels and the general serviceability of the vehicle: he is then ready to start the engines. The GUE is always started first, thus preventing a power drain on the batteries; as we have said, the GUE can be used to start the main engine hydraulically, a method that is recommended for the first start of the day, or on very cold occasions. Once the driver has started the GUE he will turn it to full revs and ensure it is charging; he will then engage the hydraulic starter clutch, and by pulling on the hydraulic starter control, will attempt to start the main engine. In fact this was never a very reliable system, and most crews preferred to start the main engine electrically.

Once the engines are running, the driver can check all the various lights and instrumentation that monitor them: the main dashboard situated in front of him will show engine revs, oil pressure, temperature, fuel, and the selected gear.

Gear Changing

The other main control for the driver is the gearbox controller: this is a small round pedal on a bracket, which is connected to the gearbox controller itself. This replaces the gear stick and does away with the need for a clutch pedal as the gear change is semi-automatic, and changes are effected by using the pedal, much as you would on a motorcycle. With the toe under the pedal a slight flick will change gear until top gear (6th) is reached; to change down, the foot is placed on the pedal and with a quick burst of revs the pedal is depressed, thus changing down the gears. There are six forward gears and two reverse gears.

An automatic change-down is included in the system so that if either the main engine revolutions drop below a certain set amount, or the driver brakes, the gearbox will automatically change down. Most experienced drivers will disconnect this feature, as it tends to take away full control of the vehicle from them; though needless to say, when the vehicle is presented to the REME for inspection, the cable is in its correct position.

Because the transmission is semi-automatic it very easy to carry out gear changes, and as a result – and more importantly – this reduces driver fatigue. In one instrumented trial using the Mk 4 Chieftains in the US, the driver was recorded as carrying out a gear change every six seconds: imagine that with a manual gearbox and clutch! There is a very slight delay in the gearbox as it reacts to the signal sent to it for a gear change, which is why Chieftain always seems to be jerking when it is viewed on film.

Braking and Accelerating

The next control across from the gear change pedal is the brake pedal, located traditionally in the centre as in the family car; the only difference is that it is large enough to place both feet on. Finally the accelerator pedal, too, is just where you would expect to find it; it is linked to the fuel injection system by a hydraulic line, and not by rod-type linkages.

Steering

Unlike a car, most tanks do not have a steering wheel to control direction: instead the driver has two steering levers, one on each side of his seat. To steer the vehicle in forward motion he pulls the required lever and the tank will turn in that direction; also, the gear he has selected will determine the radius of the turn, the lowest gear giving the tightest turn. Thus first gear gives a turning circle of 3.2m (10.4ft), and sixth gear a circle of 30.7m (100.9ft).

As we have seen, the gearbox has six forward and two reverse gears, the latter known as high and low; there are also two emergency gears that will move the tank forwards or backwards. Although very slow – approximately 3kmph (2mph) – this will allow the vehicle to move under its own power instead of depending on a tow – though if any great distance has to be covered it will be boring, to say the least: the author can vouch for this after driving what seemed like for ever in BATUS in 'emergency forward' to an area that had been designated for a pack lift on his vehicle.

Batteries and Projectiles

The two banks of batteries and projectile racks effectively take up the remainder of the space in the cab. There are six 12v 100ah batteries on the vehicle, four of which are situated in the cab, two each side of the driver; these are kept in special stowage to try to prevent water and dirt getting to them. They are charged by the generator on the GUE, by the main engine generator, or by both generators charging in parallel. The remaining two batteries are located in the rear of the turret.

The batteries' position in the driver's cab makes servicing the most awkward task imaginable, and to remove them for replacement is a major undertaking. The introduction of low maintenance batteries, similar to those used in a car, has helped.

Situated above the battery racks on either side are stowage racks for five rounds of 120mm ammunition each. The driver will pass this ammunition into the turret during a lull in fighting to help replenish the 'at-hand' stocks.

The Driver's World

We can see from this brief description that the driver's world is fairly cramped, and pretty much isolated from the rest of the crew. Nevertheless his job is as important as any other member: first, it is his responsibility to pick the safest tactical route without having to be guided at all times by the commander. He also has to try and provide the smoothest ride possible, to help the gunner when he is having to fire on the move. When stationary, he can help the turret crew by looking out for the enemy, as his location lower down can sometimes give him a better picture of the ground in front. This is especially useful during range periods were targets are 'puffed' by a small explosive charge, since the driver with his limited view forwards – as compared to the turret crew – would quite often be the first to pick up the flash of the charge going off.

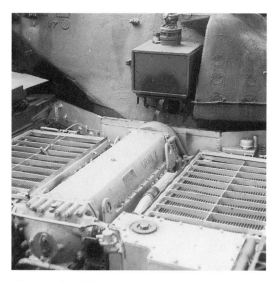

Showing the L60 fitted into the vehicle; notice that the radiators now lie flat, and how little space there is. (Tim Babb)

Showing the layout of the L60 auxiliary generator and gearbox. The radiators are shown in their right position for servicing on pack removal. (RCMS Shrivenham)

THE ENGINE AND TRANSMISSION COMPARTMENT

The engines and transmission are located in the rear of the vehicle: within this space the designers have crammed the main engine, the gearbox and the GUE, plus oil and fuel tanks for 195gal (886l) of diesel fuel. Access to the various components is by a series of heavy engine decks over the rear part of the hull: four of these cover the GUE side, and four cover the main engine air cleaner; the main engine itself is covered by what is know at the 'T-piece'. This is a T-shaped cover running from in front of the transmission decks to the turret ring; it has two armoured covers set into it, and it also acts as a support for the armoured decks in the closed position. The transmission compartment is covered by five armoured covers: two of these can be opened to carry out maintenance, the other three have to be unbolted before they can be removed.

Layout of the Engine Compartment

The GUE and main engine covers are opened by simply lifting them up and lowering them on their hinges to rest on supports on the hull; if not lowered sufficiently they make a very distinctive sound.

The first components we see are the twin radiators of the main engine. Unlike a car, when the Chieftain engine is lifted out, the radiators and all the subsystems come out with it: this is called a powerpack system. It was designed to speed up the replacement of worn or damaged parts, in that a complete pack could be removed and a new one put straight into its place. Challenger 2 has taken it a stage further, as the whole assembly consists of the engine, cooling system and gearbox as well, in theory speeding things up even more. In practice, however, it did not work out quite so conveniently, as certain components still had to be removed from one powerpack and put in the new one.

The Main Engine Air Cleaner

With the radiators lifted out, the various engine components are now visible. Looking from the rear of the vehicle, on the right-hand side is the main engine air cleaner. To ensure that only clean, filtered air is delivered to the ME, air is drawn through the air cleaner (secured tight against the right side of the ME) and a scavenge pump.

The air cleaner is of the two-stage type, and would normally draw air in through the armoured decks; the air then enters the first stage of the air cleaner, where large particles of dust are separated by the cyclone tubes. These work on the same principle as some vacuum cleaners: the particles are directed into a dust hopper, and from there are drawn out by an extractor fan and blown into the cooling air stream within the powerpack compartment, and thence out of the vehicle.

The clean, filtered air now passes through a filter element and into the Rootes-type blower that will supercharge the air before feeding it to the engine. As mentioned above, normally the air will be drawn in via the open hatches in the fighting compartment, as this generally provides the cleanest air. This is not practical during combat, however, and in these circumstances alternative flaps will be used so that air is drawn through the engine deck covers; but this is less satisfactory because the air will not be as clean.

The Cooling System

To dissipate the excess heat generated by the ME, the GUE and the transmission, a liquid/air heat-transfer system is employed. The main cooling system has 132l (29gal) of coolant in the system. Coolant is passed around the ME system by two pumps, situated one on each side of the ME; after passing through a heat exchanger on each side of the engine, it then flows into the lower manifolds. It then rises around the cylinder liners to exit via thermostats on each side of the engine. If the liners fail, then the engine will produce clouds of white smoke – a familiar sight with Chieftain!

This is burnt coolant, and as well as giving off a noxious smell, it will also vaporize and cover the vehicle with a slippery layer of liquid. Coolant will also be fed to the GUE coolant pump from a connection on the left lower manifold.

To aid the flow of air through the compartments and over the radiators, two fans are fitted, driven by belts from the ME. Although only a minor component, the fan belts in the early days of Chieftain were causing so many problems and failing, that questions were actually asked in the British Parliament; needless to say, the papers had a field day.

In addition to being belt-driven from the ME, the left-hand fan is driven by a hydraulic motor that comes into operation when the GUE only is running, to provide the latter with an air flow. When the fans are running, they draw cool air through the powerpack decks and through the core of the radiators, and then expel it through the transmission covers. Access to top up the coolant level is through the right-hand side of the armoured cover in the T-piece.

The GUE

The GUE is located under the left-hand radiator, and its function is to provide – in conjunction with the main engine generator, when this is running – the electrical power that is required to operate the various systems, equipment and ancillaries fitted to the vehicle, and to charge the vehicle batteries. It can also provide power by means of a hydraulic pump and clutch to start the ME, and it also drives the left fan motor when the ME is not running.

The GUE, complete with its generator, hydraulic pump and all ancillaries, forms a single compact unit that is easily removed from the engine compartment. As already observed, it is running all the time that the vehicle is in use, but it really comes into its own when the vehicle is going to be stopped in one location for a long period of time, but still requires all its electrical services. To use the ME generator for this purpose would not be viable (although it can be done; but the engine revolutions need to be kept at a high turnover).

GUE Oil System
The GUE has the same type of oil system as the ME, namely a dry sump: unlike a car where the sump is directly beneath the engine, they are fed from an oil tank within the engine compartment. The reason for adopting this particular method is to save height, since with no sump, the engine's silhouette is lower. Although the GUE has its own oil system and tank, it shares the ME cooling system, and is connected to it by two quick-release hoses.

GUE Controls
The GUE is controlled from the driver's cab, thus carrying on a design from later Centurions and Conqueror. Prior to that the controls were on the fire wall that separated the fighting compartment from the engine compartment (as on early Centurions); this meant that to start or stop the GUE, the turret had to be traversed. In putting the controls in the cab, the task was made much simpler.

The controls consist of a GUE switchboard, identical in external appearance to that of the ME, and the auxiliary control box. The switchboard contains the starter button, various lights, and the generator charge button, and is situated to the left of the driver. The auxiliary control box is located by the driver's right leg on the cab floor, and has three levers located on it. These work in the following way:

The right-hand lever has a spring-loaded gate that allows it to move either fully forwards or fully to the rear: this is the selector for the emergency gears.

The left-hand lever has three positions: a rearward position, a detent halfway up the box, and a sprung gate at the very front. The rearward position is used when the GUE has just been started, when it will normally be allowed to 'tick over' for about thirty seconds. To bring it up to running, when it will be charging the

The turret boiling vessel – a boon for the crew, as it enables them to heat food. It usually falls to the loader to be head cook. (Tim Babb)

The GUE in Service

On the whole the GUE proved to be reasonably reliable in service, and it was certainly a boon when the tank was stationary for long periods as it meant that power was available for all vehicle services, including that most important article of equipment, the boiler. On previous vehicles this had been no better than a glorified electric kettle, but the model issued to Chieftain (and still in service) could deep-fry as well as boil water. This led to the tank crews showing a certain air of superiority over the infantry, as there would always be hot water in the turret, whereas the infantry would have to try and light the issue hexamine burner – not the easiest thing to do on a wet and windy day.

If there were complaints about the GUE from the crews, it would be the noise it made on first starting up. This was all right when in barracks, but on exercise when you are warm and dry in your sleeping bag, the sound of the GUE starting up, then thirty seconds later being taken up to its operating revs, closely followed by the others in the squadron, was most depressing because it meant it was time to get up.

system, the lever is moved as far forwards as it can go, to the location marked 'Normal Speed (Charging)'. The detent is used if a hydraulic start of the ME is required: the lever is pushed to one side of the gate and then fully forwards, and this increases the GUE revolutions to assist the start. Once the hydraulic start has been completed, the lever must be returned to the normal speed location.

The centre lever controls the fuel supply to the fuel injector pump: pulled back, in the 'stop' position, no fuel flows to the injector; in the forward position, fuel is allowed to flow to the injector.

The Gearbox Assembly

The third major assembly in the compartment is the gearbox: the TN 12, a combined Wilson change speed box with a Merrit steering system. As we have already discussed, this provides six forward and two reverse speeds, plus emergency forward and reverse gears.

The gears are engaged by brake bands that are applied by oil pressure from two gear-type pumps driven by the gearbox. The gearbox and the output from the main engine are connected by a centrifugal clutch: this responds to the main engine revolutions. The clutch starts to take up drive at around 400/480rev/min, as shown on the tachometer, with full engagement at 880rev/min.

Gear selection is by means of the foot-operated pedal on the gearbox controller in the driver's cab. For the forward gears, raising the pedal changes up, and depressing it changes down. The two reverse gears (high and low) are also selected by depressing the pedal, so to prevent the inadvertent use of reverse there is an electrical push-button switch marked 'Reverse' situated between the lighting switchboard and the GUE switchboard, which must be pressed before reverse can be selected. If all the main gears fail

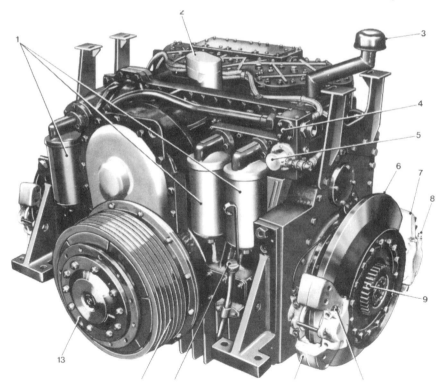

Three-quarter view of the gearbox. Notice the size of the steering disc on the left of the box. (Crown Copyright)

there is an emergency control situated on the GUE control box by the driver's right foot that allows the manual selection of second forward gear and low reverse.

Steering

As we have seen, the tank is steered by means of two levers in the driver's cab: these are connected to hydraulically operated disc brakes, each controlled by two sets of callipers. When a steering lever is pulled back, the pistons in the callipers bear against the disc in the same manner as in a car, the pressure exerted on the disc slows it down, while a differential inside the gearbox is controlled by the disc brakes. This will allow one track to speed up, and will slow the other down, so that the vehicle turns in the required direction; thus if the left steering lever is pulled, the vehicle will steer to the left.

When steering in reverse, the vehicle's response to the steering lever is the opposite to what it would be in a forward gear. Thus to steer to the left, the driver must apply the right steering lever: this slows the right track down and speeds up the left track, and so the vehicle is made to steer to the left. If emergency reverse is selected, then steering is limited to a skid turn, when one track is locked and the other carries on turning.

The Semi-Automatic Gearbox

The semi-automatic gearbox certainly makes the driver's job easier, as it was designed so to do; in previous tanks he had to depress a heavily sprung clutch pedal and move a gearstick to change gear, and there was always the risk that he might miss the gear, or he might have to make another change immediately. As we saw with the Mk 4 trial tank in the USA, the driver was recorded as changing gear at least every six seconds: obviously this could be done with a manual box, but the effort involved would be tremendous, besides which the driver would not be concentrating on his job of driving as tactically as he could, as he would be trying to ensure that all the gear changes were smooth and accurate. Today his task is even easier, as most gearboxes are now fully automatic.

Lastly there is the neutral turn, when the vehicle turns almost in its own length, depending on the type of ground. With the gearbox in neutral, the driver will ensure he has sufficient revs on the main engine, and then applies either the left or right steering lever: this will have the effect of making one track go forwards while the other will drive to the rear. This will make the vehicle pivot within its own length – a very handy manoeuvre for getting out of a tight spot where forward or rearward movement is limited.

THE SUSPENSION UNITS

The vehicle is supported on six suspension units of the Horstman type, similar to those fitted to Centurion and Conqueror. Each unit consists of a housing on which are mounted two spring-loaded axle arms; each of these carries a wheel hub and a pair of rubber-tyred, 31.6in-diameter road wheels. A track-guide roller is fitted to each unit, and the front suspension units have a shock absorber fitted to them. Each suspension unit has three concentric coil springs mounted between knife edges; these are mounted on extensions on top of the axle arms. Any upward or downward movement of the axle arms is controlled by the action of the springs that either compress or reassert themselves; to prevent excess movement, bump and rebound pads are fitted.

The front units are fitted with hydraulic shock absorbers of the double-acting type; inside they have six valves that allow the passage of hydraulic fluid, which creates the damping effect on the suspension unit. The shock absorber is linked to the axle arm by link bar. The prototype vehicles had shock absorbers fitted on the front and rear units, with the option of the centre units being fitted as well; however, these were the simple piston types, as found on a car suspension. The present fit is superior in all ways, giving bump of 6.3in (15.9cm) (one wheel rising) and rebound of 3.3in (8.4cm).

View of either centre or rear suspension units. This shows how self-containing the units are, making for ease of replacement if damaged.

The Track

The track itself consists of ninety-six links of the dry pin type, 24in (61cm) wide when new; each link is fitted with a rubber pad to help reduce wear on the roads, though these can be removed if necessary for operational needs. The track is driven by rear-mounted sprockets, and can be adjusted by the adjustable idler wheels at the front of the vehicle; the top run is supported by guide rollers, of which there is one on each suspension unit. In service, general wear and tear will cause the bores in the links to become enlarged, causing the track to become slack and running the risk of it being thrown – and if this does happen, it is a very hard job to get it back on again.

Adjusting the Track
To prevent this happening, the idler wheel can be adjusted by means of a nut that is tightened with a track-adjusting tool (really a very large ratchet spanner and an extension bar). To do this the tank is manoeuvred so that the slack in the track is at the front of the vehicle: this is one of the occasions when a turn in neutral is very useful. This makes it easier to use the track-adjusting tool, as it takes the tension of the track.

Inevitably there comes a time when the track cannot be tightened any more, and then a link must be removed; a total of six links can be taken

out, and then the track must be replaced. After removing four links the sprockets must also be replaced with ones of a different pitch – just to make things harder for the poor crew.

Sprockets and Idlers
As we have seen, the track is driven by rear-mounted sprockets 24in (61cm) in diameter, with twelve teeth per sprocket, mounted in pairs on each final drive. Each sprocket is bolted to lugs on the sprocket hub: this allows the inner sprocket to be removed easily. The track adjusters are mounted at the front of the vehicle; adjustment is achieved by a cranked axle that moves the idler wheel, thus providing tension on the track.

THE HULL: EXTERNAL FITTINGS

Various fittings can be seen around the outside of the hull. Most obvious are six stowage bins that carry the large amount of tools and equipment required to maintain the vehicle in the field, and also the crew's personal kit and rations. Two of

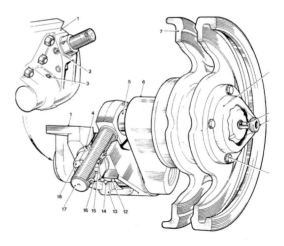

Showing how the idler wheel is used to adjust the track; the adjusting spanner is placed over the nut (18) and tightened, drawing the axle arm forward and righting the track. (Crown Copyright)

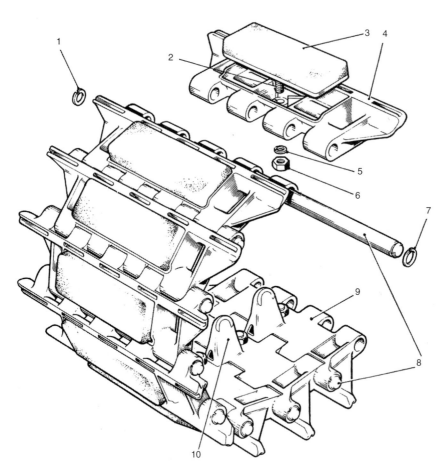

1 Circlip
2 Retaining bolt
3 Rubber pad
4 Link grouser
5 Lock washer
6 Nut
7 Circlip
8 Track pin
9 Track pin plugs
10 Horn

This shot from the handbook shows the make-up of the track and how it is joined together by the track pin and retaining clips. (Crown Copyright)

these bins are mounted on the catwalk on the forward part of the hull, and two on the rear (see Appendices for a list of their exact contents).

Other fittings include light clusters at both front and rear; and also situated on the rear hull plate is the infantry tank telephone box, used by the infantry to communicate with the tank commander when he is closed down. Unfortunately the infantry always manage to forget that when a tank moves from cover it usually reverses out of its position, and of course who is hiding behind the tank? This results in the sort of scenes that make you wish you had your camera handy.

One very noticeable feature is a 'C'-shaped lip that runs all the way round the upper hull:

when the tank was deep wading a rubberized cover would be attached here. Also situated around the hull are four hooks, where the guy ropes of the wading tower would be attached. On later vehicles the lip has been ground away from about the rebound rail to the rear of the vehicle, as the wading tower is no longer considered a requirement; with the lip ground flush at the rear of the hull, water and spilt fuel can run off the hull much more easily, thus helping to prevent the flood that would otherwise head straight for the driver's cab at the first dip in the ground. In those days, if the fuel caps had not been tightened down securely after a fuel replenishment, then the poor driver was guaranteed a diesel bath.

THE TURRET AND FIGHTING COMPARTMENT

The turret and fighting compartment is a complex area; most significantly, it contains the main armament – which, after all, is the very reason for the tank's existence.

The fully armoured turret is situated in roughly the middle of the vehicle, and it is capable of all-round traverse whether under full power, emergency power or by hand. In its original shape it was unique in British service for being the first battle tank to dispense with the heavily armoured external mantlet. This was done for several reasons, the main one being to try and reduce the tank's total weight: armour protection had to be compromised somewhere, thus the decision to dispense with the mantlet. As a result the turret front became well sloped and very narrow, producing in fact a much better ballistic shape: formerly a strike on the mantlet risked immobilizing the weapon system.

Turret Armament and Equipment

Besides carrying the main weapon the turret also carries the 7.6mm co-axial machine gun, multi-barrelled smoke dischargers (MBSGD) for local protection, an efficient NBC pack, a commander's machine gun – and the three remaining members of the crew. Like the hull, the turret itself is a combination of conventional rolled armour welded to a cast section. Looking at it from the rear, we can see the No. 6 NBC pack running across the full width of the turret rear; earlier marks had a very different system that was much smaller. This provides protection against NBC attack and can also provide cool air to the crew.

In front of this are two access panels, the left-hand one being hinged and allowing access to the two turret batteries; these are identical to the type, and are fitted in the driver's cab. Also accessible from the location is the rubber filling tube for the turret water tank. The right-hand panel covers the

metadynes, which are part of the powered gun control equipment. In front of this panel is the location for the IR detector stalk, fitted to give the crew warning when they were illuminated by an IR source; it was linked to a control box by the commander.

On the control box are three buttons that relate to front, left and right: by pressing each of these in turn until a buzzer sounded, the commander could obtain a rough idea of were the viewing source was located. If the three buttons did not trip the buzzer it was assumed that viewing was from the rear. Whilst admirable in concept, it was never widely used in its intended role, and most pictures showing it fitted are usually just PR shots. Although on rebuild the control box was removed, for some reason the mounting for the stalk was often left in situ.

In front of the IR stalk mount and the commander's cupola is an armoured cover: this protects the pressure relief valve that is part of the NBC system.

The Commander's Cupola
The main feature of the turret roof is the commander's cupola: in fact there are two basic cupolas in service. If the vehicle has been modified, then it will be fitted with the vision cupola no. 15 Mk 2; the other version is the no. 15 Mk 1.

The cupola is capable of all-round manual traverse, and is fitted with nine periscopes for all-round vision. On later marks these periscopes have a sloping head to reduce the reflection of sunlight from them. Earlier versions have an upright head, though both versions are of one-piece construction; the very early cupola periscopes were designed in two parts, and always leaked when it rained.

The Commander's Sight
The cupola also mounts a commander's sight: depending on the model issued to a particular vehicle, this can be either x10 or x15 magnification, and is used for identifying and laying on to targets. Both versions have an x1 window to

allow the commander a wider view, also a vertical or sloped head variant may be fitted. Both the cupola sights and the main sight are equipped with heated demisters and a wash/wipe system. In the early versions the main commander's sight could be dismounted and an IR night sight fitted in its place; later on a II sight was developed, but was only on limited issue, if at all. Perhaps if Chieftain had had to soldier on, it might have been given a combined day/night sight.

Cupola Visibility

Also mounted on the cupola, on the right-hand side, is a spotlight with IR/white light capability; on the left-hand side is the commander's 7.6mm GPMG that can be elevated and depressed from under cover, and is traversed by means of rotating the cupola. Less clever was the fact that to load or clear stoppages, the commander had to expose the upper half of his body from the cupola. On later marks of vehicle the commander's single hatch, opening to the rear of the cupola, can be secured in one of three positions: fully open, vertical or umbrella. To achieve this, a locking pin in the hatch engages in a hole in the commander's sight position, leaving the hatch at an angle: the commander can therefore see out, but has overhead cover. The vertical position was obtained by adjusting the removable catch arm and changing its setting.

Looking down into the gunner's station: clearly visible in the centre of the picture, from left to right, are the elevating hand wheel, the firing handle and the power controller. (Author)

The Loader's Station

To the left of the cupola are the two hatches for the loader: these are set into the turret roof at an angle across the turret. To the left of the forward hatch is the loader's periscope, for use by the loader when the tank is closed down to help in giving all-round observation; it has no magnification, but can rotate 360 degrees. The main join between the cast and plated parts of the turret is just in front of the cupola and loader's hatches: it shows up as a deep groove running across the turret, and can be seen very easily.

The Gunner's Station

In front of the cupola is the armoured sight hood that protects the gunner's sight. It is equipped with an armoured shutter that is controlled by the gunner from his station in the turret.

Situated to the left of the sight hood is the light projector for the muzzle reference system; this makes it a simple task for the gunner to check the relationship of the gunner's sight to the main armament. First he lines up the gun with markers in the turret, then presses a switch that will allow a beam of light to be projected from the light projector. This will be reflected from a mirror mounted on the end of the main armament, and then back into the gunner's sight: by checking the image created by the reflected light, he can adjust his sight if required.

It is a very simple and extremely useful system; before this, if it was suspected that a loss of sight and gun relationship had occurred, the only way to confirm it was to stop firing and carry out a full boresighting procedure – not a very viable option during a battle.

Turret Equipment

To the left and right of the turret are situated the smoke dischargers: each can hold six smoke grenades, and a further twelve spares are carried on the vehicle. They can be fired as one bank of six or both together, and are controlled by two

buttons at the commander's location. When fired they will provide a quick local smokescreen that hopefully will mask the vehicle long enough for it to back its way out of trouble.

Right at the front of the turret we can see the long barrel of the 120mm main gun and the barrel of the co-ax situated above it; when the RMG was still carried, it would have been mounted co-axially to the left of the main gun.

To the left and right rear of the turret are located two stowage baskets: these are to carry the multitude of things that a tank crew acquire, such as ration packs, oils, grease, water, and of course the crew's personal kit. Forward of the right basket is a large bin known as the commander's bin; this was always a favourite place for stowing the crew's sleeping bags, as it would keep them waterproof and safe.

In front of the commander's bin an armoured box is welded to the turret side; on its top is a metal and rubber antennae base for the Clansman radio aerial, while inside is part of the Clansman tuning system. The left basket at one time had a metal stowage box fitted inside to hold ten APDS rounds; thereby increasing ammunition stowage. This was not a popular use for it, however, as it took up valuable space in the basket, and it was more often used for personal kit; but with the introduction of TOGS a different basket was fitted that included a small stowage box mounted on its rear; the same also happened to the left basket.

The Searchlight and Night Vision System

On the left turret wall can be found either the IR/white light searchlight, or – more commonly now – the two armoured boxes containing the TOGS night vision system. As its name implies, the searchlight could be used either in conjunction with the vehicle night sights (IR,) or in the white light mode. When developed it was 'state of the art', but it soon became rather surplus to requirements, with the vehicle depending more and more on mortars or artillery illuminating rounds for

TOGS tank: looking at the commander's station. The black handle on the left of his seat is a hydraulic pump that allows him to raise and lower his seat. (RCMS Shrivenham)

night-time battlefield illumination. It did sometimes serve to deter the German drivers, who used to think that they owned the road, no matter what else was on it: a quick blast of 2kw of white light used to produce a remarkable effect.

It has now been largely replaced by the TOGS system: this is based on thermal imaging and gives a much better picture under more adverse conditions; it also means that the commander and gunner do not have to keep changing day sights for night sights, then back again.

Stillbrew Armour

Finally the outside of the turret and the area behind the driver's hatch was altered radically in the early eighties by the introduction of an add-on armour package known as Still-Brew: this covered the frontal arc of the turret and dramatically changed the profile. It consisted of armour plate bonded to thick rubber backing and bolted to the turret with thin plates: the latter were used to blend it rather more cosmetically into the turret profile.

INSIDE THE TURRET: THE LAYOUT

The layout inside the turret follows the traditional layout for British tanks, with the commander on the right, the gunner below him, and the loader/operator on the left of the turret. We shall now look briefly at each crew station and see what tasks have to be carried out there, and what equipment each crewmember has, to help him carry out those tasks.

The Commander's Station

The commander, as we have seen, is located within the cupola: this can be traversed through 360 degrees and is also capable of contra-rotation; furthermore his seat can be pumped up to give him a head-and-shoulders view from the cupola. Within his station there are the controls for the fire control system computer, and for the TOGS system, there is also the commander's TOGS viewer, the range readout display, and the commander's firing controls and power controls; the latter will let him take over a shoot if necessary from the gunner. He also has controls for the cupola mg and spotlight, and for the wipers and heaters for his optics.

Whilst looking after all this equipment he will also have to talk on the radio, navigate, control the gunner and loader, tell the driver where to go, and issue fire orders; and if he is a troop leader he will also be controlling the other two tanks in the troop. So all in all, the commander has a very busy time.

We shall look more closely at the commander's equipment in Chapter 6, when we shall see how it all comes together to engage a target.

The Loader's Station

Located across from the commander is the loader, who probably has the most uncomfortable seat on the tank: a very small square of metal padded with foam and covered with PVC, and removable to allow access to the charge bins beneath it. The loader's immediate area is predominantly occupied by three large charge bin containers, with one more forward of him; these contain either one APDS/APFSDS charge or two HESH/smoke charges, each in its own compartment within the charge bin. The walls of the containers are hollow

and filled with anti-freeze at a pressure of 7lb/sq/in, so if a container is penetrated, a stream of coolant will be forced into the bin and will extinguish any flames. Each container has it own plastic twist-and-lift lid to prevent dirt or moisture getting in, and in bad weather they are also covered in a plastic cover.

All these containers are below turret-ring level; the main armament ammunition is stored literally everywhere – as we have seen, even the driver has ten rounds in his cab. The major load is carried in projectile racks that are located at the rear of the turret and along the turret sill; these can hold all types of 120mm ammunition securely, but easily accessible. Above the projectile rack are the radios, and what these are and how they are fitted depends on whether the tank is being

Showing one of the charge containers for storing the Bag charges. This is the ready round container from the front end of the loader's station. (Author)

used as a gun tank, a control tank (SHQ) or a command tank (RHQ). Gun tanks fitted with Clansman will have two VCR 353 VHF radios; both the control tank and the command tank will have two VCR 353s, and one VCR 321 HF radio, and will probably carry an 8m mast.

As well as all the 120mm ammunition there are 7.6mm ammunition boxes stowed all around the vehicle, and most marks will now have two large trays that hold 2,550 rounds for the co-axial mg. Other controls include heater switches, and the main control for the NBC system allowing the choice of full NBC or just ventilation. Also located on the loader's side immediately behind the 120mm is the boiling vessel; as described earlier, this enables the crew to heat food and water within the turret.

Most of the space between the loader and the commander and gun is taken up by the breech of the 120mm. A small shield is pulled to the rear when the gun is to be fired – and this is the only barrier that stops the loader from falling behind the gun, so he must be constantly alert so as to save himself from this situation. In the author's experience most loaders cope very well, and seem capable of hanging on for grim death no matter what is happening to the tank.

The Gunner's Station

The last crew station is that of the gunner, and this one is definitely not a job for the claustrophobic as his only normal means of access is via the commander's cupola. This means that if the commander is injured in any way, then it is hard for the gunner to escape – though in an emergency he could possibly get out by crawling over the gun and climbing out through the loader's hatches.

The Gunner's Field of View
To his immediate left the gunner has the mass of the 120mm gun cradle, from which he is protected from injury by a fibreglass shield. In front of him is the sight mount: this is bolted to the turret roof and linked to the gun cradle, and fitted to it is one of the marks of TLS, giving him a x10 view of the target. It is also fitted with a x1 unity window, allowing him a wider field of view than if he were using just the x10.

The main purpose of the sight is to enable the gunner to determine the range to a target accurately. The read-out for this appears in his left eyepiece, and either a firing button on the sight or a foot pedal operates the laser. In an emergency the laser can be replaced with a conventional day sight, and if the situation is deteriorating, a x7 telescope is also provided.

The optics are all provided with heaters and washers; these are controlled from the lighting and control box by the gunner's right thigh, allowing him control of interior lights, washers and heaters.

Activating the Armament
To the right of the control box is the power supply for the laser: this is armed by a key, and the key itself was treated as if it were a weapon, so to lose it was a serious offence – that is, until gunners found out that, with a little juggling, an electrician's screwdriver would do the same job, so they could leave the key in a safe place and use the screwdriver instead.

To the gunner's right hand is his powered controller: a fixed handle with a grip switch and a small, rubber-covered movable dome on the forward face. With the power kit running, the gunner would squeeze in on the grip switch, thereby activating the switch, then by moving his right thumb on the dome he could traverse and elevate under powered operation. The commander had a similar controller, but on pressing his grip switch he could override the gunner. In the event of the power kit failing, or for tactical reasons, a hand traverse handle is provided; however, even though it has a fine and a coarse setting, it is a very hard job to traverse the turret using it – although it does serve as a useful punishment. There is also an emergency power mode that can be selected by the commander;

Specification – T72

Crew	Three
Combat weight	44,500kg (40 tons)
Length	Gun forward 9.53m (31.26ft)
Width	Over skirts 3.59m (11.78ft)
Height	2.222m (7.29ft)
Road speed	60kmph (mph)
Range	480km (300 miles); with long-range tanks fitted, 550km (342 miles)
Engine	V-12 multi-fuel 840hp @2,000rpm
Transmission	Hydraulically assisted, seven forward and one reverse
Armament	1x125mm, 1x 7.62mm co-ax and 1x 12.7mm AA
Ammunition	45 main rounds including six ATGW, co-ax 2,000, and AA 300
Armour	Turret 280mm (11in) approx., nose 80mm (3in), glacis 200mm (7.8in) inclined, giving 500–600mm (20—24in)

The T72 would have been one of Chieftain's main opponents if the cold war had ever broken into full-scale war. It was armed with a 125mm main gun loaded by a carousel auto loader. Whilst being a good feature in that it allows a lower turret silhouette, this would appear to be the main reason that so many T72s lost their turrets in fighting when hit, as the carousel was located directly below the turret and when full could carry twenty-four complete rounds. Later models were able to fire the AT 11 missile through the barrel, giving the T72 a long-range AT capability. Penetration figures are APFSDS 150mm (5.9in) sloped at 60 degrees at 2,000m (6,560ft). Chieftain seemed to be able to dish out the damage and take it and survive when it did come up against the T72 in the Iran–Iraq war, and in the Gulf War when it was used by the Kuwaitis.

TOGS Chieftain: looking at the gunner station, showing just how much has to be crammed into a small space; visible at the front of the commander's controller is the gunner's TOGS screen. (RCMS Shrivenham)

this works from the batteries alone, and will provide a fixed rate of power traverse and other electrical services.

Situated centrally to the gunner is an aircraft-type firing handle that allows the gunner to select the following: main or co-ax weapons, laser, autolay, and ammunition type for the input into the computer; it also enables him to fire the weapons. Close to this handle is the box that controls the heater and light source for the MRS, and to his left are the two pointers that must be aligned before using the MRS.

The gunner's seat is located above the sixteen-bit fire control computer, while other components are located around the turret. On the floor plate he has a foot pedal that he can flick to the up or down position, to fire the co-ax when no electrical power is available.

IN SUMMARY

The inside of the turret is therefore a very crowded place, and this is before the crew have added their own personal kit – mugs, plates, respirators, NBC suits, weapons, maps and a host of other items that they will need. Furthermore, if necessary they will sleep and eat and carry out any other functions within the confines of the vehicle whilst it is closed down.

3 Chieftain in Service

Chieftain at last came into service in November 1966, and the first regiment to receive it was the 11th Hussars, stationed at Hohne in BAOR. This was a great honour for the regiment, and one repeated years later when they were also the first to receive Challenger 1, much to the chagrin of the other RAC regiments.

Chieftain had been the subject of much publicity: it had been shown off to the public several times, and it also featured as cut-away drawings in several of the boys' magazines of the day. Nevertheless, a lot of people connected with it had a great many misgivings about its being brought into service, as they were still desperately unhappy with the L60 powerpack, many forecasting that it would blight the tank's reputation. Foremost amongst these, as we have already seen, was Major General Leakey, the director of

fighting vehicles; he was overruled in a political decision, but was sadly proved right in the end.

The big day came, and the CO of the 11th Hussars has given his impressions of the regiment's first Chieftains in Col Forty's book on Chieftain. When he first saw them he thought they looked good, and very sleek and also quiet in comparison to the Centurion – though many people who have served on both vehicles would disagree with his observation regarding quietness.

CONVERSION TRAINING

Over the coming months the 11th received its new tanks in batches, as no changeover is done all at once; so for a while Centurion and Chieftain were stablemates, although the Centurions were

M60A3, Chieftain's stablemate. (Merlin Robson)

being prepared for disposal, and never really featured again in the regiment's training programme.

There are many other aspects of taking on a new vehicle besides having it in camp. New stores have to be indented for, old stock must be accounted for and returned, and fuel supplies must be adjusted – in this case more diesel was needed, and less petrol. Also the 105mm ammunition had to be replaced with 120mm, and as the tank had new optics and other secret equipment, the vehicle park had to have security wire around it. Inevitably, too, there would be a continuous stream of regimental personnel of all ranks leaving and returning from courses on the vehicle. However, the 11th coped very well, as did all subsequent regiments, and eventually found themselves fully equipped as a Chieftain regiment.

This procedure has not really changed, and indeed has happened twice since those early days of the sixties with the introduction into service of

Challenger 1 and then Challenger 2. When the author visited the King's Royal Hussars (the present-day descendants of the 11th) in Munster as late as 1996, the wire-mesh security screen was in place, and it was even secured at lunch-time, this time because of the addition of Chobham armour.

The next regiment in line for Chieftain was the 17th/21st Lancers, and the author's regiment eventually took over from them in 1969 in Sennelager, BAOR. The regiment experienced much the same sort of problems whilst settling in, although the training was probably even more intense as the unit had been on armoured cars for some time, having served in Aden and then returning to Northern Ireland. So a lot of the 'old tank sweats' had left by then; but there were still enough left to regale us very young new troopers with stories about the 'good old Cent'. To give the soldiers a source of inspiration, and as a means of helping to carry out conversion training, one Mk 2 Chieftain – 04 EB 58 – was sent to

A Chieftain on parade in Berlin, sporting unique camouflage invented by Major Clendon Daukes of 4/7 DG. (Neil Hamilton)

Northern Ireland. As the first unit to have a tank in Ireland since the training days of World War II, we felt this gave us a small claim to fame.

The tank did its job, and certainly impressed those who were to use it very soon. The regiment's last large exercise, that was always carried out on the mainland, was on Salisbury plain, where several Centurions were borrowed to teach the potential crews tank tactics, and also how to live on it. The evenings were devoted to the same subject, as a great deal had to be learned: on arrival in BAOR we would be expected to be ready for the role. It is a great credit to the officers, soldiers and instructors that that aim was achieved.

The above gives a small overview as to the problems involved in moving to a new vehicle type, and very shortly all the regiments had been through the conversion process – which did become easier as time went on. In BAOR the cycle of events for regiments carried on, since the winter months were used for trade training, leading to low-level exercises on Soltau training area, followed by a period of range firing. The culmination of the year was the major FTX, which at the time allowed the exercising troops to range all over the area, with very few restrictions placed on movement. This would soon change, however, and more and more restrictions were brought into place.

FIRST IMPRESSIONS: THE SHORTCOMINGS

Throughout this time the crews were getting to know the vehicle and to learn its good and bad points. Definitely a bad point was the unreliability of the L60; another was the lack of any form of heating in the vehicle at all. The latter led to many pairs of rubber-soled boots being inadvertently burnt, because when the tank was halted the crews were in the habit of lifting the engine decks and sitting with their feet on the engine and gearbox. When pushed to fit some sort of heating, the

---

Getting Started

Amongst other tricks the author has seen was bump-starting the squadron leader's tank which had an unserviceable starter motor: the crew would park it on the edge of a hill every night during exercises on Salisbury Plain, and in the morning when the squadron was ready to move, the 2i/c's tank would gently nudge it over the hill and allow it to roll off. It worked, but it wasn't the recommended way to do it – and what would a modern Health and Safety expert make of it?

MoD flatly refused, and even stated that it was not cold enough in BAOR to warrant the expenditure of money to develop any heating – though the same MoD fitted three heaters into Chieftain during the last years of its life. Prior to that, many weird schemes were tried, including heated suits, all of which failed magnificently. The 4/7 RDG also took over one tank from 17/21st that had an experimental heater pack fitted on the rear of the turret; this apparently worked very well till the day it caught fire: result – one new tank and no heater.

One unforeseen by-product of the unreliability of the L60 was the amount of 'bodging' that the Chieftain would take to keep it going; this included tying a length of string to the fuel injection solenoid – when it was required to start the engine the string was pulled tight, and this would lift the linkage and off it would go. Similarly the string was released in order to stop it. Crews became very adept at preparing the vehicle for major assembly lifts by REME, thus saving the latter many hours of work when they arrived.

GUNNERY TRAINING

By now the crews were getting used to Chieftain and all its quirks, and a lot of time was spent in gunnery training; after all, this was the main reason for its existence. In fact, Higher Authority were so impressed that they organized a special

Left: *Most exercises start with movement by tank transporter. This saves wear and tear on the vehicles and roads. Here, C/S 2R of 4/7 RDG loads up. (Mark Wagstaff)*

Below: *Concentration area at the end of an exercise. Note the cluttered look of the turrets, and the commander GPMG on the floor in front of C/S 23. (Mark Wagstaff)*

fire-power demonstration to show off the gun and vehicle. This was called Exercise Fire Crest and was held on Hohne ranges on 24 April 1969; in his invitation the Commander-in-Chief in BAOR described it as a 'demonstration to show the accuracy and lethality of the Chieftain tank'. Like many of the fire power demonstrations, for those invited this was purely and simply a good day out, and I often wondered how many of the visiting dignitaries realized how much work went into it so that everything happened as it was meant to.

Regiments would spend two weeks at Hohne ranges being put through their paces by their own gunnery staff and by those from the BAOR gunnery school and the Lulworth School, and were graded on their performance; as the ranges were also one way of gauging a regiment's overall standard, it was very important to them to achieve an excellent grade on this. Prior to this the crews would spend several periods each day in the classroom and at the simulators, learning all the various drills required for the ranges.

Above: *A familiar sight: the REME FV 434 version of the FV 432 removes a gearbox from a 4/7 RDS Chieftain on the Soltau training area, BAOR. (Paul Kay)*

Below: *If all else failed, the dead tank could be winched onto a tank transporter for its homeward journey. (Paul Kay)*

Ready to be ammo-bashed. These are sealed boxes of SH/PRAC waiting to be opened. (Author's collection)

The endless chore of 'ammo-bashing': the packing cases and practice SH and DS/T can be seen. The troops are all being kept at it by WO2 Barry Boothroyd (Bootsie) 4/7 RDG. A sharp eye has to be kept, because if totals did not tally then all the boxes would be offloaded and checked – not a fun thing! (Author's collection)

Ammunition Bashing

Those who have never opened a container of tank ammunition would be surprised at just how well it is packed. Once unpacked, the ammunition would then be loaded back onto the trucks ready to be distributed to the tanks, and all the empty boxes would be sealed up again and loaded onto other trucks to be taken back to the bunkers. But before this could happen there was 'chitting', when each container had to be inspected as being empty, and a signed 'free from explosives' certificate – or 'chit' – placed into it. This chore usually fell to the sergeant major or one of the SNCOs, and was fairly straightforward. If, however, any ammunition was found in a container when it arrived back at the depot, then all hell was let loose on the poor unfortunate whose name was on the certificate.

Crews today have the advantage of all the sophistication available to Challenger 2 training, and they would not believe how crews trained then. In a building on camp would be one or two classroom instructional models known as CIMs: these were facsimiles of a real turret, but built of mild steel with large cut-out portions so the class could see what was happening in the turret. The gun could be loaded and fired, and would recoil all under hydraulic systems, thus allowing all turret drills to be taught. To simulate the firing of the main gun, a .22 rifle was fitted on a bracket linked to the gun so that it would follow the main gun in elevation and depression (as it used to be done on Conqueror and Centurion). Later versions became more complicated and were hard to calibrate. Moving targets were pulled across the range by means of electric motors and wire traces; these were often shot apart, and then the whole lesson would stop whilst the wires were replaced.

Primitive as it may seem to today's computer-generated images, it did actually work – but the crews also put a lot of work into it, and quite often spent time on it outside working hours. According to Cpl Danny Budgen, a commander in those early days:

We would do classroom work during the day, then after 1600, when normally we would think of going home, the troops would rotate through the CIM for turret drill; and this was not helped by the regiment having only the one CIM. The period of training was very intense due to the fact that this was to be the first gunnery camp since converting to Chieftain. As might be expected, there were all the usual moans and groans – but it paid off, with the regiment achieving an excellent report. After that I never experienced such a high level of gunnery training again.

Gunnery Camp

The gunnery camp was one of the highlights of the year, and a 'dream trip' for the bull of a sergeant major. All the tanks would be lined up on the firing point at an angle to the front edge; this allowed maximum access to the charge bins in the turret for replenishing ammunition. Behind this would be ammo compounds, a smoking area and a briefing area, all meticulously marked out on the ground in white mine tape on stakes. The SQMS would have put up a marquee, and if he was enterprising enough would be selling egg rolls and sweets, crisps and coffee or soft drinks – all profits to the squadron fund, and thus benefiting everyone. In the briefing area would be a blackboard on which the squadron gunnery instructor would outline his brief for the day's programme.

Gunnery camp involved a lot of hard work and shouting, but when you actually came to fire that 120mm and saw the flash as your round hit a hard target, it was all suddenly worthwhile. The drivers were probably the worst off, as they had nothing to do most of the time, so were always commandeered for that most hateful chore, ammunition bashing: this involved collecting the ammo from the bunkers by truck, then offloading it and unpacking it.

On the Ranges

Many lessons were learned on the ranges, probably the most important being how to keep the bag charge dry; very often either the charge container had leaked and this had not been noticed until a charge landed in it with a wet-sounding noise, or the bin lid hadn't been closed and rain had come into the turret and soaked them. This was one of the biggest problems in the early days; later on, the solution to keeping them nice and dry was to make the charge outer casing from nitro-cellulose – the charges on Challenger 2 are made in this way.

Another problem was that if water were allowed to seep into the D/ST rounds, when they were fired it tended to act like a shock absorber and prevent separation of the petals and pot, thus making the round inherently unstable. This produced some amazingly erratic flights down-range that were applauded by the crews for their sheer entertainment value, but certainly not by the gunnery chiefs.

Experience taught crews the importance of rigorous attention to detail when servicing: they had to follow the book to the letter. There are several tales concerning crews that became lax in their servicing routine, and suffered the consequences: for example, firing the muzzle bore sight down-range because it had been left in the barrel instead of being stowed, and no one had noticed during the action drills. This usually turned out to be a bad day for that crew. Another crew left oil in the barrel, and after firing, the pressure of the rounds forcing their way up the barrel had compressed the oil so much that it had bulged the end of it. Result: that crew quickly learned how much work was involved in changing a barrel in the field.

CHIEFTAIN'S ENGINE PROBLEMS BECOME POLITICAL

Meanwhile field exercises carried on, but they were still plagued by problems with the L60; in fact the situation became so bad in the early seventies that all Chieftains were grounded. Thus troops on exercise were obliged to find other ways of passing the time while Parliament debated the major issue of Chieftain fan belts. The 4/7 RDG ended up running a series of exercises that involved map reading and tasks of ingenuity: for instance, collecting a set number of wasps in a bottle. It was a very hot summer so the troops enjoyed the break, but in all honesty it was a ridiculous state of affairs for tank soldiers to have to occupy themselves in this manner. Later on the MoD laid the blame on the drivers, accusing them of poor maintenance; but this was no more than an easy way out for the government, and to save face, and quite rightly they were to be proved wrong.

Following on from this episode, in 1978 a sub-committee of the House of Commons technical committee made a report that praised the range-finding and gun on Chieftain as first class, but confessed to being greatly dismayed that such a potent system should be continually let down by the engine. Following this report a programme code-named Sundance was drawn up to rectify the major problems, namely the failure of cylinder liners, gear casing and fan pulley casing. To a great extent this programme did sort out most of the problems and a few more besides, and produced a fairly reliable engine; as mentioned elsewhere, the author had one of the first 13A packs fitted, and it ran with no leaks or problems for two years.

It is interesting to observe that at the time Leyland, who manufactured the L60, brought out a sales brochure advertising the Sundance pack as a 'new engine', and extolling its virtues to the extent of stating that 'its use in Chieftain MBT has proved it to be the most reliable MBT power-plant currently in service.'

MORE TRIALS AND TRAINING AND NEW BUILDS

The circle of exercises usually revolved around the Soltau training area (now returned to the Germans, and recovering very well) and the major FTX. Soltau usually consisted of low-level

The view from a driver's cab as tanks advance. (Paul Kay)

Typical German countryside, as can be viewed during the major FTXs during the training year. (Mark Wagstaff)

training, building at troop level and so on right up to squadron level, and finally finishing in a regimental exercise. As already mentioned, the major FTX usually took place later in the year, and was the culmination of that year's training for the brigade. At one time these exercises would be for three weeks, but they were soon cut to a fortnight, with no tracked movement at all over the weekends.

Tanks would deploy on these exercises fully stowed with everything that could be carried to make the crews' life a little more comfortable and bearable, especially if they were stranded due to component failure. It should be said here that, although the L60 does have a bad reputation, in some ways it was rather unfair because of course there were engines that ran well, but those are never remembered. In fact a tank was just as likely to be brought to a halt because of problems with the gearbox and the aux gen. Although aux-gen problems could be overcome by running the main engine at high revs, this meant that the electrical generators that ran off it were also brought into use, and because of the noise, and the fact that the

Fun Making Training Films

Chieftain had by now been accepted by its crews, and its service life and its crews' life merged quite well. Furthermore, aside from the usual run of regimental life, it was sometimes called on to carry out other duties, such as trials or making training films. This could be deadly boring, but it could be fun, too. On one occasion a film was being produced for the Royal Engineers, and the idea was to blow a hole in a track on Sidbury hill on Salisbury plain, and drive the tank into it to show how an armoured vehicle could be stopped. So the hole was dug and the tank was driven into it – but two things had not been taken into account by the sappers: one was that this tank had a particularly powerful engine; and secondly, the driver, Cpl 'Spiv' Baker of 4/7 RDG, wanted to prove that he and his tank were more than a match for any engineer. So out of the hole he drove, much to the consternation of the said engineers, who put more explosive into the hole and tried again – and again the tank came out. It took four attempts before they succeeded. They also tried to bog it in a river – but sure enough, out it came, flattening the camera in the process.

What appears to be a well stuck tank. In fact just after this photograph was taken it drove out of the mud, much to everyone's amazement. (Author)

A naval Chieftain? Call sign 1A of 4/7 DG cruising up the River Avon during the making of an MOD film. (Author)

driver had to be in the cab to keep the accelerator depressed as no hand throttle was fitted, it could never be anything more than a stop-gap.

By 1969 the next new build mark was coming into service: this was the Mk 3, which had an improved aux-gen, 650bhp engine, the Mk 2 version of the no. 15 cupola, oil-filled top rollers, axle arms and track adjuster. Following on from that was the Mk 3/3: this had the 720bhp engine, a low-loss engine air cleaner, and the extended-range graticule for the RMG. Around this time, and in tandem with Mk 5 production which was the last new build for the British army, the rear of Chieftain changed shape with the transmission decks no longer lying flat but at an angle; this was to allow for the expansion box for the main engine exhaust to be mounted on top of the gearbox.

FOREIGN SALES

Although Chieftain had been receiving rather a bad press, the government was still keen to make foreign sales; these were needed to help fund improvements to the UK fleet for the future. In the early sixties the British government had lost possibly its best customer in the Israelis because of its blinkered tactics after the Six Day War, preferring to comply with the policy dictated by the Arab states, who then gleefully held the country to ransom over oil. As will be seen later, this lost a vast amount of data that had been gained by the Israelis during the desert trial they conducted with two Chieftains.

Most arms-buying countries at the time still relied on the USA market for their equipment, as it was plentiful and very cheap; so trying to sell a high tec and expensive weapon system such as Chieftain was always going to be difficult. But it was very important for the UK economy, because a big order would secure jobs in the two tank-manufacturing sites at Leeds and Newcastle, as the UK order would be completed by the early 1970s. Then in 1971 the Shah of Iran placed an

A Chieftain being literally blown out of the ground in Canada after being frozen in.
(Clement Laforce DRES)

Whoops! A tank of 4/7 RDG sinks in the mud at Batus. A Centurion ARV can be seen
trying to recover it. (4/7 RDG magazine)

order for 707 Chieftains: the Mk 3/3P and 5/3P, the 'P' standing for 'Persia'; also included in the order were a number of bridgelayers and recovery vehicles. This order was completed by 1978. Iran had also taken delivery of 187 further Chieftains known as FV 4030/1. These had more fuel, better mine protection, electronic control of the gear change to make the driver's job easier, and additional shock absorbers on the rear suspension unit.

In 1974 Iran placed an order for 125 Shir 1 and 1,225 Shir 2, to be delivered from 1980 onwards; but in 1979 this was cancelled on the orders of the new rulers of Iran following the fall of the Shah. Eventually an order was taken from Jordan under the name of Khalid, for FV4030/2: basically this was the front of Chieftain and the rear of Challenger, so that the Challenger powerpack and layout could be fitted in Chieftain. FV4030/3 went on to be the basis of Challenger 1, as used by the British Army; this filled the gap left by the cancellation of the MBT 80 project, which had meant there was no firm replacement for Chieftain.

Navigating with TOGS

On one of his last exercises, the author vividly recalls being the troop sergeant for a troop of 17/21st tanks involved in training future troop leaders; he had been away from tanks for a few years, and was acting as operator for a very confident officer. He remembers thundering along through woods in pitch darkness, the commander using TOGS to navigate, and the author using II binoculars to help watch for obstacles – and observing that not so long ago, an exercise like this would have been unthinkable.

In August 1981 Oman took over twelve ex-British Army Chieftains on long loan; these were eventually sold to them, along with fifteen new-build vehicles, named the 'Qayd Al Ardh'. These were known to ROF as the Mk 15 Chieftain, a situation that sometimes causes confusion when it is a question of identifying the various marks. These were delivered by 1985; they were equipped with the Nanoquest sight that incorporates the Ferranti-type 520 laser range finder.

Chieftain in service.

The effect of a Chieftain firing DS/T at night. (Author)

These sales helped to restore the tattered reputation of Chieftain; and all the time it was being progressively upgraded with the latest technology.

CANADIAN PROVING GROUNDS

One of the hardest proving grounds for Chieftain was the vast prairie known as BATUS (British Army Training Unit Suffield) in Alberta, Canada. This was set up initially by Lt Col William Le Blanc Smith of the 4/7RDG and a small team, many of whom enjoyed life in Canada so much that they married and settled there. The idea was to provide a training ground where the Army could carry out combined arms exercises with live fire and movement – something that no European training area could offer. The Alberta prairie was leased initially for ten years – and we are still there now. The training value is immense, and it also provides employment and funds for the local region.

A battle group will spend at least six weeks in BATUS; the first few days are spent in deploying and taking over the equipment, then three weeks on the area doing live fire exercises, then back to the camp to clean and service the vehicles ready for hand-over. This means that the vehicles are really hammered for the ten months that they are in use, and regretfully a lot of the cosmetic attention that would be lavished on them in UK or BAOR is just not possible due to the limit on time. What it does achieve, however, is equipment that is well run in and used – indeed, some say that this is the best way to look after vehicle.

What is certain is that keeping them in a hangar and only taking them out every few months is not good for them, especially engine seals and gaskets. To illustrate this fact, regiments used to seal their war reserve tanks in a large plastic enclosure that was kept at a constant temperature and humidity: this was called the dri-clad system. Once every year the batteries were fitted and the engines run up – and sure enough, a common fault would be seals blown somewhere in the system. So it appears that being driven hard may do them good.

A particularly good thing about BATUS training was that all a vehicle's systems would be used, all day and probably all night as well, unlike a normal exercise when equipment such as the weapons would not be used.

Probably the main opponent for Chieftain: the T72 with reactive armour blocks and a 125mm gun with auto-loader. (Merlin Robinson)

The Russian T64, one of the enemies that the Chieftain may have had to face if war had broken out. Note the damaged spotlight next to the gun. (Merlin Robinson)

CHIEFTAIN CONTINUES TO BE UPGRADED

Throughout the late 1970s and early 1980s Chieftain continued to receive new equipment that was designed to enhance it and prolong its life until a decision on a replacement could be made. By this time it was proving to be a fairly reliable vehicle, most of the problems with the engine having been solved; but it was still a dirty tank to work on. It was eventually fitted with a thermal optical gunnery system known as TOGS, and this gave it a truly twenty-four-hour capability.

The end for Chieftain was very double-edged, as it was being forced out slowly by Challenger and the conventional forces treaty Europe (CFE), which required the signatories to destroy set amounts of military equipment. Thus Chieftain was the ideal weapon system to destroy and this happened very quickly, followed by yet another reduction in the armed forces, and more Regimental amalgamations; as a result, fewer tanks were required.

CHIEFTAIN OUT OF SERVICE

At the time of writing the last Chieftains are still giving sterling service to the British Army as bridgelayers and AVRE (of which more in a later chapter). But these will soon be consigned to the scrapheap, with only a lucky few going to museums or to enthusiasts for preservation. For all the criticism that has so often been levelled at Chieftain, it is interesting to note the outcome of a survey carried out on an internet site recently: people were told to imagine themselves in a pre-determined time frame, and asked which vehicle they would choose to be in, in a war situation – and surprisingly the majority said 'Chieftain'. My own favourite answer came from an American, who said: 'Chieftain had the looks that said "I don't have to move, I am big enough to sit here and slug it out with you!" '

BUT FOND MEMORIES

In the end the UK crews developed a soft spot for Chieftain, and the author believes that if it had been called to face the hordes of T62s, 64s and T72s, it would have given a good account of itself – and in doing so may have stopped things getting any worse. But for whatever reason, it never came to that, and we should be thankful. Nevertheless Chieftain has seen considerable combat in the hands of other armies.

CHIEFTAIN IN COMBAT

The Fall of the Shah

Chieftains' first skirmish was during the fall of the Shah, and if they had been used more aggressively the revolution might well have had a different outcome. However, Iranian Army Chieftain tank commanders seemed only too ready to surrender their vehicle intact, standing on their turret waving flags. Sadly that seemed to be the general attitude for the army.

Chieftains were next used by Iran in defence of their country in the war with Iraq. It

An Iranian Chieftain after being hit by APFS-DS from a T72. Apparently the crew survived, although 'shook up'. Notice how neat the exit hole is. (Crown Copyright)

The more serious side of tank warfare: an Iranian Chieftain, probably penetrated twice – just one of those hits would have killed the crew. (Tank Museum)

was very hard to judge exactly how equipment had fared in this war, as both sides were relatively untrained for the modern, fast-ranging battle that we as Europeans are used to examining. In 1981 the Iranians launched a counter-offensive at Susangard; but at the end of the day the battle had been won by the Iraqis, leaving 200 Iranian tanks on the battlefield. None of the war reports describe any large-scale tank versus tank battles: more often there was a skirmish that resulted in a victory. For instance, one Iraqi officer proudly showed off his capture of an undamaged Chieftain that he claimed to have hit on the turret from 200m, killing the crew but not damaging the vehicle. One can only assume that all the crew were opened up and were killed by shrapnel from a rocket grenade. The vehicle was then driven back to Iraqi lines.

The outcome of the war is well known. The Iranians lost a great many of their vehicles, and these ended up in a captured vehicle park in Baghdad, amongst them at least thirty-one Chieftains, most totally undamaged. Iran had started the war with nearly 875 Chieftains, but by 1988 this number had declined to around 300, partly due to the heavy servicing load, coupled with the UK's refusal to supply spare parts, including engines – although some sources claim that parts were supplied.

Iraq presented Jordan with a gift of about fifty Chieftains, but this rather embarrassed the Jordanians, because although they had supported the Iraqis, they were really trying to play the middle road – so a gift like this was not really wanted. Charles Perkins tells me that when he was last in Jordan a few years ago, he saw a boneyard of armoured vehicles, including Chieftains, near the central tank refurbishment facility. The Chieftains had been cannibalized, and were sat there slowly deteriorating; however, Charles' Jordanian contacts were very disinclined to talk about the vehicles, perhaps because they did not want Iraq to find out that their gift had been left to rust away.

Showing Chieftain can do it. (Tim Babb)

Leyland L60 Sundance Engine	
Type	Six-cylinder, direct injection, water-cooled, opposed-piston two-stroke
Bore	117.48mm (4.63in)
Stroke	146.05mm (5.75in)
Capacity	19 litres (1,160cu in)
Max rating	750bhp (net) @ 2,250 crankshaft rpm
Max torque	1,540lb/ft (net) @ 1,500/1,600 crankshaft rpm
Compression ratio	16.2 to 1
Firing order	1, 6, 2, 4, 3, 5

The L60 is a vertical, water-cooled, six-cylinder engine of 19-litre capacity. It utilises a twin crankshaft layout using conventional rods for each piston. The upper crankshaft is coupled to the lower one by a series of gears, and the starter ring and output shaft are driven by one of the gears in this train. At the front is an auxiliary gear train which drives the roots-type scavenge blower, the lubricating pump, fuel injection pump and the generator. The in-line, twelve-element injection pump is fitted with a hydraulic governor, and feeds two injector nozzles for each cylinder. The engine oil is provided from a dry sump where the oil is not in a sump under the engine as in a car, but in a separate oil tank within the engine bay, to save space. Oil is circulated around the engine by means of a high capacity, gear-type oil pump. An oil cooler and centrifugal filter are also part of the system, along with conventional filters.

The Gulf War

The Chieftain's last combat must have been during the Gulf War, when the Kuwaitis stood against Iraq. Due to Arab pride it is very hard to obtain the full and true story of what happened with the Kuwaiti armour. Murray Hammick of International Defence Review visited the Gulf prior to the coalition invasion, and here are some of his comments on the Kuwaiti Chieftains:

We visited a Kuwaiti armoured unit, equipped with a mixture of Chieftain and M8 that had been delivered after the Iraqi invasion. The Kuwaitis showed a great affection for their Chieftains: originally they had about 150, of which at least fifty made it from Kuwait. They praised its ruggedness, and its ability to take hits well. The Barr and Stroud laser impressed them and allowed them to engage Iraqi armour at long range (7,000m+) – at least, it was implied by a senior officer that APDS was used at this range, though this was difficult to confirm.

The L60 came in for criticism, but it was added that it was quite reliable. The team drove a Chieftain at 40kmph (25mph) over the desert, and none of the familiar white smoke was visible, suggesting that the 'drive 'em hard' theory mentioned earlier might be correct. Ammunition supply was good, with the vehicle bombed up with both natures of ammunition. The hardest thing the team found was trying to obtain an accurate picture of the actual involvement in the fighting. The crews were very enthusiastic in their replies to questions on combat, although the consensus of opinion was that the T62 opened up like a flower when hit with APDS. They were able to offer a number of lessons learned the hard way, that in spite of the excellent armour on Chieftain, one crew had been knocked out by an RPG7 hit on their idler wheel.

IN CONCLUSION

This, then, will probably be Chieftain's last foray into combat, although nothing is ever certain, especially in that area; and Chieftain still soldiers on – but not for too much longer, one would imagine.

4   The Role of the Crew Members

A tank cannot operate efficiently on its own: as a single unit it becomes vulnerable to all manner of attack. From this requirement has evolved the infantry/tank co-operation that was developed back in the early days of World War I. And although much rivalry exists between the two arms, both know that on a modern battlefield they each need the support of the other to survive.

THE ARMOURED REGIMENT

The way in which an armoured regiment is organized has seen various changes over the years since the end of the war, largely because personnel numbers have been gradually reduced by successive governments; obviously with each reduction the regiments have had to reorganize in order to make best use of their remaining manpower. So how does this affect the crews, and the way in which they are organized?

Within the British Army regimental system the Royal Armoured Corps is formed from the descendants of the old cavalry regiments and the Royal Tank Regiment, the latter being the first to use the tank in World War 1. Each regiment is broken down into squadrons; these are the armoured equivalent of an infantry company, although the numbers are vastly different between the two. Each squadron is then broken down into troops, and within the troops are the individual crews.

The organization of squadrons and troops is quite firmly established, but regiments still manage to include their own regimental idiosyn-crasies. It might only be the way something is worn, or in a job title, but it immediately distinguishes that unit, and it would be a great loss if these were ever to be banished by the bureaucrats.

THE TROOP

The troop, then, is the basic unit within the squadron, and will normally consist of three tanks. In the late seventies, however, the 4/7th, among others, tried a variation of this, so that 1st and 2nd troops had four tanks, and 3rd and 4th had three. This turned out very well for the two troops with four tanks, because if one tank was out of action for whatever reason, it meant they still had a full unit of three; this gave them an enviable flexibility. Whereas if the other two troops lost a tank, they immediately became less efficient in what they could achieve with only two vehicles.

There are twelve members in a tank troop: the troop leader, the troop sergeant, the troop corporal and a lieutenant corporal; the rest are all troopers. The troop leader is usually a second lieutenant or lieutenant, though sometimes it may be a staff sergeant, who would be known as a TSM or 'troop sergeant major' (this being a very good old cavalry rank). The troop leader is responsible for everything to do with the troop, although this is always in conjunction with the troop sergeant, who is the real power behind the throne.

This is because a young officer will come to a troop, stay a couple of years, and then move on; whereas the sergeant will be there a lot longer, and may well have risen through the ranks

77

within that troop. He will also know all the tricks of getting the best for his troop.

The troop corporal will be responsible for many of the administrative tasks necessary for running the troop, and his role is important because he is the link between the officer and the SNCO, and the soldiers in the troop. Responsibility will also be given to individual troopers for matters to do with gunnery, radio and driving: these will be soldiers who have completed their various courses at a class one standard, or whatever the current equivalent is (the army is always changing the title of their qualifications), and each will be in charge of keeping the troop leader and the troop up to date on all matters pertaining to his trade. If the lieutenant corporal is a radio operator he will usually find himself operating as the troop leader's operator.

The troop itself will become a very close-knit group: to some extent it may be likened to a small family within the framework of the larger regimental family.

This is by no means a firm categorization of a troop, but I do believe it is fairly typical of who does what within a troop. We will now look at the individual crew members in more detail, and their role within the turret.

STARTING UP: THE ALLOCATION OF TASKS

The vehicle commander has the ultimate responsibility for the vehicle and all the crew beneath him; whatever checks or drills have been carried out by the crew, if one of them has failed to accomplish any task or detail as he should have done, then the 'buck' stops with the commander. This is obviously in addition to any tasks within the troop beholden to his position as commander.

Before he can give the order for the systems to be started up, the commander has to satisfy himself that all loose kit is stowed away, that no

---

The Wide Horizon Concept

The most impressive troop that the author has ever served in was during the eighties, when he took part in an exercise to prove what was then called the 'wide horizon concept'. One of the aims of this exercise was to practise the battlefield replacement system of casualties in both men and equipment. For this exercise tanks from the 4/7th were seconded to the 2nd Royal Tank Regiment – an experience for all concerned, although I like to think a good one.

Towards the closing phase the author's troop, which was operating as a four tank troop, lost its troop leader, then its sergeant, leaving as survivors the author, who then held the rank of corporal, and a corporal from RTR. The numbers were then variously made up: first, by the arrival of a major from the United States Army, who two days previously had been teaching in Bovington before being called up and whisked to Germany. Then a tank from the armoured delivery squadron turned up, commanded by a trooper with a crew from four different regiments. Later in the day yet another tank appeared, this time from the 17/21st Lancers and commanded by a 2/lt; but the best was yet to come, for on the scene appeared a Chieftain AVLB, complete with bridge. The Royal Engineer corporal commander explained that he had been ordered to attach himself to us, as there was nowhere else for him to go.

This now meant that we had five Chieftain gun tanks with commanders ranging in rank from major to trooper, plus a bridge-layer – so it was most certainly different. The major's solution was to split the troop into a heavy and light section, with the AVLB trailing the light section; the heavy section consisted of the major and the two corporals, while the rest made up the light section. For five days we paraded around the exercise area and – surprisingly – proved very good, tactically; although the logistics sometimes horrified people: for instance, when we turned up for a replenishment of rations and fuel, the admin. staff were expecting a normal tank troop, and instead they were greeted with this strange set-up.

But all good things come to an end, and eventually the exercise drew to its conclusion, and we all returned to our units. A year late the author was on a course at Bovington and met up with the American major, who said that that had been the best armoured fun he had had for a long time.

---

stowage bin lids have been left off, no engine deck covers are open, all weapons are correctly fitted, and that all crew members are safely at their stations. This is very important, because the risk of injury and damage is obviously much greater once under power; the turret in particular is capable of bending weapons and crushing unsuspecting limbs.

STARTING THE ENGINES

Once the commander is satisfied that all is in order, he will tell the driver to start up the engines, communicating with him by means of a live i/c system. 'Live' means that the boom mike on the crew member's helmet does not need a button push in order to talk into it: as long as i/c is selected on the various radio boxes at each station, it will function. This is a vast improvement over earlier systems, where the headset and microphone were separate items. Various cables link the system from the driver's cab through to the turret, so it was important to find some way of ensuring the system continued to function even when the turret was traversing. This is achieved by means of a rotary base junction located at the centre of the turret. In its simplest form it consists of two components, one fixed on the hull floor, and the other located on the turret floor. Inside are electrical contacts that transmit power from the moving section (turret) to the fixed section (hull): without this, there would soon be a very large knot of cables.

The driver will start up the aux-gen first, then the main engine; once the aux-gen has come on line, then the gunner can start switching on the powered laying equipment. This is controlled by two switches on the powered laying-control panel above his right shoulder; once the equipment is running, he will carry out what is known as the 'six switch test'. This confirms that various safety switches are functioning, and it also ensures that a condition known as 'creep' has been trimmed out of the system. Creep occurs when

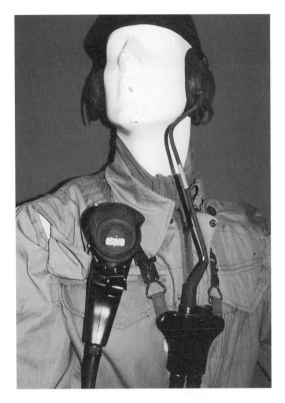

This is the earliest headset and microphone that AFV crews would have used. This is the commander's version, with a sector switch on the microphone. The crewman's was similar, but without the sector switch. These gave no protection to the wearer's head. (RCMS Shrivenham)

Trouble Shooting

On one occasion after a firing exercise and having cleaned the weapons, a turret crew stowed the GPMG in one of the charge bins, but mistakenly placed it barrel down. The commander was not with the vehicle at the time: he was attending a briefing for their move back to barracks, so the crew's mistake went uncorrected. Thus when they next traversed the turret rear, they bent the mg in half. It was the commander who was the first to be in trouble, because he was responsible for the crew; but needless to say, recriminations further down the line followed swiftly.

the grip switch is pressed: if the system is running correctly, then no movement should take place; but if the turret creeps left or right, then it must be trimmed out.

Setting Up TOGS and the Radio

Once the gunner is satisfied that the gun kit is running correctly, he can then, in conjunction with the commander, carry out the various tests that are required if IFCS and TOGS are going to be used. TOGS is used a great deal because it can pick up heat sources during the day or night; so for example, if an enemy is hiding in a wood with their engine running, the TOGS system should be able to pick it up.

While the commander and gunner are carrying out their checks, the operator will be checking his radios, and making sure that all his BATCO codes are up to date. This is a system of numbers and letters for encoding messages for security. He will be checking frequencies

A very useful piece of equipment, if looked after: the issue petrol cooker and its cooking pot. (Author's collection)

Head Cook and Bottle Washer

The loader has to double as head cook and bottle washer whilst the crew are in the vehicle, and watching a loader make a brew and sandwiches whilst rattling and rolling across country has to be seen to be believed. It would be like a veritable horror show to an environmental health officer who tends to panic at the sight of a mere cockroach. One wonders indeed what they would make of the assuredly very grimy, diesel-smelling hand that at regular intervals would reach from the loader's hatch and proceed to pass to the commander and crew a sandwich that might once have been white bread, but now bore the operator's black, grubby handprint. But we all lived like it, and are still here to tell the tale.

that will be used later, and definitely – unless it is a firing period – will be making sure that the boiling vessel is switched on, and also that lunch is in, so that it will be ready when needed.

Buried deep in his cab, the driver will be keeping an eye on all the gauges and warning lights to make sure that everything is running well. If he is to be driving closed down, then he will be reclining his seat and adjusting his steering levers, before finally settling himself down so that he is comfortable and has good vision from his sight.

ON THE MOVE

With all systems that will be required for the day now running, the vehicle is ready to move off. The commander will pass instructions to the driver over the i/c system: these may be formal and straight from the book, such as 'Driver, advance!', but usually he will use the driver's nickname or Christian name, depending on the level of familiarity tolerated. So the driver can concentrate on his job, and to avoid continually having to talk to him, the commander will also give him an indication of where to go: thus he might point out a feature of ground ahead, or refer to somewhere they have been earlier, or even give instructions to simply 'follow the tank in front'.

Whilst on the move the operator will be leaning out of his hatches – but never more than to the extent of head and shoulders, in case of snipers; also, if the vehicle for some reason turned over, he would then have half a chance of getting back inside. The forward-facing hatch gives him somewhere to rest his clipboard, used for writing down messages. He will also be checking to the left and rear of the vehicle for any possible contact with the enemy.

The gunner will have been made responsible for checking out a certain field of view; this will tie in with areas being scanned by the rest of the troop, to ensure that the maximum area was covered. He will scan slowly and methodically from left to right and back, and will be looking through his x1 window or the TOGS viewer.

The commander meanwhile will be map reading: it is important that they always know where they are, because if contact is made with the enemy, the commander will have to pass the grid reference back to the troop leader, who will then pass it back to SHQ. He will also be keeping an eye on the crew and the direction of travel, as well as listening to the radio and taking down any information that he thinks may be of use to him later.

Arriving at the Chosen Destination

Once the tank is nearly at the area given to the driver, he will slow it down whilst awaiting further instructions from the commander – and that will depend on the commander's next intention. If the tank is to take up a fire position to the front, then it becomes a team effort: the commander will point out where he wants to go, the driver will change down into a low gear, and the gunner will start scanning through his X10 eyepiece.

There are three fire positions that the commander can adopt: hull down, turret down, and

track up (the drawing should explain these), and it depends what action the vehicle is to take, as to which position is adopted. The driver will approach the selected location in low gear and minimum revs; this is to minimize the smoke from the L60. Once the gunner is happy he has a good field of view, he will tell the driver to halt; if they are to be there for any length of time the main engine will be switched off, leaving only the aux-gen running.

MOVING OFF: 'FIRE AND MANOEUVRE'

Once they are ready to move again the driver will start the main engine; he will try not to use the accelerator as a sudden burst of revs will produce a very large cloud of white smoke, guaranteed to give away their position.

To leave its location the tank is always reversed out, along the tracks it made coming in. When in dead ground the commander will order it to turn either left or right, and from there it will carry on reversing, before moving off – still in dead ground – and swinging back onto its desired route. This might seem a lot of trouble just to move from one position, but a tank never advances straight over a ridge from a fire position: this is because while they have been sat looking for the enemy, the enemy may well have spotted them, and will just be waiting for the tank to come in a straight line towards them. Following the above procedure and by setting off in 'dead' ground hides the direction the tank will actually be taking.

This type of manoeuvre is known as 'fire and manoeuvre', and its prime aim is to ensure that no tank in the troop moves unsupported, for while our tank was moving to the position earlier, the other two were covering it from a bound behind. This is the basis of all troop movement, and it can be carried a stage further at squadron level, with a troop watching while a troop moves.

THE REPLENISHMENT AREA

At the end of the day the tanks need to refuel, and to top up with ammunition if on operations or ranges. This service is provided by the SQMS and his trucks, and they will set up a replenishment area where the tanks can come through and collect everything they need, including water and rations. There are several ways of carrying this out, but it is not within the scope of this book to explain them: they are best left to the tactics books. Suffice it to say that the most popular method is to line up the trucks in a wood, hopefully on a track, and then call each troop through in turn. The whole operation is meticulously timed, and must be carried out with no lights and a minimum of noise, as tanks are very vulnerable when completing this task.

To take on all the stores required and get them stowed needs the combined effort of the whole crew. This operation is carried out at the replen. site after collecting all the stores and refuelling. The tanks pull into an area between the last but one truck, and there they stow all the kit taken on board. When they leave the area they will go to an RV point until the troop is all together again; only then will they move off.

ORGANIZING A DEFENSIVE POSITION

The tanks can now either carry on with the operations throughout the night, or they can go into a squadron hide or a troop hide. These are locations where the tanks can literally 'hide' from the enemy. The area chosen may be a wooded area, though if there was a building large enough to hide all the vehicles that would be ideal, due to the fact that it would also conceal their thermal signature. To move into and occupy a hide is not a simple task, and certainly not a case of simply driving in and setting up camp. The enemy will be well aware that the troops will be setting up a hide, so they will leave 'stay-behind' troops in likely areas. These will remain hidden for quite a

A tank crew's nightmare: this troop's hide has been discovered by an infantry tank-hunting team, and they have used a smoke grenade to represent a hit from an anti-tank weapon. (Tim Babb)

Casualty evaluation drills being taught (although the 'casualty' seems happy enough). Note the soldier on the turret holding the rope that will have been used to lift the casualty from the turret. These are TA soldiers from Royal Wessex Yeomanry. (Tim Babb)

long time, and will only disclose themselves once the hide routine is running and most people have gone to sleep.

Needless to say, the sudden eruption of grenades, explosive charges and machine-gun fire will cause havoc, particularly as this is bound to happen when it is very dark and people are more relaxed, and many casualties can be expected; also the vehicles may well be badly damaged. As can be imagined, this type of tactic could have a huge impact, particularly if instead of a troop of tanks it was the regimental or squadron command structure that was attacked.

To avoid this type of attack, any area likely to be occupied by the 'stay-behind' enemy will have to be cleared, and if this has not already been done by troops from the squadron, then it will have to be tackled by the troop itself. This is not easy, given the limited amount of manpower within the troop. However, there are several ways

this can be achieved: the troop can follow 'the book', or they can produce their own SOP for dealing with it. One such solution was for the three tanks to cover the area while the troop sergeant and corporal, plus one other crew member, dismounted and, covered by the guns of the troop, would clear the area.

Once this task was completed, the troop sergeant would allocate an area in the hide for each tank to move into, and this they would do, normally by reversing in, though sometimes a track would allow access from another direction. Whichever way the vehicles entered the hide area, it was important to have a clear route out from it in the event of being attacked.

Once all the tanks are in situ, their engines are switched off, and the crews accomplish their tasks with well drilled efficiency: a good troop will set up hide with very few commands, as each crewman knows his appointed task:

The gunner will traverse the gun over the front to left or right, and fully depress it: this helps to lower the silhouette, and makes erecting the camouflage net a lot easier.

The commander's GPMG is removed and stowed in the turret (to be replaced when all the camouflage is complete), and the commander's and loader's hatches are closed, to prevent anyone falling through when battling with the camouflage net.

The drivers will be out on the track trying to flatten and cover up the earth they have displaced whilst manoeuvring into the hide – this is important, as the sight of freshly churned earth could very easily give away the troop position.

While this is going on, the loaders will remain in the turrets on radio watch; they will also be preparing the evening meal that will have been in the BV for some time so that it will be hot, and thus avoid the need to run the aux-gen.

By this time the commander and gunner will have started to hang the large camouflage net. In the early days of Chieftain, any old lengths of wood would be used to act as props to hold up the net to break up the outline, and it was a common sight to see these tied on the back of the NBC pack or along the bazooka plates.

In the Event of Attack

Once the drivers have finished their task they will come and give a hand with the net; generally they take the place of the vehicle commanders, who then make their way to the troop leader's tank to receive his orders concerning the hide. These will cover sentries, both patrolling and chemical; radio watch; policy on light, fires and noise; and what action to take in the event of being attacked, for example by ground troops, air or chemical. He will also point out the emergency RV (the point on the ground a couple of kilometres away where the troop would reassemble after being attacked).

If the troop has to break out of the hide, each tank will break out individually, because this actually makes it harder for the attacker. Attacking a tank that is quiet and still in the dark

is not too alarming, but one that is moving and moving hard, and is not bothered what gets in its way, is a terrifying experience that can tip the odds back into the troop's favour. However, no matter who wins, that hide has been compromised and must be abandoned; furthermore the troop will lose a lot of their kit if they have not stowed it away for the night, as there is no time to stop and recover it.

Setting Up the Camouflage Net

Depending on the level of operations or training, some or all of these duties may need to be carried out. It may be that the night can be spent non tactically, except for a guard.

Once the briefing is over, the commanders will return to their own tanks and help in finishing the camouflaging of the tanks. With today's sophisticated vision equipment, it is hard to hide the tank completely, but it is essential that the crew can make the tank blend into the natural background so that no suspicions are aroused, prompting the casual passer-by to look more closely. The issue of carbon-fibre camouflage poles certainly makes this task easier: these come in a bag in sections that can be joined together like a large fishing rod; they can then be placed over the tank, resembling an igloo once assembled. It is then a relatively simple matter to pull the net over the poles, and certainly involves a lot less effort than before, when the net would catch on anything and everything, causing tempers to run very short.

Once the net is up the hatches can be opened, and the commander's GPMG will be remounted; however, the operator must be careful that no light escapes from the turret, and that all the sights have a blackout shutter fitted to prevent light shining through the optics.

Settling In for the Night

The final task before relaxing will be deciding where to sleep. At one time crew members would

This picture shows crews after a major exercise. It also shows how good a table the Bazooka plate makes; the soldier kneeling down is opening the issue petrol cooker. (Author's collection)

The tank bivouac strung from the side of a tank; it could also be strung between two trees, and was simple to put up once you had mastered it. (Author's collection)

go to the turret rear and fully elevate the main armament, and drape the tank sheet over it: this made a rough and ready tent, and was very warm. However, for various reasons apparently of health and safety, this is not allowed any more.

Crews can opt to sleep in the open under the tank sheet, or in the crew bivouac, a very well designed piece of equipment that can be put up in many ways; it has ties on it, so it can be fixed to the side of the tank (but never the front or back in case the tank rolls during the night). It can also be suspended from two trees if it is not possible to get near the vehicle due to trees or bushes.

Once it is erected, then personal kit and sleeping bags will be laid out; these are always put in a set order so that even in the dark a particular member can be woken up without disturbing anyone else. This will be the same in all three tanks, and may well be part of the squadron's SOPs. With a little bit of effort and ingenuity these bivvies can be made quite comfortable; nevertheless the CVR (T) version is highly valued because it has a sewn-in groundsheet, thus mak-

ing it far more waterproof. Quite often the driver will opt to sleep in the cab, as many drivers prefer the reclining seat to the dubious pleasures of Mother Earth.

With the hide set up, the crew can now eat. This is also a good opportunity for the commanders to brief their crews on the drills for the hide, and to alert them as to the plans for the next day. Once the meal is finished it should be standard procedure to clear everything away and stow it; then if the vehicles do have to crash out, very little kit will be lost. However, what is actually done depends on the individual situation, and quite often rather than stowing everything away, it will all be set up for the breakfast meal; some crews find that lowering one of the bazooka plates to the horizontal position makes for an excellent table.

Showing a tank from 9 C Sqn 3 RTR with the Cpl commander cooking breakfast on the petrol cooker on Soltau training area, summer 1982. (Tim Babb)

These officers and soldiers from Royal Wessex Yeomanry are dressed in full combat kit whilst at Bovington for their introduction to Challenger 2. (Author's collection)

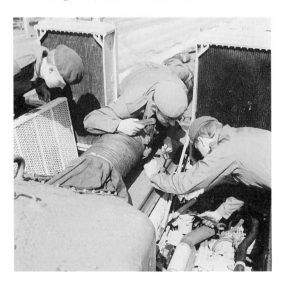

This crew from the Royal Hussars are wearing the standard issue denims for this period of maintenance. (Crown Copyright via Tim Royall)

With all tasks complete, the troop will try to get some sleep – though once again, how long depends on the task for the next day. Nevertheless, everyone will make the most of what sleep can be taken.

MORNING: MOVING OUT

The first indication that it is time to get up will be the sound of the aux-generators (if allowed) revving up to provide power for the BV that will turn out the breakfast meal – usually sausages and beans in tins. Generally the person who has the last watch lights the cookers for their crew. Most crews have a privately purchased gas cooker to supplement the issue petrol one. If time allows, the average crew likes to 'go to town' with breakfast, and a 'full English' is not unusual – crews will also buy rather more luxury items to supplement the issue rations. Food is usually cooked in a shift system so that no one is hanging around doing nothing: if not eating, you can be washing or cleaning your kit, or checking the tank.

Once everything has been washed it is then stowed away ready for the move out of the hide. The troop sergeant will check round the surrounding area for any rubbish and personal kit, and will take account of all the troop's personal weapons; once he is satisfied that all is in order, he will inform the troop leader that the troop is ready to move out.

Once the troop moves out, the whole cycle of events starts again, and continues until the end of the exercise.

IN SUMMARY

This account is assembled from the recollections of several ex-crewmen on how things were done in their various regiments. Some units will do all of the above, while others will do only some of it; but the general outline is fairly standard of how a troop will perform in the field.

DRESS AND PERSONAL EQUIPMENT

The type of uniform worn on the vehicle will vary from one regiment to another, but it will all be standard issue. The options for wear on the tank will be either denim overalls or full combat kit, and both have things to be said for and against them. The overalls evolved from those issued during the war: these were made of denim material and were very strong, with plenty of large pockets and places to stow as many map pens as you might need. On the down side they were not fire proof, although they would not burn easily; and nor were they waterproof. Today's overalls are made from a polyester material that in a fire

---

Designer Baskets

When a member of the management team visited the author's regiment, two particular complaints were levelled at him: the first was how useless were the then current rear wings and bins. They were proving too flimsy, and were easily ripped off by debris carried up on the tracks, thus necessitating renewal after every exercise – so obviously this was taking time and money that could be spent better elsewere. He then explained that this was actually in hand, and they would be replaced with a better item; and very shortly afterwards, the new wings and bins started to arrive.

The other complaint was that the basket on the left of the turret was too small for all the equipment it had to carry. His answer was to ask for certain items to be laid on the hangar floor, and then he asked if the basket could carry them. Of course the answer was 'yes', whereupon the designer explained that in the first instance these same items had been placed on the floor of his office, and he had been tasked to design a basket to carry them – and that is what he had done. Having now seen, however, what the crews actually had to carry, he promised to see what improvements could be made; and once again, in a short space of time the larger baskets appeared – and later on, another basket was even fitted to the right side of the turret.

---

will melt and stick to the skin, the pockets have been reduced to the minimum, and again they are not waterproof: enough said! The advantage of denims is that they are designed to be worn in a dirty environment, and so are ideal for use in armoured vehicles, especially one such as Chieftain that seems to be forever leaking.

The combat kit, too, has things for and against it: again, it will not burn easily, and it, too, has plenty of pockets – but it isn't waterproof, either.

Until recently, when the army started to produce some reasonably effective clothing for its soldiers, what was worn under the tank crew's uniforms was very much up to the individual. Commanding officers would have certain standards of dress, but these were always interpreted very liberally. A favourite item was the polo neck jumper in regimental colours; and in the early seventies the 4/7 DG crews all had to purchase a regimental cotton scarf in a blue colour (though this soon faded to blue/grey). Again until recently, there was never any decent waterproof or foul weather clothing issued to crews, which led to all sorts of tops being adopted, ex-Bundeswehr being a favourite. Other prized items were the parkas that the stores staff always managed to have on issue, but not for the crews – though somehow the crews managed to 'obtain' them. Other items worn were the standard issue greatcoat cut down to three-quarter length, the original 'pixie' suit from the war and a brilliant piece of clothing if a bit heavy when wet.

Problems of Heating

One of the problems in the early Chieftains was the total lack of heating. However, during Chieftain's first years in service, crews were quite regularly selected to complete questionnaires on the vehicle, and to point out faults, solutions and ideas that could improve it: these went to the project manager, and surprisingly, good results were quite often the outcome.

So having taken on board the various complaints about heating, a solution was to be placed

These grimy-looking crews from 4/7 DG are wearing the Mk 3 NBC suit, and the new crew helmet can be seen quite clearly. (Mark Wagstaff)

A mixed selection of uniforms to try and keep warm. The soldier on the tank is wearing a quilted jacket liner from his parka; one soldier is wearing his headcover, and the rest denims and parkas. (Author's collection)

on trial: this involved fitting a control on/off box at each crew station, and the issue of a special heated suit. This consisted of a one-piece quilted undersuit, of material similar to the combat kit liners then on issue. Within the suit were cables that ran to insoles to be placed inside the boots and gloves; the top of the suit had a roll-neck top.

On top of this was worn the normal over-clothing; the lead for the cables exited from one of the overall pockets, and once its wearer was in the vehicle, this would be connected to a coiled lead that was itself connected to the control box. The suit was meant to act as extra insulation, and if the individual crew member felt cold, then all he had to do was switch on the control box, and the electric elements in the boots and gloves would warm up and keep him warm. In actual fact probably the only time this looked good was when it was on the drawing board, for in the great tradition of failures, this really triumphed.

For some reason it had been decided not to include a basic rheostat to control the temperature, so you ended up with crews with very hot hands and feet as the elements warmed up – but with no control on the temperature, things just got hotter and hotter. The gloves could be removed and allowed to cool, but there was no way that the boot insoles could be taken out whilst wearing the boot. The other major problem was that the connector that joined the suit to the lead from the control box was meant to be a quick-release type so that if a crewman had to bale out it would not restrict him. Well, it may have been many things, but quick release it was not. Whilst the theory was appreciated by the crews in that it showed that someone was trying to do something about keeping them warm, this was not the answer, and the project died a very swift and grateful death. It is worth mentioning that a similar system is in existence today for use by motorbike riders.

Waterproof Clothing

The issue of decent waterproof clothing for AFV crews is something that is long overdue. In the early seventies a one-piece waterproof suit was issued that on the face of it was very good: it was a one-piece zip-up and had lots of pockets. However, it did not have a good capability for venting the body's heat, so you could end up

Larkspur, the type of radio fitted before Clansman. This is C42, and a crewman's head-set and microphone are hanging from it. This is in a Landrover, but the radio is the same. (Author's collection)

getting just as wet wearing it as not wearing it. The drivers found one very good use for it, and that was to wear it when doing any major changes such as power packs, as it helped to keep them reasonably clean. The Barbour Coat Company did well when they introduced a version of their famous wax jackets in a DPM material: here was something that was sturdy and waterproof, and PRI shops within units sold plenty.

Footwear

Originally crews would have worn the issued DMS (direct moulded sole) boot; an ankle height, leather boot with a rubber sole. It came to notoriety during the Falklands war when it proved how useless it was, having the waterproof properties of a wet sponge. It is most likely that these would have been worn in conjunction with gaiters, though not by all regiments; they were the same as those issued during World War II, and consisted of a canvas gaiter about 6in (15cm) deep, with metal buckles and leather straps. These would be worn over the top of the boot with some sort of elastic around them, so that the bottom of the overalls/combat kit could be tucked in; this was a lot neater than just wrapping the gaiter around the end of the trouser.

Officers in some regiments were allowed to purchase jackboots: fleece-lined zip-up boots, and the trouser ends were tucked into the boots. These were extremely comfortable, and very easy to take on and off – a distinct advantage at night. Since then the Army has had several different versions of boot, but all based on a high combat boot, and these now are proving to be a vast improvement over the early DMS boot.

Headwear

During the early days the ubiquitous beret was worn with the headset from the Larkspur radio system, but this combination offered the protection of an eggshell to head and hearing. However, once the Army realized that it needed to protect

This shows the first 'bone dome'; it was not very popular as it was very heavy and got in the way when trying to view through the optics. It was, however, a step in the right direction. (Author's collection)

The next helmet was much better as the headset could be detached if required. Notice the control box around the crewman's chest. This is the commander's version and it allows him to select which radio to talk on; he could connect it to a lead attached to a radio box in the turret. Crewmen had a simple push-to-talk box, their set selection being carried out by fixed boxes in the turret. (Author's collection)

vehicle crews from the noise generated by an armoured vehicle, several ideas were trialled. One of these was the first version of what is known as the 'bone dome'. This was trialled by several regiments during the mid-seventies, and was eventually accepted into service – but with great reservation by the crews. The system consisted of a fibreglass-type helmet shell, fitted with headsets that gave audio protection to the wearer; it also had a boom microphone fitted to it. This allowed the commander or any of the crew to talk on a live i/c system without having to hold a microphone all the time.

The main complaint against the system was that the helmet was heavy and hot to wear, and this caused the ears to sweat a lot, making it particularly uncomfortable. Also the helmet was so big that a gunner or commander had to tip it back on their head to be able to look into the sight, otherwise the helmet fouled the sight brow pad. These were some of the faults that were picked up on the trial, and it is disappointing that they were evidently ignored. However, providing better communication and head protection was a step in the right direction.

With the introduction of Clansman, things stayed as they were for a while regarding the helmet; then a new one was introduced. It consisted of two parts: the headset and the Hemet shell. The headset is the current Clansman headset with fittings added so that it can be attached to the helmet shell. The shell is a much smaller item than its predecessor: it does not cover the ears, nor does it reach so far down the nape of the neck – but what is important, it allows the crew to use the optics without too much trouble. It is made of a similar material to the standard issue infantry-type helmet so can offer some ballistic protection, and is attached to the headset by means of press-studs, so if it is damaged it can be removed and replaced very easily – unlike its predecessor, where the earpieces and the boom microphone were built into the helmet.

A whole new range of radios is planned to be introduced starting around 2002, and it is my

belief that even more changes to the audio equipment will then take place. One idea will be to try and remove the need for a cable linking each crewman to his control box, and instead using maybe IR or similar technology .

A Weapon for Self-Defence

Finally, each crewman is equipped with a personal weapon for self-defence. Also, should the crew have to abandon the vehicle, according to the tactics book, steps should be taken to remove the commander's GPMG and as much ammunition as can be carried. The practicalities of doing this under fire are dubious, but it is a worthwhile weapon to have, if somewhat awkward to carry. There are three reasons why it is the commander's GPMG that is taken, and not the co-ax GPMG: first, it is mounted outside; second, it has a pistol grip fitted and a carrying handle; and third, a butt can be fitted to it. Hand grenades are also available, and 6 are carried.

Each crewman used to be issued with a 9mm Sterling SMG, but this brought its own problems; the main one was that the gunner had to stow his on the loader's side, so if the vehicle had to be evacuated, it stood a good chance of being left behind. Today, however, the crew have two SA80 rifles and two 9mm Browning High Power pistols as personal weapons, which means that each crewman can now keep his own weapons close to him. The driver and loader are issued with the 5.56mm SA80, and the commander and gunner with the 9mm Browning pistol; they are also given a shoulder holster in which to carry it, so it is at hand at all times.

Other Kit

The only other kit that the crew carries will be in the baskets and bins, and will consist of their sleeping bag, sleeping mat, spare clothing, washing kit, and any other luxury items that they think will be required.

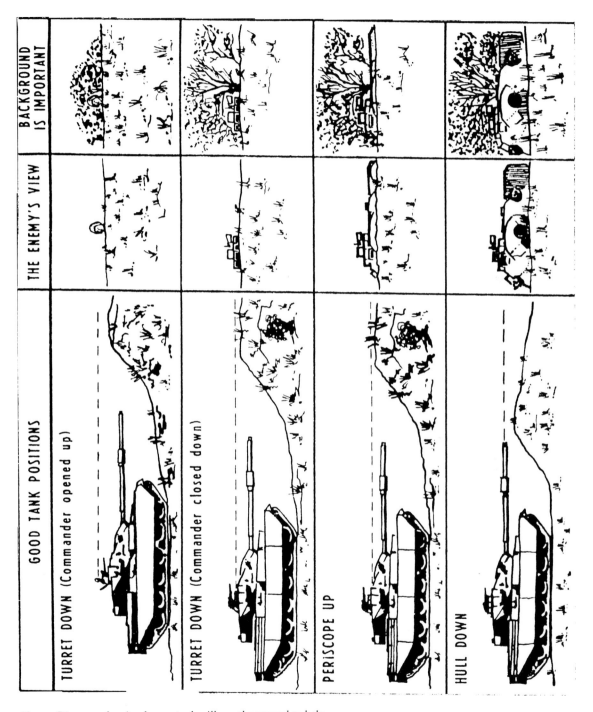

Above: *Diagram showing how a tank will use the ground to help protect itself. (Crown Copyright)*

Dug in Chieftain. (Tim Babb)

IN CONCLUSION

As we can see, the requirement for a tank crew is quite complex, and it is a life style all on its own; furthermore, we can only guess at how the job will evolve in the next twenty years.

However, for the time being I believe that a tank crewman who had landed on D-Day would be very much at home with today's crews; although a great deal has become 'hi-tech', he would still recognize large parts of the life-style.

5   Weapons

There are three main criteria that all tank designers work to: firepower, mobility and protection. Each of the major tank-producing countries would quibble about the order of importance amongst these three, but there is a cartoon from between the wars showing what might happen if any one of them is allowed to take precedence: thus we have a tank with a multitude of guns, armour so thick that there was no room for anything else, and a powerplant the size of a vehicle. Clearly there has to be a compromise: but at the end of the day, the aim is to get the tank and its gun onto the battlefield with good protection and the mobility to move swiftly around the scene of action.

THE TANK'S *RAISON D'ETRE*

The main reason for a tank being on the battlefield is the tremendous firepower it can bring down, and its use in shock action. Even with today's sophisticated 'fire and forget' anti-tank missiles, it still takes a very brave operator to remain in place long enough to fire that missile when a tank is looming down on his position, probably laying down speculative mg fire at likely locations. Thus the tank exists on the battlefield to kill enemy armour quickly, regardless of the range or whether the vehicles are moving or stationary. Nowadays it must be possible for that destructive power to be used as effectively at night as it can in daylight, since the twenty-four-hour battlefield is with us now and for the future.

The tank is therefore adept at destroying enemy armour, and it also fulfils many of the other tasks that abound on the modern field of combat. These might include destroying enemy APCs, reconnaissance vehicles, soft skin transport, and the infantryman in a foxhole in the ground. Furthermore it must be able to protect itself against sudden attacks. In this chapter we will therefore be looking at the weapon systems that have been used in the past, those that are currently in use, and those that were projected for Chieftain.

WHAT GUN?

To begin with the WO were not particularly concerned as to what calibre weapon Chieftain carried, as we have discussed: if we look at their requirement again, all it stated was that 'the new vehicle must be capable of carrying a weapon of sufficient calibre'. That really left the way open for the designers, since at the time there were just two options: Conqueror with its 120mm gun and long-range brass cases for the propellant, which were nevertheless very large and awkward to handle; and Centurion with its twenty-pounder gun. The latter, however, was soon to be equipped with what has proved to be one of the best tank guns ever produced, namely the 105mm, eventually adopted by many countries including the United States and Germany.

It was felt that, while 105mm would prove adequate, it had to be balanced by what the opposition was likely to come up with, in which case 120mm was thought to be preferable; but it was not acceptable as long as the propellant was contained in the brass case.

On 30 December 1954 the WO had decided that a liquid propellant gun was to be developed, and two types were envisaged: one was to be a bi-fuel gun in which fuel and a oxidant were

Right: *A sectioned view of the chamber showing the bag charge and a sectioned APFSDS round. Notice that the rifling does not start until just in front of the round. (RCMS Shrivenham)*

Below: *A sectioned view of breech ring and block, clearly showing the vent tube on the end of the FNA, the obturators and the base of the bag charge. (RCMS Shrivenham)*

injected into the chamber and spontaneously ignited; the other was to be a single fuel injected and ignited from an external source. But as we have seen, the technology of the day did not allow these ambitious weapons to proceed.

Instead the designers turned to a more traditional weapon in the rifled gun – although the twenty-pounder had proved its worth, it had reached the end of its development life. Similarly, there was no denying that the new 105mm gun was proving to be a world-class weapon, and would eventually go on to equip the tanks in Japan, the USA, Germany, Switzerland and India. But whilst this was an impressive feature, the designers had to look at least ten years ahead to what armament Chieftain might be called upon to face, and to come up with a weapon that could defeat all foreseen enemy systems.

The Bagged Charge System

The calibre finally chosen was that of 120mm – and the reader may be forgiven for thinking that this decision can't have taken a great deal of effort, as that weapon had been around for several years, in Conqueror. But the trouble with the gun in Conqueror was that the charge was contained in a very large and heavy brass case, and quite apart from the problem of its great weight, the size precluded a large bombload of ammunition being carried. This, and the failure of the liquid propellant guns, led to the production of a bagged charge system. Whilst not a particularly new idea – it had been in use with the navies of the world, and in artillery pieces for many years – its introduction into an AFV was at the least novel.

One immediate saving over a tank using conventional cases was that of space saved. For ease of production, the cases used for APDS, HESH and smoke were all the same size; only the propellant quantity was different in each type. Another reason for their having to be the same size was that on firing, the expanding case created the obturation needed to seal the breech.

Sealing the Breech

With a bagged charge, the whole system – projectile and charge – would be disposed of, the projectile along the barrel, and the charge consumed. The first problem was how to seal the breech; traditionally weapons using bagged charge propellant had the interrupted thread type of system. This was where a threaded plug fitting into a chamber sealed the breech, and the action of the threads forced it tight, thus effectively sealing the weapon. But whilst a proven system, it was totally impractical for rapid loading within the close confines of an AFV, especially as some loading would be carried out whilst the vehicle was moving. The system finally chosen consisted of two inserts – one in the rear of the chamber, and one in the face of the breech block; they are controlled by cams, so that there is no metal-to-metal contact during the opening and closing of the breech. The only brass case present in this system is a .625 cartridge known as a 'vent tube', and used to ignite the bag charges when they are in the chamber.

In-Built Fire Prevention

Those traditionalists opposed to the proposed introduction of the bagged charge reacted with all

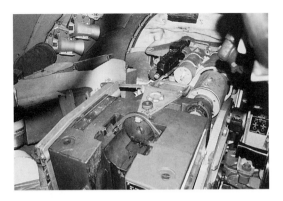

Interior shot showing the location of the co-ax. The silver bin to its left holds the ammunition for it. Notice how the breech ring seems to fill the turret. (RCMS Shrivenham)

sorts of sensationalist tales of horror: to listen to them, the whole Chieftain fleet was likely to explode, rather like the Royal Navy warships at Jutland. In fact nothing could have been further from the truth, as the charges were contained in their own individual cells within a charge container, and the whole container was double-walled; this allowed the standard anti-freeze in use at the time to fill the void under a pressure of 7lb/sq inch. This meant that in the event of a round penetrating the tank, any shards of metal that punctured the charge container would release the coolant under pressure and this would immediately flood the individual charge, thus putting out any fires and helping to prevent an internal explosion. In films taken of these trials it was shown to work very well, and the system served Chieftain until its final withdrawal from service.

Years later, trials were again carried out, and it seems that the system did not have a lot to offer as Challenger 1 Mk3 had armoured bins to protect the charges. Charge bins were never a popular item as far as the crew was concerned, as Dave Reardon, a long-time Chieftain crewman in the loader's side, recounts:

The problem with the bins was always one of coolant leaks, and if you allowed a bag charge to get wet during a range period you were dead

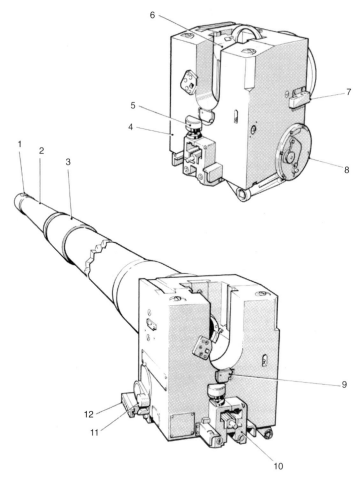

1 Muzzle reference mirror
  mount
2 Barrel
3 Fume extractor
4 Breech ring
5 Release plunger
6 Breech block
7 Anti-rotation key
8 Gearbox
9 Firing needle assembly
10 Vent tube loader
11 Actuating shaft spigot
12 Anti-distortion key

Drawing showing the main components of the 120mm gun. Notice the breech ring that the breech block fits into. (Crown Copyright)

Left: *The charge bins. It can be seen how flimsy the lids appear. The centre container holds an APDS charge, while that on the left holds a fresh charge. (RCMS Shrivenham)*

Right: *This shows clearly the GPMS and RMS barrel. The GPMS is fitted with the early flash hider, the cone-shaped part at the end of the barrel. (Mark Hayward)*

meat if the gunnery instructors discovered it. There was also a plastic closure lid which would fall off as soon as you looked at it; they were always getting caught in the traverse, and when you carried out loading drills, the seconds spent closing the lid were seconds wasted in loading.

One advantage of the system was that it did help to save space within the vehicle, because you could place two HESH/smoke charges in one container – using conventional cases it would have been two separate rounds. The weight saved was therefore also considerable.

THE ORDNANCE BL 120MM TK L11 A1-5

The weapon eventually chosen was a 120mm-calibre rifled gun, the Ordnance BL 120mm Tk L11 A1-5. The L11 A1 barrel was the original weapon fitted to the early vehicle, followed by the L11 A2, which was the most commonly seen version. This is recognized by the large fume extractor and the untidy appearance of the rear thermal sleeve, which was never secured behind the fume extractor, as it should have been. This was because it was necessary to peel it back to allow the gun to be fitted into the earlier version

Commander's 7.62mm ms of intent is how the ammunition box is fitted to the mount. Later versions had ammo stowage fitted on the cupola, either as a single bin or a large one that could hold several boxes. The tubes welded to the sights are used to hold coloured flash indicating various states of readiness when on the range, for safety reasons. (RCMS Shrivenham)

of the gun crutch. The later and final version was the L11 A5; this is recognized by the smaller diameter fume extractor and the forged upstanding on the muzzle to accomodate the mirror for the MRS. The L11 A2 and 5 were the main production versions. The gun as originally issued was capable of firing three types of service ammunition: APDS, HESH and smoke; in addition, a practice round for both APDS and HESH was issued, and the gun could also fire canister and illuminating rounds, although neither was ever issued. In later years the gun was capable of firing APFSDS as well.

The 120mm gun is made up of several components, with several more as part of the whole system. The barrel is a single forging that has been autofrettaged, a process to induce strength

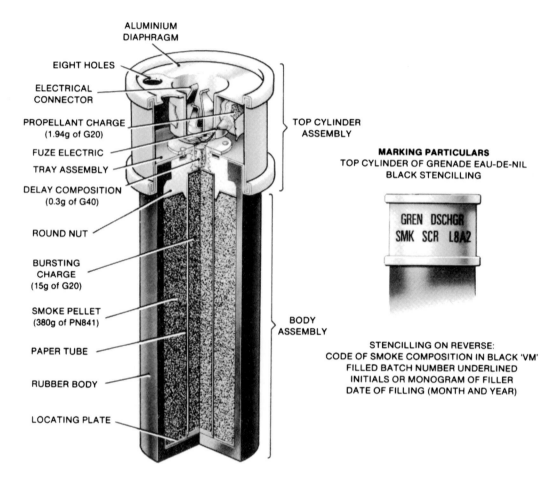

ALUMINIUM
DIAPHRAGM

EIGHT HOLES

ELECTRICAL
CONNECTOR

PROPELLANT CHARGE
(1.94g of G20)

FUZE ELECTRIC

TRAY ASSEMBLY

DELAY COMPOSITION
(0.3g of G40)

ROUND NUT

BURSTING
CHARGE
(15g of G20)

SMOKE PELLET
(380g of PN841)

PAPER TUBE

RUBBER BODY

LOCATING PLATE

TOP CYLINDER
ASSEMBLY

BODY
ASSEMBLY

MARKING PARTICULARS
TOP CYLINDER OF GRENADE EAU-DE-NIL
BLACK STENCILLING

GREN DSCHGR
SMK SCR L8A2

STENCILLING ON REVERSE:
CODE OF SMOKE COMPOSITION IN BLACK 'VM'
FILLED BATCH NUMBER UNDERLINED
INITIALS OR MONOGRAM OF FILLER
DATE OF FILLING (MONTH AND YEAR)

The construction of the L8 smoke grenade. The L5 and L7 are similar, except that their cases are all metal. (Crown Copyright)

with lightness. It is a rifled weapon with one turn in eighteen calibres. A third of the way along the barrel is a fume extractor: as it implies, this removes fumes after firing and prevents them from entering the turret. Also fitted externally along the length of the barrel is a two-part thermal sleeve; this helps prevent barrel droop due to the constant change in temperature endured by the barrel, especially when firing in cold weather. The rear of the barrel passes through the turret aperture and is located in a cradle, with trunnions that allow full elevation and depression. The rear of the barrel is fitted with interrupted threads to

allow the fitting of the breech ring, which contains the breechblock; the ingress of dust and water is prevented by a canvas mantlet fitted externally.

MACHINE GUNS

The Chieftain also carries two 7.62mm machine guns for close-in protection, AA defence, and for engaging soft skin targets such as trucks and infantry. One gun, the L8, is carried in the co-ax position, which means that it will follow the main gun in elevation and in traverse. The other, the L37, is mounted on the commander's cupola, as we have seen, and with very little trouble can be dismounted and used in the ground role. Both guns are 7.62mm calibre and are fully automatic, air-cooled weapons capable of high rates of fire. The early guns could achieve a rate of fire approaching nearly 1,000 rounds per minute; this was found to be too high, however, and they were subsequently modified to about 800–850rpm.

The co-axial mounting is on the top left of the gun cradle; most of the weapon is inside the turret, and the part of the barrel that protrudes outside it is covered by a flexible canvas mantlet. Internally a splash curtain extends across the mounting as far as the recoil buffer. The gun is loaded from the left, with ammunition of the dis-

integrating belt type: this means that as the gun is fired, the belt will break into individual links, thus taking up less space than a conventional canvas belt; also the rounds do not fall out of this type of belt as easily as they do on a conventional belt. Depending on the mark of vehicle, it can be fed from two boxes of 200 rounds, or a large bin containing 500 rounds.

The gun is cocked by a mechanical cocking lever operated by the loader, and is fired either electrically by the gunner or the commander, or by means of a foot-operated Bowden cable operated by the gunner. On firing, the links and cases fall down a link exit chute where they are stored in a canvas bag known as a 'capacious container'; this is removable for emptying. In early vehicles the passage of links caused a lot of problems, as

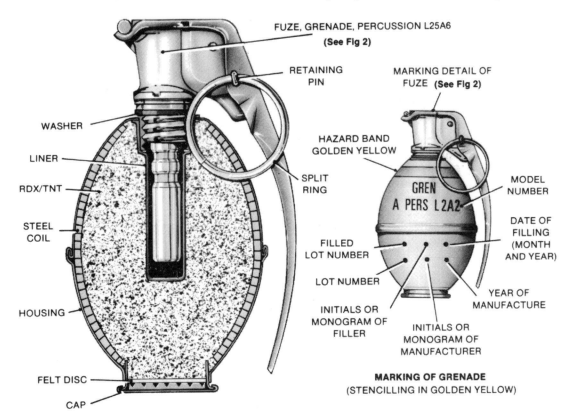

This is the current hand grenade issued to the AFV crew. One cannot help thinking that if the crew is using grenades, something has gone very wrong. (Crown Copyright)

they tended to jam up and cause stoppages.

The commander's mount can be one of three: the Mounting 7.62mm MG L37 No. 10 Mk 1; the Mounting 7.62mm MG No. 2 Mk 1; or the Mounting 7.62mm MG No. 8 Mk 1. The No. 10 Mk 1 is the latest version, and in elevation can reach nearly vertical; all the mounts are similar in construction, with just minor modifications between them. Basically they consist of a light steel cradle pivoted at the rear on two trunnions; the gun is held in at the front by a pull/push-type pin, and at the rear a pin engaging in two lugs. The right-hand side houses the cocking gear: this is nothing more exotic than a slide that engages against the cocking handle on the weapon, and is connected to a rubber handle inside the turret by

a wire cable. The electrical solenoid that fires the gun is located to the left of the cradle. The mounting is elevated and depressed by means of a handle inside the cupola, which also has the firing switch built into the handle.

The weapon can be fired and controlled from under cover of the cupola, but reloading and the clearing of all stoppages must be carried out with the commander's upper body exposed. This problem had to a certain extent been solved in the experimental cupola No. 21: in this, the commander would have an indication as to when the last few rounds were being fed through the gun, and he would then be able to clip another belt onto the end, as ammunition was stored in the cupola. In this model however, there was no provision to

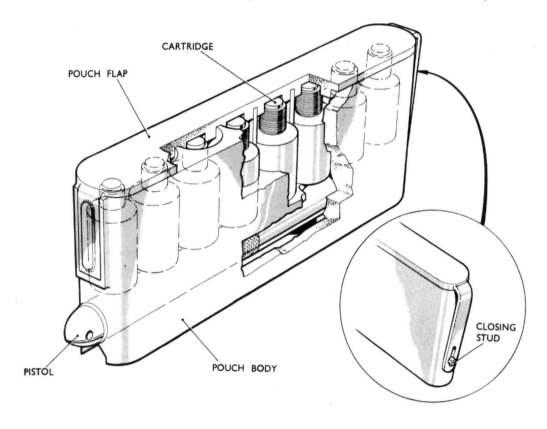

Drawing showing the layout of the individual signal kit. This same kit is used by hill walkers; the only difference is that the case is red, not green. (Crown Copyright)

catch the spent cases and links when the weapon was fired, so the turret very quickly became covered in brass cases.

SMOKE DISCHARGERS

The Chieftain is also equipped with two multi-barrelled smoke dischargers, located on either side of the turret front and each holding six smoke grenades. On vehicles manufactured before Stillbrew armour was fitted, the dischargers' mounting brackets were fixed to the turret. With Stillbrew armour fitted, one of the brackets had to be hinged to allow access to the engine decks. The early dischargers had an approximate lateral spread of 1,812mils, while the later ones have a spread of 1,800mils at a range of 60m (200ft).

Three types of grenade can be fired: the L5 white smoke and L7 green smoke will burst at the 60m (200ft) point, whilst the L8 white phosphorus will air-burst at approximately 30m (100ft). The dischargers can be fired either together or individually. The dischargers are fired from two buttons at the commander's station, giving a shot of six or twelve grenades as required.

The purpose of the dischargers is to provide an immediate short-term smoke screen at short range for self-protection, such as might be needed when, for instance, the tank came round a corner of a road and met an enemy position head on; then he would fire the grenades, and very quickly reverse and assess the situation. The burst of smoke might be just enough to throw an enemy gunner momentarily off guard while he made good its escape. As soon as the L5 and L7 leave the dischargers, smoke starts to be produced; for the L8 it takes 0.75secs of flight before smoke is produced.

A canvas cover is pulled over the dischargers when they are not in use, and twelve spare grenades are carried as reloads.

HAND GRENADES

In addition to the tank weapons, hand grenades were also carried; originally these were the old Mills bomb no. 36 of World War II vintage, but these have been replaced by the hand grenade HE L2A2, of which six are carried. This is the type of grenade as seen in countless films, where you pull out the safety pin and throw it, and if everything works, the resulting explosion should be capable of causing casualties up to a distance of 19m (62ft). Like all explosive devices, the effects of the grenade can be increased or decreased by the type of ground it explodes on; thus, if it were to explode on hard ground, then the lethal radius may be increased to 190m (620ft).

Comparison of British Tank Weapons

	Conqueror	Centurion 3	Centurion 5	Chieftain
Name	Ordnance QF120mm L1A1	Ordnance QF 20 pr Mk1	Gun 105mm Tk L7A1	Ordnance BL 120mm TK L11 A1–5
Calibre	120mm	84mm	105mm	120mm
APDS	1,433ms	1,430ms	1,480ms	1,370ms
APFSDS	N/A	N/A	N/A	1,530ms
HESH	762ms	600ms	730ms	660ms
Smpke	N/A	250ms	620ms	660ms
Barrel weight	6,578lb (2,984kg) complete	1,660lb (753kg)	1,644lb (746kg)	3,919lb (1,778kg)

THE SIGNAL PISTOL

There was also a standard issue signal pistol that fired 1in illuminating cartridges available in four colours; each had an embossed mark on the round's closure, so that the user could identify which cartridge was being loaded even in pitch darkness: thus red had a cross, green a triangle, yellow a circle, and the illuminating cartridge a dome. These were fired from the signal pistol one at a time.

The pistol was broken open in the same manner as a shotgun, and the cartridge inserted; the firer then pulled back the hammer, took aim, and fired; and to eject the spent case the weapon was again broken open. Twelve cartridges were normally carried on the vehicle, in any combination of colours.

The Signal Kit Pyrotechnic Pistol

In later years the signal kit 16mm pyrotechnic pistol replaced the standard pistol, both for ease of use and cost effectiveness. The kit is identical to that available from survival shops in the UK, except the military version is to be found in a green container and the civilian variety is sold in a yellow one. It provides a lightweight, compact signal kit in a plastic weatherproof container; this holds eight cartridges and the hand-held pistol. Kits are available either as red, white or green flares, and again, the embossed marking appears, but this time on the plastic container.

The flares are screwed onto the pistol while this is still in the pouch; once attached, they are withdrawn from the pouch, and to fire them a spring-loaded hammer is pulled back on the pistol and then released, thus firing the cartridge. The used cartridge is removed, and if required the whole process can be repeated. Once the wallet is empty it can be handed back in, and eventually it will be refilled and reissued, thus helping to keep the cost down.

PERSONAL WEAPONS

There are also personal weapons carried by the crew; in the early days this was the 9mm sub-machine gun known as the Stirling, a descendant of the famous Sten gun of the war years. It was only designed as a short-range weapon, but it was felt to be of more benefit to the crew than the pistols that were once carried by tank crews. Sixteen magazines of 9mm ammunition were carried for the crew's SMGs, and if they had to bale out, it was expected that if possible they would also take the commander's GPMG. This was one of the reasons that it was designed to be fitted in its mount complete with bipod and pistol grip; the crew then only had to worry about the butt and boxes of 7.62mm when they baled out. However, most of the crews that I interviewed met that suggestion with a resounding 'no way': it was a good idea, but just not practical if you were baling out under fire.

6 Gun Mounting, Sights and Controls

In the previous chapter we took a look at the weapons carried on board the Chieftain. If the 120mm is to be used efficiently within the turret, and if it is to retain its accuracy, it has to be carried in a special mounting. So in this chapter we shall look at the weapon mounting and its associated equipment, and the sights that are used to observe and to lay the gun.

THE GUN MOUNTING

The gun mounting is designed to allow an elevation of 356 mils above the centreline, and a depression of 178 mils; all round traverse is obtained by rotation of the turret either by power or by hand. The cradle has a trunnion fitted on each side to support it within the turret.

For the first time in a British tank no external armoured mantlet is fitted; however, a canvas mantlet cover is fitted externally, with a splinter-proof splash curtain located inside the turret at the forward edge.

All movement vertically and horizontally is by means of rack-and-pinion gears, and is achieved by electrical power, or manually using a duplex controller (early) or a thumb controller (late) for the powered mode, and the elevating and traverse hand wheels for the hand mode.

We will now consider the components that are located on or around the mounting, and that form an integral part of it.

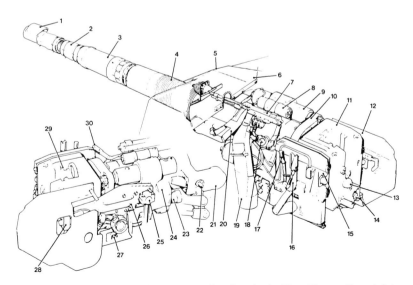

Drawing showing all the major components in the gun mounting from both sides. (Crown Copyright)

The cradle being refurbished, clearly showing the buffers and mounting trunnions. (Pilkington Optronics)

Comparison of gunner's sights with an early 9-dot ranging gun sight on the left with a laser sight on the right. (Nigel Montgomery)

The Cradle

The cradle is of round construction, and is supported within the turret by the trunnions; these sit within needle roller bearings. The cradle is machined to accept the recoil system, the loader's firing guard, the SA bracket, the anti-rotation bracket, and a mounting for the co-ax machine gun.

Liners

Within the cradle, phosphor bronze liners are fitted to ease the gun's movement as it recoils and runs out; they are grooved to help retain the lubricant that is supplied via grease nipples. The front liner is fed from a pipe from the nipple block located on the left rear of the cradle.

Gun Depression Stop

This is a block welded on top of the cradle; in conjunction with a pad on the turret roof, it acts as a depression stop – and it should be said that the forces that can be placed on this area if the vehicle is moving across country can be tremendous. The author has seen a parka that had been left draped across the cradle with four neat holes punched into it, where the depression stop has met the upper portion.

The Buffer Housings

These are areas machined on the cradle to help locate the twin buffers that are part of the recoil system; they are prevented from rotating by anti-rotation bolts on the outside of the housing.

Anti-Rotation Bracket

The cradle is fitted with an anti-rotation bracket: this has a line cut into it to receive a key secured to the breech ring, and the whole assembly prevents the gun rotating in the cradle during firing.

¾ view of the gunner's tank laser rangefinder sight giving some idea of the bulk of the sight. (Nigel Montgomery)

Recuperator

The hydro-pneumatic recuperator is also part of the recoil system, and is located on the underside of the cradle.

Semi-automatic Bracket

Bolted to the left side of the cradle, this houses the semi-automatic (SA) cam and the breech-closing lever. There is a groove in the cam that engages with a stud on the gun and forces it to rotate during run-out: as the gun moves forwards, this action will automatically open the breech. Pulling the breech-closing lever will disengage the cam and allow the torsion springs that control the breech-block to reassert themselves and close the breech.

Of note is a modification designed by S/Sgt 'Charlie' Chase of the 4/7 Royal Dragoon Guards: he felt that, with the loader holding the next projectile, the ergonomics of holding the

107

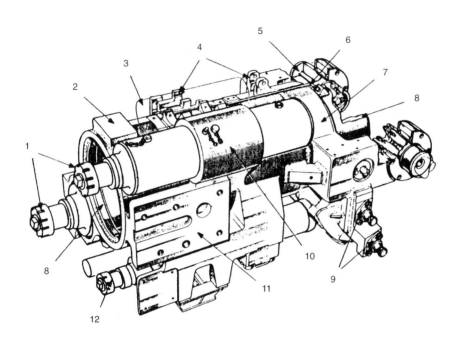

1 Gun nuts
2 Depression stop
3 Replenisher
4 Co–axial MG mounting
5 Trunnion
6 Lubrication feedpipe
7 Gun cradle
8 Front liner
9 Gun control linkage spigots
10 Buffer housing
11 Anti–rotation bracket
12 Recuperator

The 120mm cradle showing the main components (the front is to the right).
(Crown Copyright)

A not-often-seen view of the cradle. Visible are the co-ax mount, the vertical handle painted red is the breech closing handle, while the silver one behind is the breech opening handle.
(RCMS Shrivenham)

round and trying to close the lever could be made better. He did this by having the cam modified so that the action of closing the loader's safety guard released the cam and closed the breech. This modification became known officially as the 'Chase mod', and was fitted to the CAT Challenger 1 vehicles – and if nothing else went right, at least the breech was easier to close!

The Loader's Firing Guard

This is a two-part component bolted to the SA bracket; as we have already seen, it is provided to prevent the loader moving behind the gun when it is loaded. It is also part of the firing circuit, and the weapon will not be able to fire without the guard being in place, except on emergency circuits. The loader will set up the guard by pulling it to the rear, when a spring-loaded locking lever will engage with a recess in the fixed part of the shield. As the gun recoils, a cam strikes the locking lever on the guard and releases it, and the shield is then automatically returned to the open position.

The Replenisher

This component does exactly as its name implies: it acts as a replenisher for the main buffers. It is located to the left of the right-hand buffer. It is fitted with a filler plug and an indicator to show how much oil is contained inside.

The Recoil Indicator

A two-part component located on the right-hand gun shield: it consists of a bracket and a slide, on which is a pointer, and the loader must pay attention to this during firing. During recoil, the anti-rotation key hits the slide on the breech ring; if the gun is recoiling too far, the slide will be knocked further back than its correct location, in which case the vehicle may have to cease firing and the problem be investigated – though this will, of course, depend on the situation.

The Vent Tube Loader

As we have seen, split ammunition is used for the gun, and while most people will describe it as two-part ammunition, there is in fact a third component needed to complete the chain of firing: this is known as a tube vent electric .625 L1A4. There are fourteen of these held in a magazine beneath the vent tube loader, located on the breech ring at the rear.

The vent tube provides the ignition for the igniter at the bottom of the bag charges. During the initial loading drills, the loader will pull back on the rammer on the vent tube loader, which will be held to the rear, then by striking the plunger on top of it, a vent tube will (hopefully) be loaded into the breechblock. When the breech is closed, this tube will be carried up and will engage in the firing needle assembly.

When the firing circuit is completed, the vent tube will be ignited, and a flame from the tube will travel through a channel in the breechblock and ignite the charge. As the gun recoils, the spent vent tube is ejected into a special catcher, or onto the floor – this being the only part of the ammunition that is not consumed.

The Recoil System

We have mentioned in passing some components of the recoil system: now we shall see what part the system plays in the mounting. The main purpose of having a recoil system fitted to the gun is to absorb the recoil energy created by firing. It also returns the gun to the run-out position after it has fired and recoiled; it controls the length of recoil achieved after each firing; and it maintains the gun in a fully run-out position, no matter what angle of elevation is applied.

The system consists of two hydraulic buffers, the recuperator and the replenisher, attached at various points to the cradle. The buffers are located in the cradle at roughly two and eight o'clock, and are fitted with filler and drain plugs. At the rear of each piston is a large nut that is secured to the gun yoke. The recuperator has an oil and air system within it, which is used to assist the gun to the run-out position. The recuperator accepts the excess of oil that is displaced by the buffers during firing: the oil gets hot and expands; this causes an increase in pressure, which is relieved by allowing it to flow into the replenisher. Once the system has cooled down, then the oil will flow back into the system from the replenisher.

On firing the gun is driven backwards, and this movement is controlled by the oil in the buffers becoming compressed, until the gun is brought to a halt. During the recoil phase oil will be displaced from the high-pressure cylinder in the recuperator, and the piston in the cylinder will move forwards, compressing the air in the cylinder. After recoil has been brought to a halt by the buffers, the compressed air in the recuperator reasserts itself, driving the piston back; and as the piston is also attached to the gun yoke as well as the buffers, it will return the gun to the run-out position.

The Breech and its Associated Mechanism
The forward and backward movement of the gun has the effect of automatically opening the breech. The breechblock and its associated mechanism are located within the breech ring. As we have seen, the breech is opened automatically once firing has taken place, but initially it must be opened by hand; in early vehicles this could only be achieved by the use of a breech-opening tool (BOT) that fitted onto the breech ring. This consists of a handle linked by a chain – similar to that used on a bicycle – to a drive socket, which fits over a corresponding shaft on the actuating shaft. Rotation of the handle on the tool clockwise turned an actuating shaft that controlled the breech; further rotation brought the cranks that controlled the breech dead centre over the top, and broke the mechanical lock, thus starting to release tension on the torsion springs that helped close the breech.

Continued rotation caused the block to fall to the open position; the handle is now turned in an anti-clockwise direction, which will bring the breech up to the load position. Once this position has been reached, the tool can be removed and stowed.

As can be seen, a lot of effort was needed to open the breech using the breech-opening tool. Later models had a breech mechanism lever (BML) fitted: when pulled to the rear and downwards, this opened the breech to the loading position; the handle was then brought back to the vertical position, where it was retained.

Fume Extractor

This is located about a third of the way down the barrel: it is 546mm (2in) long, with a diameter of 226mm (1in); it covers eight ports drilled in the barrel, and it acts as a pressure vessel. Once the gun has been fired, the projectile travels right through the bore of the gun: some propellant gases will enter the fume extractor through the eight ports, and will build up a pressure in the extractor cylinder. They will remain in the cylinder until the projectile has left the barrel. When this happens, the gas pressure in the bore will fall below the pressure within the fume extractor, and the trapped gases will re-enter the bore; this causes a flow of air from breech to muzzle, with the result that the gases are forced out of the muzzle.

THE GUNNER'S CONTROLS

We will now look at the controls available to the three turret-crew members, and consider how they are used to fight the vehicle. We will also be comparing the earlier marks of vehicle with the latest (TOGS) to see what has changed (the drawings and photos should help). The gunner is situated on the right side of the gun and below the commander; this makes it easier for the commander to place a well used, size 10 combat boot into the gunner's back when he gets it wrong.

A sectioned view of the fume extractor. Notice the angular cutout at the top of the barrel; this allows the gases into the extractor, then when the round has left the barrel, the vacuum that has been created collapses and the gases are vented out through these holes in the direction of the muzzle. (RCMS Shrivenham)

The Gunner's Sights

The gunner is equipped with two sights: a periscopic sight – this could be either a pure optical sight or the tank laser sight (TLS) which protrudes through the roof – and a sight unit that is basically a telescope. Both these sights were used for direct fire. Later marks supplemented these with the 'thermal observation and gunnery sight' (TOGS).

Early marks of Chieftain had the gunner's sight AFV no 32 Mk2: this was very similar to the later marks of sight issued to ranging gun-equipped Centurions. This was then replaced by the sight periscopic AFV no. 38 Mk1. Both these sights were of a similar construction, with a monocular eyepiece for use during engagements, and above that, a unity window of x1 magnification that gave the gunner a general view of the outside world. Both had a ballistic graticule designed to work with the RMG; basically the

sight graticule was made up of various markings in the form of split circles with a dot in the centre.

Also at the edges were vertical and horizontal lines, used to engage moving targets, and as a reference point to help the gunner judge the fall of shot. The gunner would lay the centre of the first circle around the target, then a burst of three rounds from the RMG was fired, then the gunner would move up to the next circle until all four dots had been used. The RMG's fall of shot determined the final range given by the commander.

This was a very quick and reasonably accurate method of determining the range to a target; prior to this the commander had either had to guess accurately (not very easy), use a main armament round or, in the case of Conqueror, the range finder in the fire control turret. The limitation was the RMG's range of fire, which was about 1,100m (3,600ft). To rectify this a new sight was issued, the sight periscopic AFV no. 59 or 69; together with modifications to the RMG barrel and extended range ammunition, the range was improved to 2,000m (6,560ft).

The main change to the sight was the replacement of the four-dot graticule with a nine-dot pattern; the gunner would still fire the four bursts, but the commander controlled any use of the remaining dots. Totally against the gunnery schools' teaching, a good crew would let the gunner get on and fire all the bursts, the commander stepping in as soon as he spotted the fall of shot. The problem with this method was that the commander could easily lose count of the fall of shot, or which burst was which, since at the longer ranges several bursts of three rounds might be in the air at the same time. Nevertheless, if you could make it work it was slick and effective.

The major difference between the 59 and the 69 sights was the fact that the 59 sight had an adapter collar fitted so it could be mounted into the no. 39 sight mounting: this had been adopted so the tank laser sight could be fitted. All the gunners' sights were of x8 magnification.

The Sight Mounting

The sight mounting is bolted to the turret roof by means of a mounting plate; it is suspended by two trunnions, to allow it movement in the vertical plane. On the right of the mounting is a large locking lever to secure the sight in the mounting, and on the left is a lug connecting a hollow link bar to the gun. This bar is filled with anti-freeze to prevent any movement due to extreme temperature: such movement would cause distortion and place the sight out of alignment. The coolant is continually pumped around by the link-bar pump; this is controlled by a switch on the gunner's lighting and controls box. Also on the right side is a connection for another link bar, this time connected to the commander's projector reticule image.

Sight Protection

Above the opening above the sight mount is an armoured hood to protect the head of the sight

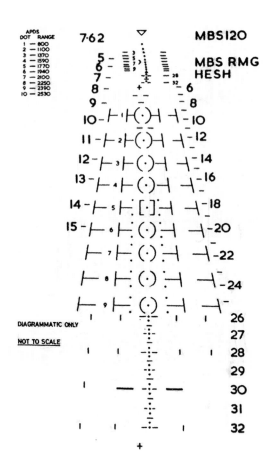

The nine-dot sight. Notice that dot five is a square; fire was controlled by the commander from five to nine, although the gunner could still use dots one to four as before. (Crown Copyright)

fitted; on the front of the hood is a glass window to prevent the ingress of rain and moisture. The window is fitted with a heater for demisting, and a wash and wiper system, all of which are again controlled from the gunner's lighting and control panel located on the turret to his right. The hood also incorporates an armoured shutter that can be lowered, firstly to protect the sight, and also to shut off any light escaping via the sight optics at night if the turret lights are on. A handle to the right of the sight mount controls this cover.

The Sight Unit

The gunner is also equipped with a sight unit AFV: there are several different marks, reflecting the same changes as for the periscopic sight. It provides the gunner with an emergency sight should his main sight become damaged; it has a magnification of x7. It is located to his left shoulder, and the viewing head is visible from outside as a very small aperture below, and to the left of, the main sight hood. The unit has a control head that houses the adjusters for the graticule, and is connected to the sighting head by means of a bearing that allows rotation when the gun is elevated or depressed. The main housing is an optical link between the front and rear housings; the rear housing contains an eyepiece for the gunner, and is provided with an eyepiece heater that is controlled by the same switch as used for the main sight.

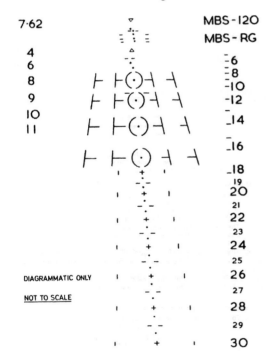

The original four-dot sight for the RMG. The dots referred to are in the split circles, and the gunner would lay the dot on target, then fire, moving through each dot till a strike was observed. (Crown Copyright)

The Graticule

The graticule would be that of the main sight: the telescope was a most unreliable piece of optical equipment, and it always took a long time to bore-sight it. It also always seemed to be the case that having adjusted it so that it was spot on, as soon as the gun was elevated or depressed, then the sight unit would lose all relationship with the gun. Because of its location and mounting, if a rubber bung was not fitted, dirt and moisture could enter and damage the head, or even cause it to seize. The sight was meant to be removed at least once a month by a REME instrument technician; however, this rarely happened, since the poor technicians had many other jobs to do, and not enough time to spare. Usually before a firing period there was a mad panic to ensure that all the units worked; then things would slow down, until the yearly inspection of vehicles came around again.

The Tank Laser Sight

In the early 1970s the Chieftain was issued with its first tank laser sight: the No.1 Mk 2. However, this was at the expense of the ranging gun: this was removed and the aperture in the turret welded over, and its ammunition space utilized for other stowage. Whilst both the tactical and the technological benefits were appreciated, many crews felt that it was a big mistake to remove the RMG. Their feeling was that, if it had been converted back to an MG and provided with the correct ammunition, it would have given them a cost-effective weapon to deal with light armour. It would have been excellent for engaging targets that the GPMG could not deal with, but which equally would have been a waste of a HESH round; however the decision was taken, and would not be changed.

Whilst by today's standards the issued laser sight would seem crude, it was a giant leap forward for the crews. For the first time a tank commander could sit in his fire position and accurately range on to locations where the enemy was expected to appear. Prior to this, all he had been able to do was hope that he could estimate

113

accurately from the map, or use information from a previous engagement, or even register using the RMG – although the latter would give away the tank's position. So the use of the laser was a major advantage in producing accurate range figures for static defensive positions.

How the Laser Sight Works

The lasers used in Chieftain are all ruby rod lasers, and although there are many versions that could be fitted, the basic design is the same for all the laser sights used (see the appendix on technical specification). The sight consists of an alloy body that contains the x10 and x1 optical system and the laser transmitting system. The head of the laser is a right-angled prism, secured to the body by four screws.

On the rear of the body is a x1 unity window: this gives the gunner a broader outlook than viewing through the x10 eyepiece. The window is fitted with a blackout shutter. Also visible in the window is a circle that defines the field of view of the x10 eyepiece.

The x10 eyepiece is of the fixed focus type, and is fitted with an eyepiece heater; to the left is another eyepiece that allows the gunner to read the range readout and other data, including the type of ammunition selected, and the type of laser pulse being used. The sight is adjusted with two graticule adjusters, in the same way as the RMG-type sights.

The sight is equipped with a trunnion tilt mechanism: this allows the prism upon which the graticule is etched to swing in its mounting and find a vertical position, even if the whole vehicle is canted – in fact this can compensate for the vehicle being on an angle of 178 mils. When not in use, the mechanism must be locked in place with the locking lever provided on the sight.

The lever controlling the boresight mark in/out check – already discussed – is located to the right of the x1 window.

On the lower left of the sight is the flash button that can be used to fire the laser; on early vehicles this was the only means of doing so. Located on the lower right is a laser filter that fits into the x10 eyepiece, and this must be used if it is suspected that the enemy is subjecting you to any device using laser range-finders.

Bore Sighting

With the introduction of the laser, a method evolved that would allow the gunner to check accurately the relationship between the axis of the bore of the gun and his sight. Initially this was done as the first duty of the day, by placing an instrument known as a 'muzzle bore sight' into the bore of the main armament. This is basically a Y-shaped shaft with two spring-loaded plungers on the leg of the Y; it is pushed into the bore, with the plungers locating it firmly. The object end has a rubber-coated head that contains a right-angle prism.

The person who was going to carry out the bore sighting would stand on a convenient oil-drum or such-like so that he was level with the bore sight, ensuring that he did not hold on to the barrel, or lean on it, at any time during the procedure. Then by means of a set sequence of commands, the person looking through the bore sight would lay the aiming mark in its graticule onto the centre of the bore-sighting screen.

This was a screen erected at 1,100m (3,600ft) down-range; painted on its surface was an outer surface with a central aiming dot. Once he was happy that the gun was laid on, the gunner would adjust his aiming mark by means of graticule adjusters on his sight, until it, too, was in the centre of the bore-sighting screen. The gunner would also adjust the sight unit at this time, and the commander would adjust his projector reticule image: so now, all three aiming marks were laid on centrally to the screen. This procedure would also have been applied to the RMG, when it was fitted, and it would have been provided with its own bore sight.

Adjusting the RMG could prove to be a frustrating business, as the loader would adjust the RMG mounting cradle for line and elevation, and then lock them up. He would then try to cock the gun: if this proved impossible, it was generally because a condition known as 'crossbind' had happened, when adjusting the cradle caused the gun body to twist – and the solution? Start again – great fun if it was raining.

Bore Sighting in the Field
The procedure just described was always a feature of ranges: an average of fifteen tank crews all bore sighting at the same time, and all using the terminology approved by the RAC gunnery school – the effect can be imagined. This system had been in use for many years and was considered sufficient, although it was realized that the gun's accuracy would deteriorate during the day due to the continuous shock of firing. However, once guns were shot in using calibrated screens, it soon became apparent that their accuracy in fact fell off far more rapidly than had at first been thought.

I remember when our tank was shot in for the CAT competition; all the drills just described were carried out to the letter. We then fired our rounds at a calibrated screen, and were given adjustment figures to put on our sights by the gunnery staff in the control tower. Eventually we were so well adjusted that all the rounds were going through the centre of the screen – which is just what we were trying to achieve. However, when firing had finished we were told to place the bore sights back into the guns and see where the bore-sight dot was now, after adjustment by fire. To our amazement the dot for our tank just touched the top left of the screen – a result that definitely provided food for thought.

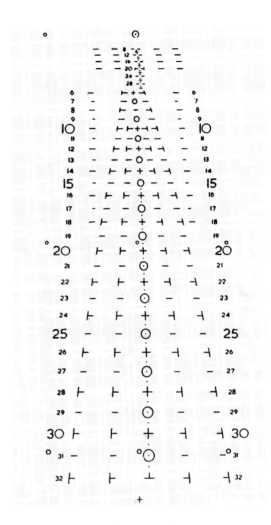

A typical TLS graticule pattern. Compare this to the IR night-sight pattern. (Crown Copyright)

UPGRADING THE SYSTEM: A NEW BARREL

I am quite sure that the authorities knew about this problem, since they had been working on a solution that would enable the crew to adjust the sights after every round if necessary; inevitably this would give them confidence in the accuracy of their gun. Thus as part of the upgrade of the vehicle a new barrel was fitted: the L11A5. The main

A troop of Chieftains with the commander carrying out the bore-sighting procedure. The person doing this would have to balance on an oil-drum so as to be level with the muzzle. (Paul Kay)

external differences were the more compact fume extractor, and a forged upstanding at the muzzle end; this held part of the new muzzle reference system (MRS) that was designed to combat the problems discussed above.

The Muzzle Reference System

The MRS provided, for the first time, a facility for aligning the bore-sight mark in the gunner's sight with the bore of the main armament, without the crew having to leave the vehicle and start using the bore sight whilst possibly under fire. It enables the gunner to check the gun/sight relationship at any time during firing if he suspects a fault – indeed, if taken to the extreme it could be checked after every round.

The main causes for a loss of gun/sight relationship may be the elements, barrel heat, or if the barrel or the cradle have been disturbed, such as hitting a tree or some other solid object. Using MRS the gunner can carry out an immediate check, and straightaway make adjustments to the sight settings if required.

The MRS system consists of four components: the light source, the mirror assembly, the switch box and the depression brackets.

The Light Source
The light source used is AV No. 1, a rectangular box mounted on four lugs to the left of the gunner's sight hood. Inside is a v-halogen bulb, controlled by the switch box at the gunner's station. The light is projected through a large fibre-optic fitted with a red filter so that the light projected will not be so easily visible to anyone viewing the area where the tank is. The light that is projected is shaped by the fibre-optic to conform to the MBS mark in the sight – either a circle or an inverted triangle, depending on which gunner's sight is fitted.

Mirror Assembly
The MRS No. 1 shroud mirror is made of stiff rubber, open at one end and sealed with a metal plate at the other. It covers the mirror, which will reflect the transmitted light back towards the head of the gunner's sight. The mirror is made of machined bar that is highly polished, with a reflective and protecting coating; it is mounted on a bracket bolted to the forged upstanding on the end of the muzzle. The shroud provides a dark, non-reflective tunnel.

The Switch Box
The MRS No. 1 switch box is mounted on a bracket forward of the gunner's position and

contains three toggle-type switches. The upper-most switch is the on/off switch for the light projector; it is spring-loaded so that it cannot be left on, which would be a tactical give-away. The centre switch is an on/off control for the heater in the light projector; and the bottom switch controls the brightness of the projected light.

The Depression Brackets

The two depression indicators ensure that the gun is at the correct elevation before the MRS is used. One is located on the right of the gun cradle, and the other is fixed to a bracket to the left of the gunner's position. They contain Trilux gas, so they can be seen in the dark without a light.

One further facility is contained in a lever marked MRS in/out fitted to the gunner's sight: when appropriate the lever can be moved to the 'in' position, which allows the field of view of the sight to be distorted to take in the end of the gun and the mirror.

Using MRS

If it is suspected that the gun/sight relationship has been lost, the commander can order the gunner to check the accuracy by using the MRS system. The gunner will place the in/out lever on his sight to 'in', and level the gun to the required position by aligning the depression indicators. Then he will hold down the on/off switch on the control box: this will allow a beam of light to be reflected back into the sight via the mirror on the muzzle end. The gunner observes where the light is in his sight, and if necessary will move the ballistic graticule by means of the graticule adjusters, until the MBS mark is directly over the reflected image. He can then lock release the on/off switch, and lock up the graticule adjusters; and finally he will change over the in/out switch to the 'out' position, and so be ready to resume firing. The whole procedure is completed in a matter of seconds, without affecting the efficiency of the drills in the turret.

CHIEFTAIN'S NIGHT-FIGHTING CAPABILITY

Before the introduction of TOGS, which allowed the gun to be fired almost twenty-four hours a day, night-fighting capability had been one of the requirements for Chieftain, and to that end, infra-red sights and a searchlight had been provided. Both the gunner and commander had an IR night-sight, to be used either in conjunction with the searchlight or on their own. The driver was also issued with a set of IR goggles that were worn on a harness over the issue helmet; however, these proved to be very limited in their use, and also unpopular – they generally spent most of their life firmly packed in their stowage box, only seeing the light of day for serial number checks.

The Gunner's IR Sight

The gunner's IR sight was the sight periscopic IR L1A1, and it was interchangeable with the day sight. If it was going to be used it would be fitted at last light when it would be bore-sighted in, which was not an easy task. On the whole, crews did not like using the IR sight: the image produced was never the best, and identification was always hard; moreover the shoots carried out on the ranges always gave a false impression of how efficient the equipment was, as everything possible was done to achieve a good picture. This could mean illuminating the target with the tank's own searchlight, using mortar or artillery illuminating rounds, and even heat sources on the target itself.

Another problem was that, in the morning, the crew would have to bore-sight again when they fitted the day sight back in. And even though this was a daily task, the removal and replacement of sights did not help maintain accuracy.

When not in use the IR sight was stowed in a container on the left bank of charge bins behind the driver's seat.

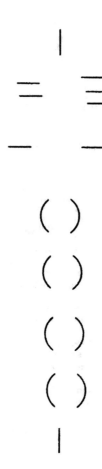

A very simple graticule pattern for the gunner's night sight. This sometimes obscured the target, but if you turned the brightness down it would disappear. (Crown Copyright)

The Searchlight Before TOGS

Situated on the left-hand side of the turret – before the introduction of TOGS – was the light projector No. 2 Mk 3 Xenon searchlight. The light was contained in a lightly armoured box, and could be used either as a white light searchlight or an IR searchlight. For white light, the outer door and then the inner IR filter were opened; for IR, the filter was closed. Normally the searchlight operated at 2kw; however, it could be boosted to 3kw by means of a button on the control box, but for a period of 10sec only.

The light was controlled by a control box situated at the commander's station. It consisted of a rotary control knob that allowed him to open the doors to use either white or IR; depression of the knob gave the boost facility. There was also a trim knob on the gunner's fixed grip that gave him a degree of trim control of plus or minus 44 mils. This was later moved to the commander's control box.

Use of the searchlight was not popular, as the tank that provided white light illumination would be blatantly obvious to even a purblind enemy anti-tank gunner. The accepted tactic would be for one tank to illuminate, and a second tank situated off to a flank actually to engage the target. However, although this was

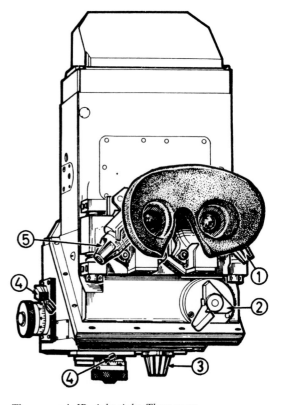

The gunner's IR night sight. There were similar feelings about this sight as for the commander's: it really was a monumental pain to change! (Crown Copyright)

sometimes practised as an exercise, it was never enthusiastically embraced, and slowly fell out of use.

Another recurring problem was the amount the searchlight jutted out over the side: quite often drivers forgot this, with disastrous consequences – as L/Cpl Simon Fletcher of the 4/7 RDG discovered during a road move to the Staple training area near Detmold in West Germany. As his tank was heading out to the area, a tank from the 15/19 Hussars – the other regiment in the garrison – was approaching from the other direction. Somehow they managed to meet, and in so doing removed both searchlights: so definitely not a case of tanks that pass in the night.

FIXED LINE AND INDIRECT SHOOTS

Besides having the optical sight to engage targets, the Chieftain is capable of firing on fixed lines, also semi-indirect and indirect. To carry out these types of shoot the gun is laid on by means of two instruments: the traverse indicator and the quadrant fire control AFV No. 14 Mk1.

The Traverse Indicator

This consists of two components: a transmitting unit and a receiving unit. The transmitting unit is located on the left side of the turret and it is connected electrically to the receiving unit. A split pinion connects the transmitting unit to the turret ring, so any movement of the turret will be transmitted electrically to the receiving unit. The receiving unit is mounted flexibly on a bracket whose location may vary depending whether TOGS is fitted or not. It consists of a dial marked with an inner and an outer scale marked in mils, and two pointers, one long and one short; these can be set independently by means of two adjusters. It is fitted with illumination, and is controlled from the gunner's lighting and switch panel.

The scales are marked as follows: the outer scale is marked in red from 0–100 mils for left rotation, and 0–100 mils for right rotation: this scale is used with the long pointer. The inner scale is marked every 100 mils, from 0–32 left and 0–32 for right: the representative colours used are again, red for left and green for right. In use the gunner would zero the scales before commencing an engagement by rotating the adjusters till both pointers read zero; then any movement left or right can be seen on the respective dials. The commander can also order the gunner to carry out a line switch by giving it in units of mils, which the gunner would apply by zeroing the scales then traversing off the required amount by looking at the dials. It was proposed to eventually replace this unit with a modern digital version.

The Quadrant Fire Control

The other component required to carry out those shoots is the quadrant fire control, bolted to a bracket on the right side of the gun cradle. It works in the following way. A clinometer – a type of spirit level – is attached to an arm that is moved whenever the range drum adjuster is moved, this action influencing the bubble in the clinometer. The range drum has two parts: a fixed drum on the left marked up in mils, and a movable drum on the right, which has a range scale, marked in metres. The movable drum is locked to the fixed drum by means of a knurled knob lock nut. A Perspex cursor is fitted over both drums so that readings may be taken.

A bulb controlled from the gunner's lighting control box illuminates the QFC when required. Scales marked on the drum are for HESH from 0–8,000 (later models are marked to 10,600). An angle-of-sight scale is also marked on the right part of the fixed drum: elevation is from 0–360 mils, in yellow; and depression from 0–80 mils, in white. A quadrant elevation scale is marked in the same way as the angle-of-sight scale, and is located on the left of the fixed drum.

Using the QFC

To use the QFC the commander will calculate the angle of sight required, or it can be measured by the QFC. The gunner will rotate the range drum until the required angle of sight is set under the cursor line. Then he will unlock the range drum and rotate the moving part until the scale reads zero under the cursor; he will then lock up the knurled nut. Next he will elevate or depress the gun as required by using his hand elevation controls, until the bubble in the clinometer is level. He may also have been directed to traverse the gun off, in which case this will be achieved by means of the traverse indicator and the hand traverse controls.

These instruments allow the crew to carry out fixed line and indirect shoots. These are quite fun,

but they do take time; furthermore they require the tank to be static for a long time, so they have to be carried out when there is no chance of the enemy closing the gap and engaging. They are also the commander's 'baby', in that he makes all the corrections, and the gunner applies them.

These techniques are only used for what are called 'area targets', such as trenches, men in the open, or transport.

CONTROLLING THE ARMAMENT

The gunner is equipped with both power and hand controls for traverse and elevation, and

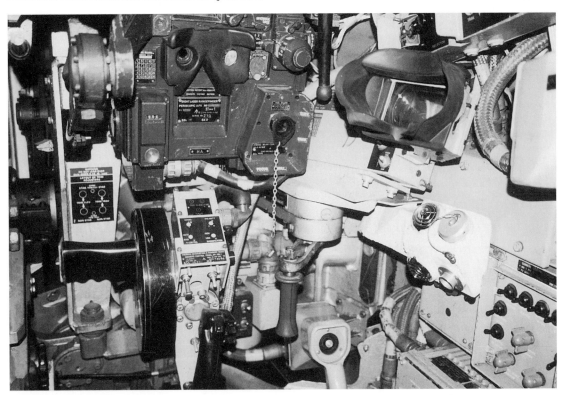

Most of the gunners' controls can be seen in the photograph including the hand traverse and elevation handles, the tank laser sight, at the bottom right is the control for power traverse and elevation. In the centre is the gunner's firing handle, containing all the switches he needs to select ammunition and fire the guns. (RCMS Shrivenham)

there is also a fixed rate, emergency traverse system that can be used by the gunner or by the commander. The hand-laying equipment consists of a hand traverse handle situated to the right of the gunner; it has a two-speed mechanism that allows coarse or fine traverse to be used by the gunner: to obtain coarse traverse the gunner must pull down on the traverse handle, and to obtain fine he must push up.

The drive from the traverse handle is transmitted to the traverse gearbox that is bolted to the turret wall in front of the gunner and to his right-hand side. From there via a series of gearings, a pinion engages in the turret rack. In the event of the barrel striking an object such as a house or a tree, a slipping clutch is built into the gearbox in order to prevent damage to the system. A dog clutch is incorporated between the traverse handle shaft and the gear train, and will disengage the hand traverse when the power-laying equipment is in use.

The Power Supply

The power for the power-laying equipment comes from the power supply unit and control cubicle located behind the commander's seat; further behind that, in the rear right of the turret, are the metadynes. These each contain a generator, which receives and transmits power from the control cubicle to the turret traverse, and elevation motors. The system also includes various limit switches: thus there are switches operated by cams to prevent the gun striking the rear of the hull if traversed in full depression. There are also elevation limit switches designed to prevent damage when the gun is approaching maximum elevation or depression; and there are separate limit switches that come into operation when the travelling stabilizer is in use.

Using the Power-Laying Equipment

To use the power-laying equipment the aux. gen. must be running and on line, and it is the gunner

who controls the starting of the powered laying equipment, from the control panel on the right of the turret and above his position.

There are various modes that can be selected: the first is 'non-stab', meaning that only powered traverse is available to the gunner; the commander, however, will have full control. With the switch moved to 'stab, full power', traverse and elevation will be available to the gunner; it must be in this position for the vehicle to move off with the gun under full stabilization. At 'trav stab', full power elevation and traverse are still available, but the gun will remain within set limits. This mode is usually employed for long approach marches, when the gun kit is required to be running, as it saves the gunner having to keep control of the gun.

To use emergency power, the commander must use a lever located on the control cubicle, moving it from the horizontal position to the vertical; this will then give a fixed rate of power, and traverse only, usually about 90sec for one rotation of the turret; in full power one rotation takes 18sec. The gunner is equipped with controls to trim out any creep that occurs within the power system.

To prevent injury to the crew and damage to the vehicle there are three safety switches: the driver's and loader's switches will prevent traverse and elevation in power mode, whilst the commander's will cut off the power supply, although the turret may still run on. The loader's safety switch will also prevent the weapons being fired.

Controllers for the Power-Laying Equipment

The commander and gunner have similar controllers for the power-laying equipment: in early models a controller known as a 'duplex controller' was fitted; later marks have a thumb controller.

The Duplex Controller
The duplex controller was a twin-axis handle with a grip-switch fitted in the handle, and the equipment could not be activated unless this

switch was kept gripped at all times. To use the controller with the equipment running, the gunner or commander would grip the handle and incline it left or right for traverse, and forward or to the rear for elevation and depression; the more it was inclined, the faster the movement. It was spring-loaded and would self-centre if released.

The two controllers were all but identical in use, the only difference being that the commander could override the gunner's controller by simply pressing in on the grip switch. This was so that he could take control, either in an emergency or to lay the gunner on to a target – as soon as he released his grip switch, the gunner would regain control.

The Thumb Controller

In later marks the duplex controller was replaced by a thumb controller: this consists of an ergonomically designed handle, again incorporating a grip switch, at the top of which is a small rubber nipple on which the thumb of the gunner/commander rests. The movement of this controls the movement of the gun and turret in very much the same way as the duplex controller did. Thus movement left and right will move the turret left and right, and forward or backward will move the gun in elevation or depression. The commander was also provided with controls that enabled him to select and fire the armament if required: these also overrode the gunner's selector switch.

The Gunner's Firing Switches

The gunner has both electrical and mechanical switches for firing the main and secondary armaments. In early marks he had a firing switch on the hand elevation wheel, and a switch on a fixed grip directly in front of him; the grip also housed a trim control for the searchlight. Both these switches could fire either main or secondary. The gunner would select the required weapon by way of the three-position switch and warning lights on the selector box located to his right. Thus in the central position the circuit was dead; with the

switch moved to 'main' and the red light illuminated, the 120mm could be fired; and with co-ax selected and the amber light lit, the co-ax could be fired.

Once IFCS was fitted to the vehicle in conjunction with the thumb controller, the gunner's fixed firing switch was changed. He could now select main or co-ax by a switch on top of the handle with a lift-up safety guard; on the forward face was a push button to tell the computer which ammunition was to be fired; and above that was the firing switch.

To the right of the armament selector switch was the laser/auto lay switch, a rocker switch used by the gunner during an IFCS engagement. There was also provision for firing the co-ax manually by means of a bowden cable – similar to a bicycle brake cable operated by a foot pedal. If this was used, then the safety switches were bypassed.

In early marks there was also an electrical foot firing switch for the RMG; this was linked to the solenoid on the RMG, which when activated would allow the gun to fire a burst of just three rounds. The gunner's selector switch had to be in the main position before the RMG could be fired. On later marks a firing pedal for the laser sight replaced this foot pedal; and if required, the laser could be fired from the sight itself.

THE COMMANDER'S SIGHTS

The commander has for his main sight a sight periscopic AV No. 37 Mk 1–4, although the Mk 3–4 is the most common issued now. The major differences in the sights are mainly in the magnification and shape. Thus the head of the Mks 1 and 2 was vertical, whilst that of the 3 and 4 is inclined; and the magnification of the Mk 3 is x15, while that of the Mk 4 reverted to x10, as x15 was found to be too powerful.

The sight consists of three castings: the upper, centre and lower. The upper casting contains the object reflector, and also a mirror that is linked to the commander's mg mounting. The centre casting contains a reflector for the injected graticule from the projector reticule image PRI, and on the left side is a magnification lever that enables the commander to select either x10 (x15) or x1. Also on the left side is the linkage to connect the mirror to the mg mount. The lower casting contains the eyepieces that are arranged in a binocular layout; they are of fixed focus, and will be either x15 or x10, and they are provided with eye heaters and a rubber facepiece.

Above the eyepieces is a unity window of x1 magnification; this gives the commander a broader view than that obtained by the eyepieces. There is also a wash-and-wipe system, controlled from the commander's control box.

In the left eyepiece a graticule pattern will be injected from the PRI when the cupola is in the line-up position. A sight periscopic AV image-intensified L5A1 was produced, but as far as the author is aware, was never issued. These sights cost about £1,000 to produce, but can now be purchased for around £50 at military fairs.

The Cupola Periscopes

Although the cupola can be traversed a full 360 degrees, the commander is provided with nine cupola periscopes; again, these vary with the mark of vehicle. The early sights were of a two-part construction and were awful things to use, as the bottom half kept moving out of alignment with the top, and this gave a distorted view on the outside world.

They were soon replaced by a one-part periscope: the AV No. 40 Mk 1–2. The only difference between the marks was that the No. 1 had a vertical head, and the No. 2 a sloping head. As we have seen, there are nine of these located in the fixed part of the cupola, of x1 magnification; they are equipped with a wash-and-wipe system, again controlled by the commander's switch box. They have a spring-loaded, retractable blind that can be pulled over the viewing widow to prevent the emission of light at night when the turret lights are on.

These sights are fitted into the cupola from outside, but in the event of one of them becoming damaged, two periscopes – AV No. 41 – are carried; these can be fitted from inside the vehicle, simply by pushing the damaged 40 sight out and fitting the 41 into its place. They can use the washer wipe system, and also have the blackout blind fitted; two of these are carried as spares in the turret.

The IR Night Sight

Along with the gunner, the commander was originally provided with an IR night sight as well: the sight periscopic AV L1A1. Confusingly it has the same number as the gunner's. While the latter was struggling to fit his sight, the commander would be doing the same – but he had to connect up the mirror linkage to the mg in the same way as the day sight, and at times this could be a really awkward job. Once the sight was in, then the performance of adjusting the graticule began, and hopefully it would be completed before darkness set in.

The Projector Reticle Image

The projector reticle image, or PRI, is located on the turret roof inside the turret immediately in front of the cupola ring. The PRI is connected to the gunner's sight by means of an adjustable linkage. Its purpose is to project into the commander's sight a graticle image similar to the one as seen by the gunner. This is because the commander's 37 sight does not have a built-in graticle pattern, and it will only work when the commander's sight is in the lined-up position. This is because the sight is mounted in the moving part of the cupola, while the PRI is mounted on the turret roof.

The brightness of the image can be adjusted from a dimmer switch on the cupola services junction box. As with the gunner's sights, the projected graticle will depend on the current state of modification of the vehicle. One useful secondary

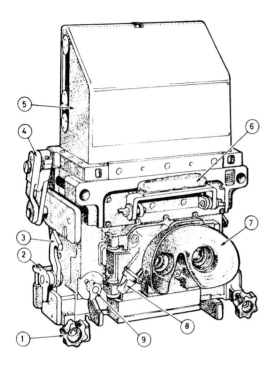

The commander's IR sight was not very popular and usually stayed in its stowage for most exercises, unless the Sqn Leader had a mind to see the system worked. (Crown Copyright)

use that the designers never imagined for the PRI was that if you lowered the lamp housing down so the bulb was exposed, it made reading that much easier as it was brighter than the turret cluster lights.

THE CUPOLA

In accordance with the rest of the vehicle, the commander's cupola has experienced several modifications throughout its time in service. The original cupola issued to the early vehicles and Mk 1 Chieftains was version AFV No. 11 Mk 2. It was very similar to the cupola on late mark Centurions, as it had split hatches that could be raised in the closed position so the commander could view outside but still have overhead protection. The optics for this cupola were an entirely different fit to the ones that we have discussed.

It was decided that for production vehicles an entirely new cupola would be produced: the AFV No. 15 Mk 1. This was followed by the No. 15 Mk 2, introduced on Mk 3 vehicles onwards. They both featured a fixed part that housed the periscopes and wipers and washers, and a movable part that had the commander's sight, mg, hatch, ammunition box and spotlight. The main difference between them was that the Mk 1 had split periscope sights that had to be inserted from inside, and outside had locking levers on top of the cupola to retain them. As we have mentioned they were not a great success.

The Commander's Hatch

This could be locked either fully closed, or opened with a type of umbrella position obtained by a locking pin engaging in the sight cover of the commander's sight. The Mk 2 had these features, but the hatch could also be retained at a 90-degree angle, giving some protection to the commander's upper body. The Mk 2 also had a much flatter and larger plate covering the periscopes, meaning that the commander had somewhere nice and flat to rest his mug of tea.

The moving part also carried the commander's mg mount, and again there are several versions of this, some having only a limited elevation, while the final version elevated to 90 degrees. The ammunition for the mg was originally carried on a bracket on the mg mount, but later, some versions had a large bin for the ammunition, allowing more than one box to be loaded. For although the mg could be laid and fired from inside the cupola, reloading had to be carried out from outside, thus exposing the commander to hostile fire. The commander has his own IR searchlight fitted on the right side on a shaft connected to the mg mount; it has a removable IR cover so it can be used for IR or white light.

Traversing the Cupola

The cupola can be traversed by hand, allowing the commander to scan through 360 degrees independently of the main turret. Should he spot a target he can train the main armament on it by moving the cupola selector lever to the forward position, and providing that the powered laying equipment for the gun is running. Thus when he presses in on the grip switch, the cupola and main turret will contra-rotate until the gun is pointing in the direction that the commander required. This was a useful but quite often ignored way of bringing the main armament to bear on a target without a lot of fuss. The drive for the contra-rotation was removed when TOGS was fitted to the vehicle.

Had Chieftain soldiered on into the next century – plans were in hand to make it last till at least 2005 – the commander's station was due for a major upgrade, including a power-operated cupola and panoramic sights.

The Night Shoot

The night shoot was always an anti-climax, with the crews hanging round or making brews to keep warm before the time came for them to fire the fantastic amount of ammo generally designated for the night shoot. This usually amounted to one or two boxes of 7.62mm and maybe three of 120mm DS/T. When the great moment came and all was ready, you would struggle to make sense of the ghostly green images produced by the IR sight. Then the mortars would burst overhead and slowly drift downwards, illuminating the range beautifully – but the next range, as the wind had carried away the parachute flares. However, you had managed to pick out one hard target, and very quickly let loose at it – and quite often would be rewarded with a fantastic shower of sparks as the DS/T hit. Then it was all over and back to camp, a hot mug of soup, and bed.

Things might have been different if the commander's II sight had been on issue, but we saw in an earlier chapter why commanders liked to steal the driver's II sight for observation when static at night.

The Commander's Controls

The commander has several controls to enable him to make use of the various facilities available to the cupola, such as the mg, the spotlight, washers, wipers and the sight eyepiece heaters.

The IR Detector and Control Box

One component from the early days that survived for a long time was the IR detector and control box. This evolved because it was felt that if we used IR, then undoubtedly the enemy would as well, and it would be nice to know when you were being observed.

Basically the detector consisted of the detector stalk and control box. The stalk was mounted on the right rear of the turret just behind the cupola; it was a flexible shaft with three photovoltaic silicon cells set in a triangle pattern on the top, and covered by an IR filter; these cells gave detection coverage over 360 degrees. If the vehicle came under observation by an active IR source, one of the cells would pick it up and cause a buzzer to sound in the commander's control box. He would then press a set of three buttons in turn, one of which would cause the light on the control box to light up. This indicated the angle the tank was being viewed from, the buttons relating to front, left and right; and if none of the lights came on, then the light source was from the rear – not very good news. Mark Davis tells me that:

> … they tried to make the system work, but the trouble was, it was so light-sensitive that it had to keep adjusting the trim control to prevent the buzzer giving false alarms. In the end we gave up, and it was only ever fitted at shows where we would tell people it was an IR alarm clock.

The Commander's Firing Controls

As well as being able to override the gunner with the power kit, the commander also has a set of firing controls that allows him to engage a target independently. Early versions only gave the com-

A Typical Engagement

Let us imagine an engagement using the RMG: the crew is mounted, and the generator and all the gun-powered equipment is running. The commander has warned that firing is imminent by the time-honoured gunnery cry of 'Action!', and this has immediately galvanized the crew into action. They will carry out set drills: thus the driver will close down, if he has not already done so; the gunner will select the lights that he is likely to require, he will ensure that he is seated comfortably, and will check that 'non-stab' is selected and that both his foot pedals are down – one for the mg, and the other for the RMG. The loader will check that all stowage is clear, that ammunition is available, that the traverse indicator drive is engaged, and that his safety switch is set to 'live'. The commander is likewise setting up everything in a state of readiness.

Once all the drills are complete, the gunner will start to 'scan': he will move the gun slowly across the designated arc, searching for targets; alternatively using x1 and x10 to identify, the commander will be using his binoculars or the 37 sight. The driver will also be observing, as quite often he can see the target before the turret crew.

Once a target has been spotted, the commander must decide instantly what type of ammunition to use, and as soon as he does so, he will use his duplex controller to start the gunner laying in, roughly, the area of the target. While the gun is moving he will be issuing his fire order: this might sound something like 'Ranging sabot tank – on'. This tells the loader to load sabot, and the gunner that they will be firing at a tank with sabot, and that it is a ranging gun shoot.

Once the gunner sees the target, he will report back: this tells the commander that he has identified the target. The loader will have fully loaded the RMG, and loaded a sabot round and charge, and closed the breech. Then he will pick up the next sabot round, pull his shield to the rear and check that his safety switch is still on 'live', then finally at the top of his voice he will report 'Loaded!'.

The gunner, meanwhile, using the hand controls, will have laid the first circle of the RMG aiming marks on to the centre of the target; and once the commander is happy that everything is in order, the gunner will stamp on the RMG firing pedal, and the gun will fire a burst of three rounds. The gunner, all the while observing for the fall of shot, will be laying the next mark on and firing it: and he does this until all four aiming marks have been used. He will then depress the gun until the APDS aiming marks are in the area of the target, and await the commander's next order.

The commander is watching for the fall of shot, and in particular for a burst on target: if that happens, then that is the range he will pass to the gunner – or if no strike, then the first burst that happens will provide the information. The commander will tell the gunner 'Sabot dot three fire' (note that the range is given in dots, and not distance). The commander also says 'fire' as he is retaining command of the shoot, which is normal for APDS; for HESH he would normally give 'go on', and this hands the shoot to the gunner.

This time we are lucky, and the round hits with a bright flash. The gunner might not see this, as quite often the heat and dust caused by firing the gun makes it hard for him to see; but if he does, he will report back 'target'. And if the commander agrees, he will issue the command 'target stop'. From there they can either carry out another engagement, or clear the guns.

Back to Basics

That was a very simple and straightforward shoot; things became more involved with the introduction of the nine-dot ranging gun sight, then laser, then IFCS, and finally TOGS. With the introduction of these systems, the training had to encompass the probability of breakdown, so reversionary modes of gunnery were taught. This may have been 'back to the basics', but it meant that the crew could still engage a target even when some or, in the worst case scenario, all of the systems were down.

mander an armament selector box, and any use of the firing handle was controlled by the duplex controller. This was not very satisfactory, as trying to make a fine lay or correction with the duplex was next to impossible, especially as the commander had no hand controls for the main turret and gun.

With the introduction of IFCS things became a little better, as the commander now had a firing handle identical to that of the gunner. He has a thumb controller with override facility, and his own range readout located to the left of his sight, that gives him the same readout from the TLS as the gunner's. He also has – as part of the IFCS equipment – the commander's control and monitor unit: this has many functions, but when firing during a full IFCS shoot it is used to enter corrections for elevation/depression into the computer.

This meant that the commander could now almost carry out the same drills as the gunner, as IFCS depended on the powered kit running to be fully operational. The only controls that the commander still did not have were hand controls, but that was considered acceptable.

The Emergency Firing Button
In the event that the gun does not fire using the commander's or the gunner's controls as described, there are two more circuits that can be used. First of all there is the auxiliary: this makes use of a firing button in a box on the right of the breech. To fire using this method, switches are made as for normal, and the commander will reach through a cut-out in the safety shield on the right of the gun, and fire it by pressing in on the firing button. Then there is the emergency circuit, fired from the same box: to activate it, the gunner must select 'emergency' on the gun junction box on his left; once that is done, the commander can then fire.

If none of these works, it would be prudent to select reverse and depart as fast as possible.

7 IFCS and TOGS

Chieftain had managed for a long time with a very simple fire control system, but this really depended upon the skills of the commander and gunner, and it was becoming increasingly obvious that technologically it was being left behind, especially as the RMG was the only accurate method of establishing a range. Even though the RMG had been uprated from the original four-dot sight to the nine-dot sight, it was felt that the system was too slow, especially at longer ranges. It was also a tactical hazard, as the tank risked revealing its location as soon as it fired the RMG. So a computerized fire control system was developed, and this was introduced into service during the late seventies.

THE IMPROVED FIRE CONTROL SYSTEM

This system was known as the 'improved fire control system', or IFCS, and was developed from the advanced integrated fire control system that had been fitted to the FV4211, the aluminium Chieftain. The system was based on the field computer used by the Royal Artillery known as FACE. It was important that Chieftain kept ahead, because whatever system was used, there was no getting away from the fact that the tank that located, identified, found the range and fired first was the tank most likely to survive.

It was also hoped that IFCS would improve the tank's facility for shooting on the move, as this was about the most imprecise method of shooting that was available. The British Army did not place a great deal of emphasis on it as a technique, usually allocating only one HESH and one DS/T round during a fortnight's gunnery camp.

But in practice the drivers were blatantly misadvised: they were normally told not to speed up until the gun had fired in order to give the gunners a better chance of scoring a hit, the theory behind this being that as we would be fighting a defensive battle, we would be static for much of the time, while it was the enemy that would be on the move. As a gunnery technique, however, it was no use whatsoever: targets could be hit, and the author has managed to do it several times, but more by good luck than good judgement.

IFCS was designed to provide a high degree of accuracy, coupled with a short response time, and to give Chieftain a fire control system that was second to none at the time. It is very debatable that this lofty ideal was ever achieved to the satisfaction of the crews, however, because even though the system solved certain problems, it in fact created several others. One of these was that it required a great deal of user time to maintain it and set it up; moreover it was not a 'switch on and go' system, but needed testing at least once in a twenty-four-hour period when deployed and the armament had been in use – which was just another burdensome task on top of all the others that an operational crew had to carry out.

HOW THE IFCS WORKS

Nevertheless, IFCS was evidently there to stay, so it is now worth taking a look at what made it tick. If nothing else, it certainly provided a whole new language of abbreviations to be learnt by the crews: if you were sitting near a table in the NAAFI or a bar and overheard a crew chatting who were learning IFCS, you might be forgiven for thinking they were talking a foreign language.

It will also be appreciated that the system certainly introduced a lot more equipment into an already cramped turret, along with the problems of equipment failure.

The system comprised three groups of components: the control group, the input components group, and the output components group.

The Control Group

First of all in the control group is the 'computer and interface unit', or CIU, located beneath the gunner's seat in the space previously occupied by the commander's IR sight. The computer performs all the calculations required to produce a solution, and it also controls the functions for IFCS, the interface allowing it to communicate with peripheral components.

Situated to the right of the commander, where once a box of 7.62mm ammunition was stored, is his control and monitoring unit: the CCMU. This

is the main control box for IFCS, and it displays information in two windows, allowing the commander to monitor inputs and outputs from the system. It will also allow him to enter information that is not provided by the sensors, or to override sensor input. He will also use it to enter corrections when firing HESH.

IFCS requires a stable power supply, and in the same way that a domestic PC is provided with a surge plug, so IFCS has its equivalent. This is located to the rear of the commander's position, and is known as the 'low pass filter unit', or LPFU. It also serves to close the system down by switching the DHSS to 'off' should the battery voltage drop below 18 volts, or rise above 32 volts.

The Input Components Group

The input components provide the data for IFCS in the form of computer programs, sensor information, and control signals input by the crew.

The CCMU: the window on top displays data to the commander; also visible is the gun position indicator. This shows the commander where the turret is facing in relationship to the hull, very handy when closed down. (RCMS Shrivenham)

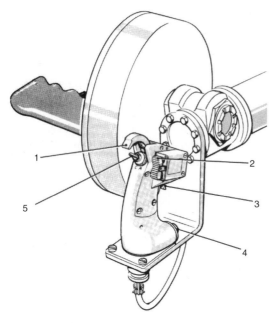

1 Armament switch guard
2 LASE/AUTOLAY switch
3 FIRING switch
4 AMMUNITION selector
5 ARMAMENT switch

The gunner's firing control handle with the elevating hand wheel behind it. The commander's handle has the same controls as the gunner's. (Crown Copyright)

Computer Programs

Like all computers, the IFCS computer needs programs loaded into it before it can carry out any of its functions. Various programs can be loaded, and like its civilian equivalent, as programs are updated, then new ones can also be loaded. One interesting program that is generally included in most suites is an 'On-Tank Trainer Program', or OTT. This projects computer-generated images representing various types of target directly into the laser sight, so crews can practise their drills without having to leave the vehicle hangar. To make it even more attractive to a generation of computer-literate youngsters, at the end of a shoot a score would be displayed, giving the gunner a percentage total.

To load these programs a unit known as 'program loading and interface control equipment' – PLAICE – is used. Once the program-loading sequence is finished, the PLAICE unit plays no further part in the operation of IFCS, and will only be used if a program needs to be replaced for any reason, or new parts fitted to the system.

The Firing Control Box Group (FCB)

In this group are the gunner's and the commander's firing control boxes (GFCB and CFCB) and firing handles. The combined use of these components allows the selection and firing of the main and co-axial armament, and they also control the signals for the charging and firing of the tank laser sight, for autolay, for ammunition selection and HESH correction routines.

The Sensor Components

The sensor components of the input group are contained in the range unit located to the right of the gunner's station: this converts the returned laser signal into readable range information that can be viewed by both the gunner and the commander.

First, underneath the gun cradle is located the trunnion tilt and angle of sight unit: the TTASU. This measures the trunnion tilt, which is the angle between the trunnions and the horizontal plane; and the angle of sight, which is the angle between the line of sight and the horizontal plane.

To provide information on the elevation of the gun, a 'gun elevation displacement unit', or GEDU, is located to the left and beneath the gunner's sight. Likewise information on traverse is also needed, and this is provided by the 'traverse displacement unit', or TDU, located on the left side of the turret and connected to the turret ring.

In the driver's cab is the sensor for vehicle motion, which comes into play if the vehicle is moving at a speed above 5mph (8kmph): then the gun control equipment will automatically discontinue autolay and activate the stabilizer. This is very reminiscent of the movement switch fitted into Conqueror.

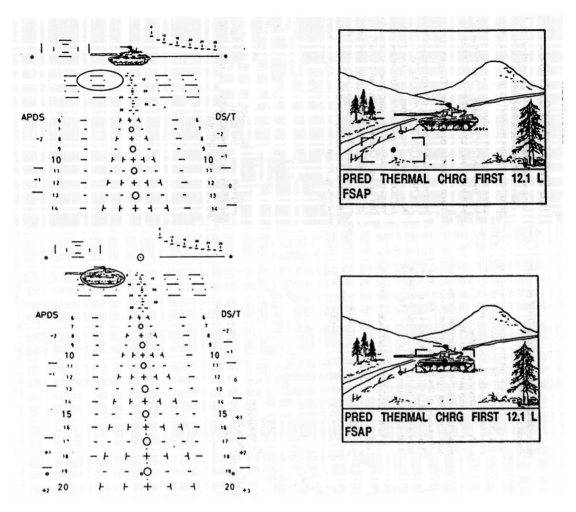

These drawings show a typical engagement: in the first, the ellipse is positioned left and below the target, and autolay has been demanded. In the next drawing autolay has taken place and the ellipse has moved the gun and turret, thus positioning itself over the target; this will automatically take in the correct aim-off required. (Crown Copyright)

The Output Components Group

This group accepts data and control signals generated by the computer, and uses them to provide gun-laying facilities. The 'aiming mark electronics unit', or AMEU, is located on the top of the range unit by the gunner's right side. In response to signals from the CIU, then through the aiming mark electronic (AMEU) and the commander's aiming mark (CAMPU), it pro-

vides an elliptical aiming mark; this will vary in size depending on the range. The AMPU is located within the TLS, and its controls are located on the right rear face of the TLS.

The CAMPU is situated to the right front of the commander's location and acts in a similar manner to the AMEU in that it provides a projected ellipse into the PRI, which is then superimposed within the graticule in the commander's sight. The commander is also

131

Short-Cutting the System?

In Cpl Dave Stones' opinion, when IFCS was all up and working, the system was very good, albeit a bit slow; but if things broke down, it became a nightmare. In fact it was his experience that even when it worked, Lulworth instructors were sometimes still not happy. He was fortunate to have a very quick and capable gunner, and an excellent suite of IFCS – but imagine his surprise when, during the day's shooting at gunnery camp, the instructor from Lulworth criticised the crew for being '...too quick, and trying to short-cut the system, and not using the IFCS as it should be used.' In Dave's words: 'To say that to us was just unbelievable, especially as we were not short-cutting the system – it's just not worth doing that. And more important, we were hitting everything that we engaged!'

Much as it really annoyed everyone concerned, it is one of those things that you just have to put behind you.

provided with a range readout unit that gives him the same laser range readout as that available to the gunner through his TLS. It also shows the nature of ammunition selected, and whether the first or last range readout has been selected.

Lastly we have the gun control equipment, which will respond to signals from IFCS to provide automatic laying and tracking facilities.

The Meteorological Probe

There was one other feature of IFCS that the British Army did not take up due to cost, and because they felt it was not required, and that was a meteorological probe. This would give information on the weather conditions, such as temperature and wind speed, but only at the vehicle end; it was perhaps for this reason that it was not taken up by the British. However, other countries use it on their FCS. IFCS could

The gunner's firing handle, the commander's and gunner's power controls, the TLS and, on the floor, the right-hand foot pedal for firing the TLS. (RCMS Shrivenham)

monitor readings such as charge temperature and barrel wear.

IFCS served the British well until a far more capable system came into being with Challenger 2, when for the first time on a service British AFV the sights were electronically stabilized. This meant that the commander and gunner had a stable picture, which also meant that the days of the gunner struggling to keep the target within the sight picture were at last over.

A TYPICAL ENGAGEMENT

In considering a typical engagement, we will assume the following: that all systems are running as they should be; that Fin (APFSDS) is being fired; and that a first round hit is obtained (any more being beyond the remit of this book). On identifying a target, the commander will decide what nature of ammunition to use: this will form part of his fire order, which he will issue as he lays the gun on the area of the identified target. The gunner will be checking that all his controls are set, and will position himself with his head against the TLS waiting for the target to enter his field of view. The loader will be selecting the correct nature of ammunition, and will be starting to load the gun. The gunner will select the type of ammunition and armament on the firing handle; this will be displayed to the commander as well, and the charge legend showing that the TLS is ready to fire will also appear in his readout.

The gunner then identifies the target, and lays the MBS onto the centre of the observed target: once he is happy he will fire the laser, and the charge light will go out until the TLS is recharged. The range will appear in the TLS for the gunner, and in the commander's range readout in metres x100 ie 21.4 = 2,140m. An ellipse-shaped aiming mark will appear around the MBS mark, and the computer will now start to perform its calculations, making use of all available data. The gunner has now pressed, and will maintain pressure on, the autolay switch on his firing handle.

The computer will now utilize the solution from the input of data, and will move the ellipse to a new location on the graticle pattern: this will indicate the range and aim off (if any) that is required. As soon as that has taken place, the computer sends out the signal to drive the gun into the correct elevation, and this will now place the ellipse around the target. Once all this has taken place, the gun can be fired; and assuming a first round hit, the commander will order the engagement to cease.

IFCS engagement using APFSDS with a first round hit

Commander	Gunner	Loader
Fin tank on	On	Loaded
Fire	Lasing	
	Firing now	
Target stop		Loaded

The above table shows the exact words that the engagement would use; also bear in mind that from start to finish this should take no more than 9sec. The gunner will report 'Lasing!' when firing the laser, and 'Firing now!' for the main armament.

TOGS FOR CHIEFTAIN

As we have seen, when Chieftain entered service it was equipped with a combined white light/IR searchlight, and the commander and gunner were issued with IR sights: but the latter took time to fit and adjust, and were unpopular. Once their novelty had worn off (very quickly), most night shoots were conducted along the 'go white, go hard' – which was fine as long as you were not the illuminating tank. It was felt that something better had to be provided, as British tanks were largely ineffective at night-fighting at that time.

The 21 Cupola and Tombola

The next step was to explore the possibility of using image intensification: this had worked well on the sights as used by the infantry, and Rank Precision Products were producing a II sight to be fitted into the new 21 cupola. The 21 cupola also mounted the first thermal image demonstrator fitted to a British tank. Known as Tombola, this was produced by Barr and Stroud, in Scotland, largely in an attempt to try and impress the Germans as the UK initiative in the Anglo/German tank venture. This collapsed, however, and for a while nothing was seen to be happening; but a new TI system was being designed by MEL for the MBT 80 project (though at the time there was no intention of fitting TI to Chieftain).

As a demonstrator model Tombola was flawed, in that the 21 cupola had to be locked to the turret; this meant that traverse could not be employed, thus negating the advantages of power operation – this was due to the fact that no slip rings were available to transmit power to Tombola. This also meant that the commander's day sight and mg were fixed in line with the main armament. {Obviously if Tombola was not to be used, then the cupola could be traversed as normal.) Furthermore Tombola could not be used to lay the weapons or to fire them, as it only indicated the gun barrel axis – and this not too accurately.

But even though Tombola had proved to be rather a pointless project, it had nevertheless convinced people that TI technology was ready to be fitted to tanks. It is not known exactly how many Tombola systems were built, but the author has the maker's plate for the serial number 001 built by Barr and Stroud; this was found at Gallows Hill, Bovington – but how it got there is a mystery.

Unfortunately for night vision, the 21 cupola was not accepted for service, and as it passed into history, so the specially designed II sight also was discarded with it. But a contract for a second II sight had been proposed by Pilkington Perkin Elmer (PPE): this called for a sight to be designed that could be incorporated in the current no. 15 cupola as fitted to Chieftain – the sight was known as Condor.

The Problems of Installing TI on Chieftain

One of the major problems of installing TI on Chieftain was to find a location for the sensor head that would enable the field of view of the sensor to follow the elevation of the gun. Many ideas were tried, and in the end the sensor was located in an armoured barbette that replaced the old searchlight housing. By 1978 the basis for a system was formed.

The next step was to decide which TI scanner and telescope to use. At that time there was only one system in the world up and running that met the necessary criteria, and that was a private venture of Barr and Stroud known as IR18. There was also the MoD funded, common module class 2 TI which had potential, but in 1978 no working model was available; also both systems were very different.

To make matters worse, 1978 was not the ideal year to try and produce a TOGS demonstrator, as FVRDE staff did not want the Tombola project belittled. The Chieftain project management was in the final stages of developing Condor, and the team responsible for the MBT did not want the night-fighting capability of Chieftain to be enhanced at all, as they feared it would lessen the case for procuring the MBT 80.

The first ray of sunshine came with the announcement of the cancellation of the MBT 80 project, and the decision to build Challenger. Of great importance in regard to TOGS development, Challenger used the same cupola as Chieftain, and the same gunner's sight. And hot on the heels of the cancellation of the MBT 80 was the cancellation of the Condor II, intended for Chieftain and Challenger. In the event, the early Challengers were issued with a 'swap' sight that replaced the commander's 37 sight – bringing back memories of the swapping of the day and IR sights on Chieftain. This sight was also planned to be issued to Chieftain for the same role, and a very few were actually issued; now you can buy them at military shows for around £50–£100.

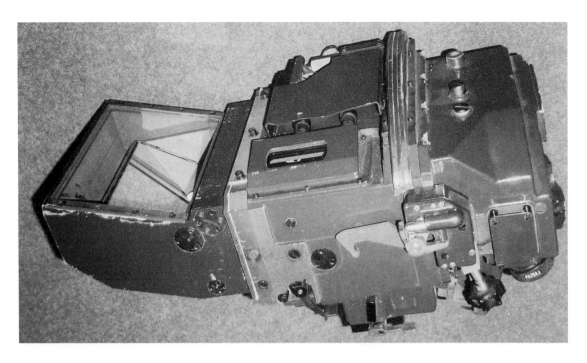

The L5 II swap sight that Chieftains nearly had issued. (Derek Hanson)

This state of affairs only lasted until Challenger was fitted with TOGS. The Condor sight was cancelled just prior to going into production, which in retrospect was a good thing, as it at least meant that TOGS was looked at seriously. At a meeting to consider the contract for the swap sight, Barr and Stroud decided that the specification required by the MoD defied the laws of physics, and told them so – and surprise, surprise! They did not win the contract to make the swap sight.

Barr and Stroud's Private Venture

There was only scattered interest in fitting TOGS to Challenger and Chieftain, as the view held by the procurement executive at the MoD was that it was not feasible to shoot aiming with TI from these vehicles. That this decision was made without a working system to examine was amazing, but not unusual for the MoD. This meant that the only way forward for Barr and Stroud was to make production a private venture. Obviously this would be a major commitment, and quite rightly Barr and Stroud wanted to know that the Operational Requirements (OR) staff and the Director Royal Armoured Corps (DRAC) would give their support if it could be successfully proved that the system worked.

A trial was therefore organized: an IR18 mounted on a tripod was set up, and tank targets were set at ranges up to 2.5km (1.5 miles). Major Bagnall-Wild, who by this time worked for Barr and Stroud, hosted this trial. After everyone had viewed the array of targets, he made the promise to return in one year with a tank-mounted TI demonstrator. The plan was discussed that evening, and the DRAC agreed to back it. But three months before the demonstrator was ready, the MoD asked Barr and Stroud to cease work on it. This had the opposite effect, however, as it convinced the company that TI on tanks was a winner: and so the venture carried on.

Lighter Moments

There were other, somewhat less formalized scenarios that clearly demonstrated the power of TI, but which could never have been dreamt up by the MoD. One evening when the tanks were waiting to deploy, a German walked past with his dog. As it passed the tanks, the dog did what dogs do, and having completed its business, moved on with its owner. Luckily they couldn't hear the laughter that followed them, as the rear end of the dog was glowing hot in the TI lens. On another occasion whilst scanning a wood for likely enemy locations, a young couple was seen driving into a secluded spot in their car, and pulling up... At first only the normal hot parts of the car glowed in the sight, but after about ten minutes the whole car was glowing hot – a suitable testimony to young love.

A Successful Trial

One year to the day the demonstrator equipment arrived at ATDU and was fitted to a Chieftain. The trial officer Maj Miller QRIH very quickly grasped the potential of the system, on his own judgement and also because of the crew's enthusiasm for it. The trial was deemed a success, and ended with demonstrations by the team by day and by night; visitors were also able to see a live display of the gunner's TI picture, at that time an innovation, though it is commonplace on the ranges today. Included in the programme was target acquisition, viewed through smoke and a large amount of live firing. The conclusion at the end was that this was a winner, and that as a gunnery system it certainly proved superior to the II sight.

Incredibly the MoD chose to ignore the trial and demonstration, and also the trial report by Major Millar, by all accounts an eloquent and forceful paper. Instead they continued to try and produce their third attempt at a II sight. But Major Davies, RHG/D at the OR, took the case to his superior, Brigadier Swindells ex 5DG, and the brigadier by all accounts took up the cudgel for TI: at one meeting he told the Procurement

staff that 'they were incompetent and useless to the soldier'. His OR staff then wrote an 'Operational Emergency General Staff' requirement for TI to be fitted to Chieftain and Challenger, and this gave Procurement no option but to agree to support TI. Thus in the space of four months the system had come from a situation where the MoD was demanding that it be stopped, to one in which it was 'an operational emergency requirement'.

It might have been hoped that Barr and Stroud would have been the prime candidates to win the contract, but the MoD wanted a 'project definition stage'. Part of the requested concept was for the TI sensor to be shaft-mounted to the gunner's sight to allow follow in elevation; also it was apparent that the MoD preferred the TICM system mentioned earlier. Procurement still had doubts about the system being good enough for gunnery, despite the evidence to the contrary. This meant that the Barr and Stroud demonstrator did not conform to the MoD requirements. But Barr and Stroud were in a good position because they had a video showing the system working, while the opposition could only offer paper studies; also they proposed the use of TICM instead of IR18. This all paid off, and finally Barr and Stroud were awarded the TOGS contract. And whilst there were many changes to come, TOGS had at least come through everything that had been thrown at it.

TOGS USER TRIALS

Several large-scale user trials were carried out to establish the best way of employing TOGS; one of these was called Exercise Dragon's Eye. The author's troop was attached to the Royal Scots Dragoon Guards as the enemy for many set-piece scenarios that took place over six weeks in Germany. Six weeks in the field might not be everyone's idea of fun, but as far as I was concerned it was one of the best exercises I have ever undertaken. The troop had been boosted to four tanks for the exercise period, though only three were in use each day, whilst the fourth was shown the scenario for the next day. Coupled with the fact that this was one of the best summers for a long time, a great deal of fun was had by all.

The aim of the exercise was to film and record crews carrying out text-book fire orders using TI. To that end the tanks were fitted with a commercial TI camera mounted on the barrel just behind the fume extractor; full Simfics was also fitted to all vehicles. Inside, a VCR was fitted and linked to the Clansman harness, and two video camera eyepieces were provided for the commander and gunner. These had a simple aiming cross engraved on them to give some semblance of sighting.

The exercise format was as follows: the three tanks and a Milan section and an infantry section would take up prepared positions, and the RSDG would then attack using current Russian tactics to try and smash through. As the enemy, surprisingly we never lost an engagement – but it was

equally surprising that the RSDG TI tanks always seemed to pick up the Milan post as soon as they entered the battle area, even though they were well concealed and dug in. This made them really despondent!

Each night the tapes were studied and the crews debriefed. One thing we found was that target recognition was not going to be so easy, but we were shown special slides taken through a TI sight of different vehicles, and this gave us a better understanding of the lessons to come.

Some of the trial was to establish where the TI head would be best located, and also the compressor for the cooling air: the TI needs to be kept cool in order to work efficiently, and compressed air is used for this. In our case the bottle was fitted just before the start of a phase and would last about one hour. When TI was eventually fitted to Chieftain and Challenger 1, in both vehicles the sensor was housed in an armoured barbette on the side of the turret, with another barbette for the compressor.

03EB87 showing the modification to the searchlight to house the thermal camera.
From this came the design for the barbette in which TOGS was housed on the Chieftain.
(Bagnall-Wilde)

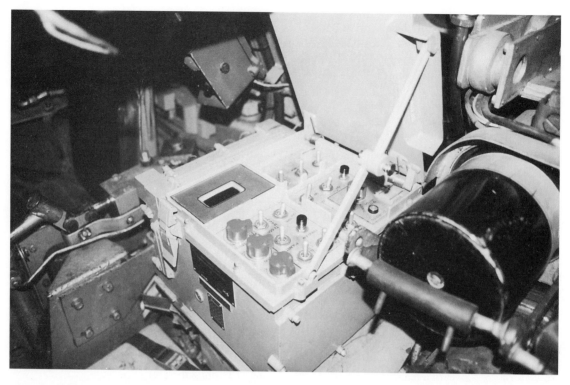

The SPU with its cover open. This gives the commander control of all aspects of the TOGS system. (RCMS Shrivenham)

At the end of Dragon's Eye I felt that for once we had achieved something that was going to be of real value in the future, and it felt good to have played even a small part in that future.

SO WHAT IS TOGS?

So after all the test and trials and exercises, once TOGS came into service, what did we get for our money? There are many components that make up the TOGS system, and to list and explain them all here would be like reading the gunnery manual; the illustration shows and names the main components, and we will just take a look at some of the major parts.

So what is TOGS? The 'thermal observation gunnery sight' (TOGS) is a thermal imaging surveillance and automated gun-sighting system that is fully integrated with the existing IFCS components. All the functions of visual sighting equipment are thermal-copied by TOGS. Both the thermal surveillance system and the gun-sighting system are divided into a number of easily replaceable units that can be changed by the user.

The most obvious feature of Chieftain TOGS can be seen in the two large barbettes on the left side: these replace the searchlight. The forward barbette houses the thermal image sensor head (TISH): this is linked to the gun, and will follow it in elevation and depression. It is located behind a glass door, and is equipped with its own wash/wipe facility; when not in use, an armoured door seals the housing from damage. Behind the TISH housing is the armoured cooling-pack housing: this contains the bottle pack for cooling, and the compressor to keep it charged.

The commander and gunner are each equipped with visual display units: these are like small television screens, and besides the TI picture various other information will be displayed on the screen, including the aiming marks, mode of operation, ammunition and messages from the built-in test equipment (BITE).

One of the more important control boxes is situated to the commander's left and above the location of the boiling vessel: the symbology processing unit, or SPU – pronounced with some feeling by the crews as 'spew' (as in slang for 'being sick'). With the SPU located here, it is convenient for the commander to operate the controls, but it leads to a loss of four projectiles. On the SPU are the controls for operating the system, and one of these allows the crew to select between 'white' hot and 'black' hot. This is like looking at a photographic negative, and then viewing it with the colours reversed; this sometimes helps to improve definition.

When using TOGS there are two magnifications that can be used: HIGH, which gives a field of view of 96 mils with a magnification of x11.5; and LOW with a field of view of 270 mils and a magnification of x4.

TOGS THE BATTLE WINNER

TOGS has proved to be very popular with the crews as it enables them to carry out tasks at night that previously could not even have been attempted. It probably had its greatest moment during the Gulf War when its performance was so good that no details of it were allowed to be given to the media. Thus while pictures of TI images were regularly broadcast, they were from aircraft, but never from the British TOGS-equipped Challenger regiments. Many crews called it their 'battle winner'. This is a fitting tribute to those who fought against outdated ideas within the MoD to bring TOGS into service, despite the MoD's seemingly reluctant attitude. Challenger 2, today's main battle tank for the British Army, carries a much improved version of TOGS, and it will be the way for night-fighting for a long time yet.

8   Variants

Chieftain is no different from its predecessors in that it was always envisaged that its hull could be used as the basis for a family of support vehicles; these would necessarily include an armoured recovery vehicle, or ARV; an armoured vehicle Royal Engineers (AVRE); and an armoured vehicle-launched bridge (AVLB). These were the vehicles that would be required to support Chieftain on the battlefield (not counting vehicles of an administrative nature).

The ARV would be required to carry out recovery tasks, and to replace the venerable Centurion ARV that had soldiered on for so many years, giving valuable service – and indeed, was to soldier on for many more, even ending up in the Gulf War in 1991. In the same way it was envisaged that the Centurion bridge-layer would need replacing due to its age, and also because inevitably a system would be needed that was capable of crossing a greater gap. It was also decided to replace the Centurion AVRE with its impressive 165mm 'bunker-busting' gun.

Whilst many would mourn the passing of Centurion in its many guises, the cold hard facts of economy and technological advances meant that it was the correct decision. Trying to maintain several front line vehicles with varying roles, and the inevitable shortage of parts as companies stopped producing spares, would increasingly become a logistical nightmare. Even today with the introduction of Challenger 2, the MoD is trying to standardize the battlefield fleet, but it is not an easy task. We have Challenger 2 as the MBT, and Chieftain as the AVRE, and likely to soldier on for a while yet – as is the Chieftain AVLB, although it is to be hoped that redundant Challenger 1 hulls may yet fill those roles and allow Chieftain finally to retire.

But things never run to plan, and so it was with the Chieftain variants; thus the gun tank went into full production, and it was decided to go ahead and produce the AVLB. This would use up some of the Mk 1 hulls initially as a conversion, while the Mk 6 would be a new build. Trials and mock-ups were produced for the AVRE – but it never progressed any further than that, leaving the Centurion AVRE in both 165mm and 105mm versions to soldier on until the Gulf War, which was its swansong.

This left the Chieftain AVRE to surface much later and in a different form, although it still fulfilled the 'armoured engineers' requirements.

THE ARMOURED RECOVERY VEHICLE

The first major variant of Chieftain was as an armoured recovery vehicle (ARV). Although the venerable Centurion ARV could work alongside Chieftain, it was realized that it would be retired from service a long time before Chieftain. In the event, however, the Centurion ARV went on to provide the main recovery vehicle for Chieftain within the armoured units for quite a long time before the introduction of the Chieftain ARV.

Vickers built the ARV at the Elstwick factory at Newcastle-upon-Tyne, with the first prototype running in 1971; it came into production from 1974. The ARV is built around the hull of the Mk 5 gun tank in that it uses the same suspension, power pack and aux gen. It is fitted with a main capstan winch with a 30-ton pull, controlled electrohydraulic, and a 3-ton auxiliary winch; the main winch has 122m (400ft) of 28mm (1in)-diameter cable, and the auxiliary winch 260m

Chieftain ARRV in the Gulf, this vehicle is still wearing the standard green/black camouflage from Germany. (Dennis Lunn)

Right: *Villich conversion. (Dennis Lunn)*

Below: *Top view of a Berlin squadron ARRV in Berlin colours. Of interest notice how every inch of space has been used. A good shot for modellers. (Andreas Kirchoff)*

(850ft) of 11mm (1/2in) cable. The power for both winches is taken via a power take-off from the main engine, and the auxiliary winch is used to deploy the main winch during recovery operations. This makes life a lot easier for the crews, who would otherwise have had to deploy Centurion's winch rope by hand.

Another feature was the hydraulically operated blade at the front of the vehicle: this could be lowered to act as an anchor, thus helping to maintain the ARV's position during a recovery operation.

As we have seen, the ARV was built on the Mk 5 chassis: it had the power pack and aux gen in the same location, and the forward half of the vehicle housed a superstructure that contained a cupola no. 17, equipped with night sight and cupola periscopes. Also, the commander's cupola was equipped with the vehicle's only weapon: the 7.62mm GPMG. The superstructure carried the driver at the front left, and the remaining two crewmen. To the left of the driver is the winch housing for both winches.

The vehicle was equipped with most items required to recover or repair a vehicle in the field, and if all else failed it could hitch up the dead vehicle and tow it by means of the 'A'-frame hole-bone towbar. This was fitted to the dead tank's towing eyes left and right, and the single connection to the ARV's tow connection. A small hand jib was situated on the left rear side to help in handling the 'A' frame; this could be used to raise the frame until it was nearly in line with the ARV tow shackle, and then the ARV reversed and hitched up. If this worked, it saved crewmen having to hold the frame while the ARV reversed, and thus helped to prevent accidents.

Around the outside of the vehicle were large stowage bins for carrying all the recovery equipment, and each crew would customize the back of the vehicle by adding various scrounged bins and other 'useful' items. Normally along the T-piece would sit the NBC filtration pack, similar to that found on the rear of the gun tanks. However, this would quite often be removed and left off, as the one major fault of the ARV was that it still had the L60 power pack and so was as prone to breakdown as the gun tanks. Leaving the NBC pack off meant less work when changing power packs, because it had to be taken off before the T-piece could be lifted.

Traditionally REME recovery crews have always tried to make themselves as comfortable as possible in the field – and who can blame them? A feature of the ARV was the canvas house

---

Clearing the Roads

The hydraulically operated blade at the front of the ARV was often looked upon as the same sort of blade as carried by the gun tank, although it was not. As a result of this, during one particularly severe winter in Fallingbostel, the 4th/7th Dragoon Guards were ordered to use their dozer tanks and ARVs to help clear the roads for the local authority. Despite telling the authorities that the ARV was really not a suitable vehicle for this task, they were ordered to carry on. So out they went, and cleared the roads, and at the time everyone was happy. But then the snow melted, and the damage that had been caused by the blades became apparent; and through no fault of their own, the regiment was never asked to perform that task again.

AVLB deploying its No. 8 scissors bridge: it can launch and recover the bridge from either end. (Dennis Lunn)

A Chieftain hull with mounting to enable it to be used for trials of different weapons, thus precluding the use of static bases. (Crown Copyright, DERA)

that always seemed to appear on the back of the vehicle. Usually built from old truck canopy frames and canvas, these shelters were a boon to the crew from a broken-down tank, providing welcome shelter from the elements – even though it made things very cramped.

The ARRV: The Armoured Repair and Recovery Vehicle

The ARVs that were sold abroad to Iran and Kuwait were equipped with a hydraulic crane and renamed 'armoured repair and recovery vehicles', or ARRVs. The British Army also adopted these, because it was found that when the Challenger 1 MBT was introduced into service, the venerable FV 434 of the REME was not capable of lifting its power pack. The ARRV was also helpful to the REME because it meant that there were now two vehicles within a squadron that could carry out major repairs. Up until then the FV 434 had coped on its own – now at least two vehicles at any one time could have major assembly work carried out on them. These ARVs were only armed with the cupola-mounted GPMG and smoke dischargers.

THE AVLB: THE ARMOURED VEHICLE-LAUNCHED BRIDGE

The next major variant that was planned from the beginning was the 'armoured bridge layer'. It was felt that this type of vehicle was of importance because of the many river crossings and other water obstacles that were to be found in the projected battlefields of Europe, should another war break out. Until then the Centurion had provided the AVLB system; however, as with the ARV, it was showing its age, and as it only was designed to launch a single bridge spanning a gap of at most 13.7m (45ft), it was felt that a vehicle that could launch a bridge of greater capacity should be designed.

Thus it was that the Chieftain AVLB came into service, equipped to launch two types of bridge. The no. 8 bridge is of the scissors type and is carried in the folded position; it is launched by means of hydraulic rams, and when laid can cross a gap of 22.9m (75ft). The second bridge is the single span no. 9 bridge, capable of crossing a gap of 12.2m (40ft). These have now been replaced by the Army's new bridging system: this

AVLB fitted with armoured bazooka plates and chain armour in the Gulf War. (Dennis Lunn)

has three new bridges, a conversion kit for the vehicle, and a high mobility wheeled truck to carry more bridge section. This system is known as the 'close support bridge', or CSB0, which is part of the bridging for the 90s (BR 90). These bridges are the no. 10, the scissors version that can span a gap of 24.5m (93.3ft); the no. 11, a single span bridge that can span a gap of 14.5m (47.6ft); and the no 12, spanning a gap of 12m (39.3ft). If necessary an AVLB can carry two of these bridges.

Design Differences

The AVLB and the ARRV, and later the AVRE, had their manual track adjustment replaced by a hydraulic track-tensioning system that is controlled by the driver from his cab, making life just that little bit easier. The track adjuster is needed because it was found that when a load was removed from these vehicles, the hull rose due to the loss of top weight and the track came under great tension; this meant that the driver generally had to slacken the track. But as soon as weight

was applied to the vehicle again the track would be too slack, and would need tightening.

The AVLB, like the AVRE, is coming to the end of its life, and it is becoming increasingly difficult to maintain it and obtain spares for it. It has been decided that the vehicles will be phased out in about 2005, and replaced by a vehicle based on a Challenger 2-type chassis: the suggested names for the new vehicles are 'Trojan' for the AVRE, and 'Titan' for the AVLB. According to Major Graham Thomas of the Royal Engineers, the crews have a soft spot for their Chieftains, and take great pride in making them work. Once the new vehicles are in service I am sure that there will be a host of new 'when we were on Chieftain'-type stories told in the NAAFI, just as the author heard about Centurion when he joined his regiment.

One chore that will not be any easier for the new AVLB crews will be that of camouflaging the vehicle, since due to its size, it takes much longer than a gun tank to cover it with net. Another awkward task is that of refuelling, as the bridge has to be raised several feet so that the crew can reach the fuel fillers: this is no easy task, especially at night when it is wet and no noise or lights are permitted.

AVRE: THE ARMOURED VEHICLE ROYAL ENGINEERS

We have mentioned the AVRE several times already, but it is a relatively new variant on Chieftain. It was originally planned to have a new AVRE on the Chieftain hull, to be known as FV 4203. In shape it was similar to the ARV and had an 8m (26ft) fixed bridge fitted. However, it was decided that it would not be fitted with a new, large-calibre demolition gun such as the 165mm 'flying dustbin' that the Centurion AVRE had used. This was mainly because there was no funding for the production of a new weapon – although in the end it did not matter, as the AVRE project was cancelled.

In the late 1980s it was felt that an AVRE-type vehicle should be produced, because when Challenger 1 was introduced, the Centurion-based vehicles were struggling to keep up during the advance. As always, the design had to be as cost-effective as possible, and this whole project landed in the lap of Capt Dave RE. The captain had been looking at ways of getting more class 60 trackway to a crossing site than was currently possible by using wheeled transport. He reasoned that if it could be placed on a tracked vehicle, then more rolls could be carried that, furthermore, were instantly ready to lay.

First he experimented with an old Chieftain hull minus its turret, then using parts from the current medium-girder bridge, and hydraulic rams from the M2 amphibious bridging rig, a working design was decided on. Production work to convert surplus Chieftain hulls into AVREs was then ordered to go ahead.

Converting the Chieftain Hulls

The bulk of this work was carried out by the engineers' workshop at 40 Engineer Support Group in Willich, Germany; this workforce produced twelve vehicles. The conversion consisted of

Chieftain AVRE with L60 pack on the jib. This is probably its own engine as it could remove it itself. (Dennis Lunn)

Above: *ARV in a rotating welding jig during conversion to AVRE status at 23 Base workshop in Germany. (Dennis Lunn)*

Below: *Production AVRE showing its crane and hampers in 'raise' position. Note also the track-width mine plough fitted. (Dennis Lunn)*

removing the turret and associated equipment from the fighting compartment, and plating it over, leaving a simple cupola for the commander. A simple top hamper of girders was erected over the whole vehicle, and the front and rear of the hamper were controlled by hydraulic rams, so that simply lowering that section of the hamper could drop the load.

The concept proved a success, and in 1989 Vickers were awarded a contract to produce an improved, purpose-built AVRE. The prototype was ready by 1991, and production ceased in 1994. The Vickers version has a new super-structure, a winch with a 10-tonne capacity at the rear of the vehicle, and an Atlas hydraulic crane.

Various Roles for the Chieftain AVRE

The AVRE can be fitted with a dozer blade similar to that used by the gun tanks or track-width mine ploughs. It was decided that mine ploughs gave the most effective method of clearing mines in a battle situation. People ask why the Army did not produce a flail tank on the AVRE chassis, and it is quite simply that the flail does not give 100 per cent success in clearing a lane

Chieftain Willich AVRE towing giant viper mine clearing system. Notice also the up-armoured bazooka plates. (Dennis Lunn)

in the time that a plough can do it. At one time an AVRE was fitted with experimental set of mine rollers, but – amongst other things – they prevented the loading or offloading of any stores on the hamper, and were discarded. The AVRE can carry pipe fascines or class 60 road-way on the hamper, or any engineer stores that might be needed.

There will still be no new demolition gun, and many view this as a serious omission because the gun is a very capable weapon: if required it can destroy a bridge very quickly, thus saving time in preparing charges and avoiding the risk of their not exploding. It can also be very useful during street fighting for clearing a building – quite literally. The American Marines were very pleased to know that 165mm Cent AVRE would support them in the Gulf War before the decision to move the UK forces was taken.

As we have seen, in the next few years the AVRE will be replaced by a new purpose-designed vehicle, thereby bringing to an end the Chieftain's service in the British forces.

It is perhaps of interest to note that all the Chieftain AVLBs and AVREs in the Gulf War were fitted with the Chobham armour side skirts as seen on Challenger 1 in the Gulf and Bosnia, and more recently on Challenger 2 in Kosovo.

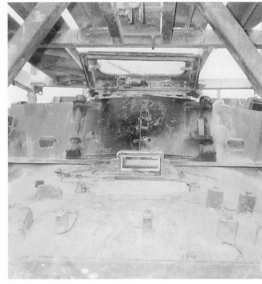

A full factory conversion to AVRE, showing driver's cab and raised commander area. (Dennis Lunn)

VARIOUS FITMENTS

Dozer Blade

All Chieftain gun tanks can be fitted with a dozer blade. The first was produced by Automotive Products Ltd, and was a fairly horrendous piece of equipment that could take up to six hours to fit. Power was supplied by an add-on electro hydraulic power pack that replaced the front right stowage bin, and always seemed to leak. The blade was controlled by an add-on joystick located in the driver's cab; it had a hinged flap to it, which was designed to give the driver an indication when it was full.

It was usually mounted on the squadron second-in-command's tank, as no one else would have it – although this was not a hard and fast rule. Most blades seemed to end up lying in a hangar, and no attention paid to them except on the occasion of regular accounting checks. If nothing else, the blade did provide a most impressive extra armour effect to the front of the tank.

It is quite probable that if Chieftain had remained in service, the dozer blade would have been replaced by a new version produced by Pearson engineering, as can be seen on Challenger 1; this is a much lighter and easier blade to mount, taking two men fifteen minutes. Whichever blade was used, it meant that the tank

could carry out such tasks as digging tank scrapes to hide in, clearing blocked routes, and filling minor obstacles.

Stillbrew

The most important variant was the add-on armour package introduced in the late 1980s. It had been felt for some time that the protective arc on the front of Chieftain was in fact quite vulnerable to some of the modern weapons on the battlefield. So a programme was instigated to try and produce an upgrade package that would protect the turret front, and also stretch to the rear of the driver's position to protect the gap between the hull and turret.

Stillbrew was originally designed by RARDE at Chertsey – the location that earlier had seen the birth of Chobham armour. ROF Leeds were involved in producing the armour, taking the project from concept to reality; this included firing trials at the armour that was mounted on stands down-range, which proved that the concept worked. Leeds and RARDE

Experimental mine rollers fitted to a Willich Chieftain AVRE. They were not altogether successful because they impede the use of the front part of the top hamper. (Dave Clegg)

The Marksman AA system. This has been fitted to a number of MBT hulls, including Chieftain. It can engage targets out to 4 miles (6.5km). The British Army did not take it up. (BAE Systems)

worked together to design the first system specifically for Chieftain: one vehicle so equipped was sent to the ranges for firing trials, and the results were well above that of the General Staff requirement.

One of the worries about fitting the new armour was that it would seriously degrade Chieftain's already stretched performance. Two tanks equipped with Stillbrew were sent to the RAC centre at Bovington, and there they carried out mobility trials consisting of half road and half cross-country. These trials showed that there was no marked degradation in performance, although there was a small loss in the power-to-weight ratio.

In 1986, twenty-three Base workshops were fitting Stillbrew packs during the vehicle's base overhaul. Many speculative ideas were mooted as to the composition of Stillbrew armour, but basically it consists of armour plate backed with rubber, the whole being mounted on brackets welded to the turret; sheet metal plate was then used to fill the gaps on the tops and sides, for the cosmetic appearance.

The Anti-Aircraft Turret

Chieftain's hull was used to carry two different types of anti-aircraft turret, neither of which entered service with the British Army, although both provided valuable information for further study. Air defence was an area that had been neglected for a long time, and not since the World War II conversion that carried twin 20mm Polsten cannon had the British Army had a vehicle capable of keeping up with armoured formations. Every system that is in use today has to stop and deploy from trailer-mounted missiles, the exception being Short's Starstreak high velocity missile system mounted on a Stormer chassis. There are many reasons why a vehicle such as 'Tracked Rapier', that entered service to a fanfare of publicity and then faded away, never lasted the course and was replaced by a tracked version.

The two versions of anti-aircraft turret that were trialled on a Chieftain were Marksman, made by Marconi Defence systems; and Sabre (a name later used for the latest member of the CVR (T) family), produced by Royal Ordnance

149

A Chieftain 900. Two of these were built, up-armoured and re-engined as demonstrators. (Dennis Lunn)

Chieftain 2000.

factories and Thompson–CSF of France. Marksman has so far only been sold to Finland, where it is mounted on a T72 chassis. Dennis Lunn, who after leaving the REME worked for Barr and Stroud, relates one of the selling points of Marksman. He says that as part of a demonstration for Marksman, a Chieftain was driven into a hangar, and about four hours later was driven out with the Marksman turret fitted and ready to use. In the end, however, the British Army took up neither Marksman nor Sabre.

THE CHIEFTAIN 800, 900 AND 2000

In 1974 the Shah of Iran ordered a further 125 Chieftains, but of a modified version: amongst the requirements were the replacement of the L60 power pack, and the fitting of a fully automatic gearbox. The engine chosen was the Rolls-Royce CV12, down-rated to 800bhp; and the TN12 gearbox was modified to a fully automatic box, as requested, to make it an easier vehicle to drive – it also meant that drivers needed less training. The resulting vehicle was known as Chieftain 800 and became the Shir 1.

In the late 1980s, ROF realized that financially it was not going to be practicable to re-equip the entire British Chieftain fleet with Chobham armour – but they considered that other users might well be interested in this option. Two Chieftains that were ex-Iranian order were converted by fitting the Rolls-Royce CV12 power pack and fully automatic TN12 gearbox, very much as in the Chieftain 800 – but this time it was rated at 900bhp, hence the name of Chieftain 900. They too were fitted with sheet-metal cladding to simulate the addition of Chobham armour: this gives the tank a very stealthy-type look. This is due to the fact that Chobham armour has to be used in flat plates – hence the angular look in all the latest generation tanks that use it. It was also intended to fit the hydrostrut suspension as a replacement for the venerable Horstman units.

Chieftain hydrostrut system. This was designed as a bolt-on replacement for the normal Horstman units, giving a better ride. (Dan Newton, via RCMS)

Smooth-Bore Gun Trials

In 1973, 05 EB 43 of A Squadron 4th/7th RDG was sent to the ranges at Kirkcudbright in Scotland along with a crew. It was fitted with a 120mm smooth-bore gun, and for several months it was used to carry out trials on that type of weapon; once the trials were complete the gun was removed, and the vehicle returned to its regiment.

This suspension had already been trialled by the 5th Inniskilling Dragoon guards, and had proved very successful. It gave a better ride and allowed faster speeds across country; it also allowed each wheel to be independently sprung.

In the event no interest was shown by any user, so the project was dropped. One vehicle – 56 MS 89 – was used as a demonstrator for the Centaur fire control system, and had panoramic sights fitted as part of the system; but it was never anything more than a demonstrator vehicle. Once the project was over, both vehicles became surplus to requirements, with 56 MS 89 going to the Tank Museum where it currently forms part of the reserve collection, and 56 MS 78 ending up on Lulworth Ranges minus its turret, awaiting its final role as a hard target. The turret has ended up on a normal Chieftain chassis as part of a test bed for BAE; it is now called Chieftain 2000.

A GAS TURBINE FOR
THE NEW MBT

After the failure of the MBT 80 project, the MoD started to look forward to producing another vehicle to replace Chieftain: to this end the 'Component Technology Demonstrator Programme' was instigated. This was basically to look at new technology that might be of use in designing the new MBT, and one of the proposals was the installation of a gas turbine into the new tank. At this time the USA had been running the M1 Abrams with a gas turbine, and many varying reports were coming back as to its effectiveness, or lack of it. To obtain first-hand user feedback it was decided to test a more modern auto gas turbine than that used by the Abrams: the unit chosen was a reconditioned Garrett GT601, and this was installed in a Chieftain hull and tested.

A great deal of work was required to fit the turbine into the hull, and after the initial running, many modifications were deemed necessary. The vehicle was accepted by RARDE for further trials, and several reports that are still classified were produced on the trial. It would seem that the aim was achieved, however, in that we now had first-hand experience of the pros and cons of installing a gas-turbine power unit in any future MBT.

It is worth pointing out that at no time was it ever envisaged to retrofit the Chieftain fleet with gas turbines, although there were plenty of rumours to that effect. In fact the Garrett unit was actually under-powered for the job, and only served as a test bed for data collection, even though the prospect is intriguing. Thus the next generation of tanks stayed with the diesel engine, leaving only America and Russia to pursue the gas turbine.

PROJECT CRAZY HORSE

This project came about in 1987 as a means of assessing the vehicles and armament that might be used by contemporary enemy forces. An anti-tank missile operator fired inert missiles at a manned up, heavily armoured Centurion weighing in at about 70 tons; it had a crew of two, and for safety it carried just one small fuel tank. It would drive along a pre-determined route allowing the missile operators to engage – but even with dummy warheads the impact could cause damage, and one Centurion had its cupola removed by the force of the missile, though luckily no one was hurt.

The development of new generation smart weapons, including those that could attack the top of the vehicle, meant that a replacement gun was needed. The requirement called for a vehicle that could be made to look like enemy MBT, and could provide a representative thermal and radar signature; also it had to be agile (20mph/32kmph). The top armour had to be strengthened, and radio control was to be installed to remove the crew from any danger.

Several vehicles would be needed to test the smart weapons, picking out their target from an array of enemy vehicles on the battlefield. Because the Chieftain was about to be withdrawn from regular service, it was an ideal test bed. The trial team however, showing the total confidence that they had in the radio-controlled project, named it 'Crazy Horse' – not out of respect to the great Indian chief, but more to do with how they felt the vehicle was likely to respond to radio control.

A surplus Chieftain therefore had its entire gun, radio and NBC system and round stowage removed; the automotive side was left intact. Hydraulic rams were attached to the original steering levers in the driver's cab, along with an indirect driver's seat in the hull centre; this was so the vehicle could be driven to an area and set up without the need for radio control. The driver used a colour monitor linked to a camera fitted where his day sight used to be. The radio control equipment used was provided by Skyleader (who had provided the equipment for the model aircraft used for low-level air defence training).

A Stormer CVR (T) was converted as a control vehicle, and in December 1988 a trial was

The gunless radio-controlled Chieftain known as project Crazy Horse. This had to be the ultimate 'big boys' toy'! (Tank Museum)

carried out at Shoeburyness, with the vehicle being controlled at a range of 6km (3.7 miles). The Stormer contained the safety supervisor, the trial officer and the remote driver, who received pictures from the camera on board the vehicle. Many safety features were built in, including a limited range fuel tank (just in case the vehicle decided to do its own thing, which could happen only too easily, as anyone who has used model radio remote control will tell you). The range of 6km proved workable, and it is expected that 10km (6 miles) can be achieved.

JAGD CHIEFTAIN: THE CTR

This is the colloquial name given to a programme of collaboration that took place between the UK and the FRG in 1972; it is better known as the Concepts Test Rig (CTR). The UK designed a vehicle with a semi-fixed weapon, and also constructed a prototype vehicle at the FVRDE: this was built to the combined specification from both countries.

The design called for a vehicle mounting a gun of typical tank calibre that could be elevated and depressed on trunnions, as in a conventional tank, but where traverse would be achieved by slewing the vehicle on its tracks. This was not a

new concept, as the Germans had used it well on the tank destroyers in World War II, and the Swedes had gone down that route with their S tank. The main ballistic protection was to be centred on the front plate; it was to be resistant to any current and projected anti-tank weapons.

The vehicle would have a three-man crew of commander, driver and loader; there was also the requirement that it could be driven in a reverse direction. In order to keep costs to a minimum, and to be able to meet the time scale required, it was agreed that the vehicle should be produced from current in-service components – and it was deemed that Chieftain parts were the most suitable.

A TN12 gearbox was modified to accept hydraulic steering, as this was the best method of controlling the gearbox when fine-laying the gun; it was also found that the TN12 could be converted to fully automatic mode. Each crew member had common steering tillers, and operated the hydraulic steering system by a push/pull Bowden cable.

The standard Chieftain suspension system was used, but the centre spring of each spring pack was removed because the system proved over-strong for this type of vehicle. Because the gun was laid by slewing the vehicle, a different steering ratio was calculated, and to achieve this

The Jagd Chieftain seen here is fitted with a dummy gun. It could be fitted with either Chieftain L60 or Leopard's MTU power pack. (Tank Museum)

the suspension units were mounted as close to each other as possible in order to maintain this ratio.

The use of aluminium presented problems, although some of these were overcome during the production of the 'aluminium Chieftain FV4211'; these qualified successes encouraged further use of the aluminium variant, with the aim of gaining further experience, and taking full advantage of the weight difference. With different ratio final drives of 2.84:1 as against Chieftain's standard of 5:1, the vehicle could achieve a speed of 64kmph (40mph). The main weapon chosen was to be the same 120mm as fitted to Chieftain, but it would be mounted in a purpose-built mantlet from armour steel, that would be bolted to the front plate.

The commander and driver were both able to lay and fire the gun, and the loader was equipped with a backward-facing vision device that allowed him to drive the vehicle in reverse. Normal ballistic protection was provided by the structure, with the front glacis plate being protected by Chobham armour; although this plate was never actually manufactured, the profile and weight were simulated by 5 tons of lead encased in a thin sheet-metal cover.

During trial at the Rotunda in Woolwich, it was found that while the laying system worked, it was neither comparable nor competitive enough against a conventional turret. The automotive trial proved that the vehicle easily met this requirement, and as it was designed to use either the UK L60 or the FRG MTU pack from the Leopard, it would have been interesting to have seen the result with the alternative pack fitted.

But the project was eventually dropped because of the poor result of the laying trial, and the vehicle was allowed to fall into a state of disuse. It wasn't scrapped as it was to be a valuable source of long-term information on protecting aluminium welds and joints against corrosion. The vehicle only covered 240 miles (386km) on automotive; however, the hydrosteer unit was subjected to much higher usage on the laying trials. But the experience gained from using this system bore fruit when it was proposed to use a similar system on the FV 4030 series that became KHALID and Challenger 1.

The only model built now resides in the reserve collection at the Tank Museum at Bovington.

KHALID: FV 4211
ALUMINIUM CHIEFTAIN

Khalid is a development of Chieftain that owes its existence to the large orders the Shah of Iran placed for Chieftain in the 1970s.

Whilst the Iranians were basically pleased with Chieftain, they wanted modifications carried out to make it even better; these included a better power pack and simplification of the driving controls. This was achieved by combining the front of a Chieftain and the rear of what would later become Challenger, allowing it to be fitted with the Perkins engine CV 12 as used by Challenger. The vehicle was to be known as Shir 2 and 1,225 were ordered in December 1974, but with the fall of the Shah the new government cancelled the order in February 1979.

In November 1979 Jordan placed an order for 274 of the vehicles, which were to be called Khalid. These were essentially the same as the Shir 2 with modifications to suit the Jordanian order. One good part of the Iranian cancellation was the British further development of Shir 2, which eventually became Challenger 1 in UK service.

Development work on an armour protection package that would become known as Chobham armour had been ongoing for some time. Then in 1969 it was stated by the scientific adviser (projects and research) that the new armour must be ready to be incorporated into a MBT by 1975 – ten years before the planned Chieftain replacement would be available.

In order to meet the short development time, and also to reduce the development and production costs, it was shown that using Chieftain components would be the best route for production. This was as long as an all-up weight of 55 tons was not exceeded: if it was, then some deterioration in performance was only to be expected.

Khalid: produced for Jordan after the fall of the Shah of Iran. The front is Chieftain, the rear is what would become Challenger, to allow the fitting of a bigger power pack. (Tank Museum)

*FV 4211 showing the sheet metal boxes
giving it the look of Challenger 1. (Tim Babb)*

Trials had already taken place against Chobham armour as part of a feasibility study linked to the MICV, and it was estimated that Chobham would be proof against the envisaged threat. It was then decided to use Chobham armour on a structure for both hull and turret. This led to feasibility studies being carried out, and these revealed that the desirable weight of 55 tons and the required level of protection could be achieved. The vehicle chosen was to be based on Chieftain components, thus earning the name 'aluminium' Chieftain. The original intention was to classify it as a Mark 5/2 Chieftain, but it was then decided that it would in fact be a brand-new vehicle, so a new FV number was issued: thus it became FV 4211.

The final details of armour protection are still classified, but suffice it to say that the designers achieved a high level of protection for the vehicle at only 1 ton penalty, the final weight being 56 tons. The first hurdle to cross was how to weld aluminium armour on this scale, as it had never been attempted before; so there was a great deal of experimentation with various methods of checking for cracks and poor welds. These included X-ray, dye penetrant and ultrasonic scans; in addition the welders were put through a period of intense training. The joints were mechanically joined, then welded, and a full-scale wooden mock-up was built and used to confirm the location of the mechanically joined plates and welds. Real or mock-up components were used in the mock-up, and eventually it was placed alongside the first hull to be produced, and components swapped. The mock-up also proved invaluable in helping the designers work out various pipe and cable runs within the hull.

The Automotive Parts

All the automotive parts were standard Chieftain Mk 3/3 production components that were modified where necessary. A standard TN12 gearbox was fitted, but was modified to give a reverse speed of 9.5mph (15.3kmph) as opposed to the service Chieftain box that gave 5.9mph (9.4kmph). The first prototype hull was built at FVRDE Chertsey and was of a fully armoured construction, including skirt plate armour. The vehicle now registered as 03 MS 13 was fitted with a Windsor turret to simulate the weight of the production turret. (The Windsor turret is nothing more than a round, hollow shell that is fitted to vehicles to simulate the weight of the turret; it can be ballasted up or down to achieve this. It obtained its name because someone once said that it looked like one of the towers at Windsor Castle.)

The vehicle was known as the Mobile Test Rig (MTR); it achieved 12,000 track miles (19,300km) on various test tracks, and it was found that component life was marginally better than that of Chieftain. However, it was felt that this was due to the hard work put in by the maintenance crews in the evenings, in order that the trial might carry on the next day. After about six months into the trial there was enough confidence in the hull rigidity to confirm its capability to carry a turret in the region of 20 tons. The second prototype, MTR2, was also ordered and manufactured at ROF Leeds, and it was this vehicle that was fitted with the first turret and used for turret development trials.

Once the development trials were completed, nine more vehicles were to be built, and these were to be designated test vehicles A-I; TV A was to be used for further trial by both ATDU and a regiment to be selected from the RAC. However, in the best tradition of British equipment trials, the nine hulls had already been built, and some of them even machined, when the project was cancelled.

Challenger's Predecessor

Only one TV was actually finished, and it was kept at Chertsey where it used as a fully kitted and stowed demonstration vehicle. It was photographed many times, and with the side armour removed it was presented as the representative of the forthcoming FV4030 series, to be called Shir Iran. This vehicle was the next step up from the up-rated Chieftain for Iran; it was to be fitted with Chobham armour and the Rolls-Royce power pack. As things turned out, it subsequently came into service as Chieftain's partial replacement, and became known as Challenger 1.

The vehicle at Bovington is thought to be TV-A itself, although no one seems too sure, but looking at it with the side armour fitted, and also the armoured side plates as used in the Gulf War, it is easy to see where Challenger came from. MTR 1 was stripped down, and parts of the hull were used for metallurgical analysis as part of the ongoing investigation into the use of aluminium armour. Interestingly the components that were used to construct MTR 1 were from a Chieftain that had been built by ROF Leeds but rejected due to the glacis plate splitting; furthermore, the registration number of MTR 1 was also taken from that same Chieftain hull. Things were not wasted, as the split hull was taken and used for other projects, as was at least one more aluminium hull probably expended in mine trials. The most striking feature of the turret would have been the inclusion of the 21 cupola in place of the no. 15 of Chieftain; also to be included was an early version of IFCS called AIFCS (advanced integrated fire control system).

THE MARK 4 CHIEFTAIN

It is the Mk 4 that is sometimes mentioned in books as having not been built, or only in project form. In fact two Mk 4 Chieftains were built:

these were sent to the Yuma proving ground in Arizona from May to September 1971, crewed by the 4th/7th RDG and 13th/18th Hussars. They had no long side bins at the rear – instead the sides were built up to provide a larger fuel capacity; they were also fitted with desert tracks. The aim of the trial, amongst other things, was to prove the increased weight of the Mk 5, and by all accounts this was highly satisfactory. The bins were filled with pig iron, and there was instrumentation fitted to record all aspects of the vehicle performance.

Sgt Chris Trigg relates that they had to pass back this information to control at set intervals, and during one phase when the vehicles were being driven in the mountains, the instruments recorded a gear change every six seconds. One wonders how that would have gone down with a Centurion driver who had to use a manual gear change all the time.

Once the trial was complete, the vehicles returned to the UK and were used to carry out different trials, including as suspension test rigs. In September 1989 it was decided that the two Chieftain hulls would not be returned to Army use, and were to be re-numbered. Thus 02 SP 96 became 00 WA 72; the fate of 02 SP 95 the other Mk4 – 02 SP 95 – is unknown.

THE 21 CUPOLA

As we have seen, the FV4211 was in the first instance designed to carry the 21 cupola, the replacement for the standard no. 15 cupola, currently fitted to Chieftain. The cupola was the brainchild of an engineer called Keller from FVRDE, probably one of the last designers who had actually served in tanks. It was intended to give the user a decent night vision capability, to introduce power traverse to the cupola, to load and fire the commander's GPMG under armour, and to provide a night watch facility. These were just some of the requirements that had to be met.

Left: *A 21 cupola minus II sight, as fitted to the FV 4211. Visible at the front and to the right of the gunner's sight is the light projector for the muzzle reference system. (Tim Babb)*

Below: *The large size of the proposed 21 cupola. Prominent is the II sight head, just waiting for the nearest burst of shrapnel to be blown away. It never entered service. (BAE Systems)*

The resulting cupola met some of them effectively, but at the cost of an increase in height and silhouette, leading to an M60-type look. It was power-operated, and also had a vertical-looking periscope for observing for helicopters, though this was a feature that many felt was unnecessary. The commander's mg could indeed be reloaded from under armour, quite a desirable feature. The gun would initially be loaded from outside as normal, but in the 21 cupola the ammo was also under armour and not outside, as on the no. 15. When the belt was nearly expended, a micro switch would sense this and stop the gun firing; then all the commander had to do was link another belt to the remains of the other, and he was ready to carry on firing.

It was also possible to set up the cupola for night scanning, with the sights acting as the sentry. The cupola would be traversed to its extreme left arc, and a limit switch would be set; the procedure would then be repeated for the right arc. The same would be carried out for elevation and depression, then with all the sights switched on the cupola could be set in motion. It would sweep within the pre-set limits, and as soon as the thermal pointer picked up a target it would halt the cupola motion, a buzzer would sound in the operator's headset, and if he was lucky he would be able to identify the target through his II sight.

That was the theory, but the trouble was that the thermal pointer was not cooled, as are modern TI sights, and it was hard to set it to pick up targets. Turn the sensitivity down to remove the problem of anything such as wild life setting it off, and it probably wouldn't pick anything up at all – and of course it worked vice-versa as well. Another electronic problem was that there was no operable memory function, so the user could not tell the system to ignore certain targets.

In the end the system was not adopted, and only a few examples were built; one can be seen on the FV4211 at Bovington when it emerges from the reserve collection. However, as always, valuable information was gained in the operation and tactical use of thermal imaging equipment, which would be of great use later when TI was installed in Chieftain and Challenger 1. One disadvantage of the 21 cupola was that, due to its size and the amount of equipment fitted, the actual space for the commander was a lot less than in Chieftain, making it a very tight fit. (It would be cruel to believe the story that the project was terminated on the decision of one rather rotund senior officer who, on seeing the space for the commander, realized that he would never fit into it.)

SIMULATORS

While not strictly a variant, the simulator did provide realistic training. Much has been made

---

The Multi-Purpose Chieftain

As anyone who has been involved with Chieftain will know, many trials have been conducted using the tank as a suitable base to work on. Such an example would be the trial carried out by the Royal Signals to lower the height of the combat radio antennae. The tip of an antenna is usually the first thing that can be seen as the vehicle approaches the edge of a ridge when viewed from the enemy's side. The solution to this was a fixed aerial that rather resembled a hula-hoop, which would be bolted to the forward edge of the turret in a flat position. Technically it apparently worked, but from a safety point of view it was a real hazard, as the crew kept tripping up on it since it was raised at least 20mm from the turret roof – that, and a wet day, and a camouflage net did not bear thinking about!

Chieftain hulls have also been used as cranes on MoD ranges. Kirkudbright has one that replaced a similar vehicle based on Centurion that fell into a pit and was written off. Shoeburyness had 02 EB 14 converted as a crane, but it has now long gone. These conversions were useful for moving heavy hard targets to various locations within the range area.

In short, Chieftain will no doubt carry on being used for many weird and wonderful purposes, even after the replacement of the AVLB and AVRE in the near future.

A privately owned Chieftain in Australia fitted with Simfire. The laser for this is fitted on the barrel with the flash-bang generator behind. (Colin Brown)

recently about the defence cuts affecting the Royal Navy, with crews having to shout 'bang' to simulate a weapon firing. For many years this was actually the case for troops on the ground when engaging the enemy during an exercise: all they could do was throw a thunderflash and hope that the umpire would award them a kill. What was needed was a system that would enable troops to engage each other and score a kill, though obviously without killing each other for real. The advent of lasers in manageable size proved to be the answer. The first systems were only for vehicles, and it would be a few years before everyone on the battlefield could be using a system that provided a kill not just of men, but vehicles as well.

Simfire

The first system fitted to Chieftain was called Simfire, and consisted of an eye-safe laser

mounted on the barrel and a flash/bang simulator on the right-hand smoke discharger, to simulate the noise and flash of the main armament firing. Around the turret were four detectors: these picked up the laser from an opposing vehicle and fed the information to the turret crew to tell them they were under fire. On the rear of the turret was a bracket holding a smoke canister: if the vehicle was hit and destroyed, the smoke canister was ignited to show that the vehicle was dead; this was later supplemented with an amber rotary

The 140mm Gun

At the time of writing there is a Chieftain hull equipped as a test bed to evaluate the fitting of a 140mm gun to a future tank. This is a calibre that is being discussed in several tank-producing nations as possibly the next weapon that will be used. At the moment it is still being evaluated, and may never see the light of day in service.

light. Also considered was a feature to close down the engines, but as this cut off the hydraulic power to the main brakes, the idea was soon discarded.

Mounted on the forward edge of the turret was the RX/TX unit and a small whip antenna: this transmitted and received information from both engaging vehicles.

After removing the loader's periscope, the cables from all the external fittings were fed down into the turret to a main control box. This was fitted to the commander's left, in place of a four-round projectile rack. The control box could be set up and sealed by an umpire, and gave the crew a set amount of ammunition. Connected to both the commander's and gunner's eyepieces were clip-on rings containing red LEDs: these were used to indicate the fall of shot; also the gun was programmed so that a time delay occurred once it had been fired, to simulate the loader loading the next round.

The system was not very popular as it took a long time to set up and to calibrate, and was of no use at all unless the enemy was similarly equipped. Having said that, when it did work, it was indicative to see how many vehicles actually survived an attack. With the system working, it wasn't often that you could attack a position and still have all your tanks left – and this is even truer with today's system, where every vehicle and soldier can be equipped.

Simfics

The successor to Simfire was Simfics, and it was developed so the system could be used with IFCS-equipped tanks. The most noticeable change was the removal of the laser from on top of the gun; instead it was fitted in the muzzle with the cables running down the bore. The flash/bang generator was moved to the forward edge of the turret, and there were changes to the control box; but otherwise the system was very much the same as its predecessor, and continued in service until it was replaced in turn by the modern DFWES (Direct Fire Weapons Effect Simulator) equipment in use today.

9 The End

The end came very quickly for MBT, hastened on by two major events: the fall of the Shah of Iran, and the unification of West and East Germany and the subsequent break-up of the Soviet Union and the Warsaw Pact.

The fall of the Shah meant that the latest derivatives of MBT, known as the Shir Iran, were left with no one to buy them, as the Ayatollah had cancelled all Western arms contracts. The British Army had been looking for a replacement for MBT as it was starting to show its age and the power pack was never going to be reliable. This was in spite of the fact that the MBT 800 had proved that a decent Rolls-Royce diesel could be fitted into an existing hull without too many modifications. This had been a conversion requested by the Shah, and it worked well. But for some reason the British government had decided not to go ahead with it, and the only MBTs that were destined for this engine were those supplied to the Shah, amongst others.

This left the much-vaunted MBT 80 project, which was going down like a stricken dive-bomber. This had been launched with a great show of praise and publicity, even to the extent of a brochure issued to every member of the RAC. The MBT 80 project would have resembled Challenger, but was unusual in layout as the main armament was offset to the left to allow room for the type of fire control equipment envisaged for it. The only example that can be seen is at the Bovington Tank Museum, where it is stored in the reserve collection at the time of writing. It is well worth seeing if possible, and trying to visualize what the final layout would have been, as only the turret shell is left, with neither Chobham armour nor simulation fitted. The hull is very Challenger-like in its appearance.

With the demise of the MBT 80 project and the reluctance to re-engine the MBT fleet, the solution seemed to be in adopting the FV4030 Shir Iran into a vehicle that could be used by the British Army: thus Challenger 1 came into being.

THE LOSERS: TANKS DESTROYED

Another by-product of the replacing of the MBT fleet meant that under the Conventional Forces Europe Treaty that had been signed by the British Government, we were obliged to destroy a certain amount of our military hardware. This was to be verified by observers from Russia and neutral observers, to ensure that all was carried out to the letter of the treaty. The treaty also allowed for inspections of bases and equipment with very little warning, although certain items that were deemed sensitive could be kept away from the team. The author observed an example of how silly all this looked when he returned to the 4/7 RDG in Detmold. On visiting the GTS where IFCS gunnery was taught, S/Sgt Kirkbride, the regimental gunnery NCO, showed him a large drape that had been provided to cover the GTS; this was placed over each one every night in case an inspection team decided to turn up during silent hours. In truth it really looked ridiculous, and a blatant indication that something special was there.

Meanwhile the government had decided that to show we were reducing our tank strength as required, the MBT fleet was being destroyed: this usually involved a charge being placed in

Awaiting its final duty, serving as a gate guard for brigade signals unit at Sennelager.
(Capt A. D. Vick)

the centre of a tank to blow out the sides and disrupt the turret; also the guns were flame cut. Once this was completed, the hulk was then placed on the ranges to be battered to a pile of scrap. True to form, though, a good number of these vehicles had been put through a base overhaul programme – meaning that they were in tip-top condition when they were destroyed. Having seen some of these vehicles after this programme, I can assure anyone that they would have not looked out of place in any regiment's tank park. According to one of the overseeing managers, this was done because the programme had been started, and it could not be terminated due to cost.

Meanwhile the Russians were doing the same thing, and thousands of T55s and T62s were destroyed. Meanwhile T72 and T64 soldiered on, and the T80 was further developed, leading to the T90. This was known in the army as 'playing the game'.

THE SURVIVORS

This time, however, many vehicles have survived, unlike Conqueror when the whole fleet seemed to disappear overnight. Many have gone to private owners; some soldier on as entertainment in corporate days out; others have ended their days in museums around the world. Survivors range from Moscow (ex-Iranian) to Canada, to the USA and Australia. It is still possible for the public to go and see a Chieftain in running order, especially during the summer at locations such as Bovington Tank Museum in Dorset, or the Imperial War Museum at Duxford in Cambridgeshire, or the annual Beltring show at the Whitbread hop farm in Kent.

Some have ended their days as gate guards outside various military establishments; others have been dropped into deep water in Scotland for North Sea divers to train on. Still others are used in recovery exercises, when they are

Chieftain 01 FD05, BD Metals, Albion Row, Byker Newcastle, UK. (SC Osfield, October 1999)

recovered by trainee recovery mechanics from the REME – once the exercise is accomplished, they are pushed back into the location to await the next recovery attempt. One interesting case is a vehicle used by the REME: basically it is shot up by machine-gun fire, mines and tank main armament, and is then used to train fitters on battlefield repairs, and how to make a vehicle usable again with limited resources.

Chieftain is also the basis of several kits for fans to build; it has even been built at a phenomenal scale of 1/8. Perhaps the most bizarre story concerns the vehicle that starred in a war comic story of a few years ago, in which a two-man Chieftain and its crew were taken from a training area in a time warp and found themselves in the middle of the Ardennes during the German offensive. It involved Chieftain versus Tiger 1, a decidedly interesting combination. Suffice it to say that the tanks came 'home' and the good guys won!

Sadly, as the pictures show, some are being slowly battered into unrecognizable piles of scrap on various ranges; others were taken to a foundry near Sheffield and smelted. But of those that survive in running order, it really is a wonderful sight to see them perform so well, and to witness the care and attention lavished on them.

Appendix I:
Vehicle Locations and Disposals

The following list has been compiled over a period of time with the help of the MoD first and foremost, and also the owners of private vehicles who have taken their tank out of storage. This has allowed me to take a few pictures, and then clamber inside to confirm the vehicle registration number. It has not been without its lighter moments, though, with one owner refusing point blank to let me even visit his tank. It turned out that he suspected me of being an MoD agent come to sieze his tank back so that the MoD could fully refurbish it and others in order to sell them to two Far Eastern countries. This was even more amusing when the two countries turned out to be Kuwait and Iraq.

To all those who helped, I can only say thank you. The following list is by no means complete, and I find that I am adding to it daily: so if you know of an MBT, please let me know. The locations given are as at the date listed; some vehicles have moved on since then, but if I tried to keep up with them all I would never stop, this also ties in with the pictures I have, so at least I know where each one was taken. I have not listed the names of the private owners, so as to respect their privacy, except where mention has been specifically requested. The mark indicated in the list is the mark when the vehicle was built, so although it may be listed as a Mk 2, it may well have finished life as a Mk11. Also if there is no entry in the location column, it is because I have no information as to that tank's final whereabouts. If anyone has any information regarding a vehicle's location, I would be very grateful to receive it.

Not included in this list are two surviving prototypes that are slowly ending their days on the range at Kirkcudbright in Scotland, although they do not appear to have been shot at for a long time; one even still has its original power pack. They are 00 DA 05 and P5. Also some vehicles were built, but never used by the British Army, as they appeared to have been taken out of the production line before being allocated a number. The census plate in the hull would seem to bear this out, as it carries no NATO stock number or codes; instead it shows only a trial-type number, such as 99 SP 33. For those vehicles listed as belonging to entertainment groups, contact details can usually be found in magazines and such like.

A very nicely preserved Chieftain in private ownership.
(Nigel Montgomery)

165

Hard target at Lulworth Range. (Author)

Private owned vehicle Five Star.

Vehicle Locations and Disposals

VRN	Type	Mk	Date	ROF	Location
00 EB 23	MBT	1		Vickers	
00 EB 24	MBT	1		Vickers	
00 EB 25	MBT	1	Dec 00	Vickers	Now AVLB at Bovington
00 EB 26	MBT	1		Vickers	
00 EB 27	MBT	1	Sep 97	Vickers	Bordon REME
00 EB 28	MBT	1	Dec 00	Vickers	Lulworth ranges
00 EB 29	MBT	1	Dec 00	Vickers	Now AVLB at Bovington
00 EB 30	MBT	1	Sep 98	Vickers	Bordon
00 EB 31	MBT	1		Vickers	
00 EB 32	MBT	1	Dec 00	Vickers	Turret Lulworth ranges
00 EB 33	MBT	1		Vickers	
00 EB 34	MBT	1	Feb 96	Vickers	Otterburn ranges
00 EB 35	MBT	1		Vickers	
00 EB 36	MBT	2		Vickers	Smelted
00 EB 37	MBT	2		Vickers	Smelted
00 EB 38	MBT	2		Vickers	
00 EB 39	MBT	2		Vickers	
00 EB 40	MBT	2	Feb 98	Vickers	Thetford ranges
00 EB 41	MBT	2		Vickers	
00 EB 42	MBT	2	Jan 00	Vickers	Sold privately
00 EB 43	MBT	2		Vickers	Smelted
00 EB 44	MBT	2		Vickers	Smelted
00 EB 45	MBT	2		Vickers	Smelted
00 EB 46	MBT	2	Oct 98	Vickers	Warcop
00 EB 47	MBT	2		Vickers	Smelted
00 EB 48	MBT	2	Dec 00	Vickers	Lulworth ranges
00 EB 49	MBT	2		Vickers	
00 EB 50	MBT	2	Dec 00	Vickers	Lulworth ranges
00 EB 51	MBT	2		Vickers	Smelted
00 EB 52	MBT	2		Vickers	Smelted
00 EB 53	MBT	2	Feb 00	Vickers	Cut up for scrap
00 EB 54	MBT	2	Nov 96	Vickers	Lulworth ranges
00 EB 55	MBT	2	Jul 96	Vickers	Private, Shrewsbury
00 EB 56	MBT	2	Oct 98	Vickers	Warcop ranges
00 EB 57	MBT	2		Vickers	
00 EB 58	MBT	2	Dec 00	Vickers	Lulworth ranges
00 EB 59	MBT	2	Aug 99	Vickers	Aldershot Museum
00 EB 60	MBT	2	Dec 00	Vickers	Lulworth ranges
00 EB 61	MBT	2		Vickers	
00 EB 62	MBT	2		Vickers	
00 EB 63	MBT	2		Vickers	Smelted
00 EB 64	MBT	2		Vickers	
00 EB 65	MBT	2	Feb 98	Vickers	Warminster ranges
00 EB 66	MBT	2		Vickers	Smelted
00 EB 67	MBT	2		Vickers	
00 EB 68	MBT	2		Vickers	
00 EB 69	MBT	2	Jun 00	Vickers	Privately owned, USA
00 EB 70	MBT	2	Nov 96	Vickers	Lulworth Ranges
00 EB 71	MBT	2		Vickers	Smelted
00 EB 72	MBT	2		Vickers	
00 EB 73	MBT	2		Vickers	
00 EB 74	MBT	2	Jan 00	Vickers	Castlemartin ranges
00 EB 75	MBT	2		Vickers	Vickers Factory
00 EB 76	MBT	2		Vickers	Smelted
00 EB 77	MBT	2		Vickers	Smelted
00 EB 78	MBT	2		Vickers	
00 EB 79	MBT	2		Vickers	Smelted

00 EB 80	MBT	2	Feb 98	Vickers	Thetford ranges
00 EB 81	MBT	2	Oct 98	Vickers	Warcop ranges
00 EB 82	MBT	2		Vickers	
00 EB 83	MBT	2		Vickers	Smelted
00 EB 84	MBT	2	Jun 00	Vickers	Salisbury Plain
00 EB 85	MBT	2		Vickers	
00 EB 86	MBT	2	Feb 98	Vickers	Warminster ranges
00 EB 87	MBT	2	Dec 00	Vickers	Lulworth ranges
00 EB 88	MBT	2		Vickers	Smelted
00 EB 89	MBT	2	Aug 99	Vickers	Lulworth ranges
00 EB 90	MBT	2		Vickers	
00 EB 91	MBT	2		Vickers	
00 EB 92	MBT	2	Feb 98	Vickers	Thetford ranges
00 EB 93	MBT	2	Nov 96	Vickers	Lulworth
00 EB 94	MBT	2		Vickers	Smelted
00 EB 95	MBT	2	Nov 96	Vickers	Lulworth
00 EB 96	MBT	2		Vickers	Smelted
00 EB 97	MBT	2	Nov 97	Vickers	Bordon
00 EB 98	MBT	2	Oct 98	Vickers	Warcop ranges
00 EB 99	MBT	2	Aug 99	Vickers	Lulworth ranges
01 EB 00	MBT	2	Nov 96	Vickers	Lulworth ranges
01 EB 01	MBT	2		Vickers	Smelted
01 EB 02	MBT	2		Vickers	
01 EB 03	MBT	2	Dec 97	Vickers	Withams dealer
01 EB 04	MBT	2	Oct 96	Vickers	Highland Park
01 EB 05	MBT	2	Oct 97	Vickers	Helston, Devon
01 EB 06	MBT	2	Mar 00	Vickers	Private Manchester
01 EB 07	MBT	2		Vickers	
01 EB 08	MBT	2	Jan 98	Vickers	Withams dealer
01 EB 09	MBT	2		Vickers	
01 EB 10	MBT	2	Dec 00	Vickers	Lulworth ranges
01 EB 11	MBT	2	Feb 98	Vickers	Thetford ranges
01 EB 12	MBT	2	Nov 98	Vickers	East England Tank Museum
01 EB 13	MBT	2		Vickers	
01 EB 14	MBT	2		Vickers	Smelted
01 EB 15	MBT	2	Jan 98	Vickers	Withams dealer
01 EB 16	MBT	2	Dec 00	Vickers	Lulworth ranges
01 EB 17	MBT	2	Oct 98	Vickers	Warcop ranges
01 EB 18	MBT	2	Dec 00	Vickers	Lulworth ranges
01 EB 19	MBT	2		Vickers	Smelted
01 EB 20	MBT	2		Vickers	
01 EB 21	MBT	2		Vickers	AVRE Conversion
01 EB 22	MBT	2		Vickers	
01 EB 23	MBT	2		Vickers	
01 EB 24	MBT	2	Jan 98	Vickers	AVRE Ashchurch
01 EB 25	MBT	2		Vickers	Smelted
01 EB 26	MBT	2		Vickers	Smelted
01 EB 27	MBT	2	Nov 96	Vickers	Lulworth ranges
01 EB 28	MBT	2		Vickers	
01 EB 29	MBT	2		Vickers	Smelted
01 EB 30	MBT	2	May 98	Vickers	RCMS Shrivenham
01 EB 31	MBT	2		Vickers	Smelted
01 EB 32	MBT	2		Vickers	Smelted
01 EB 33	MBT	2		Vickers	
01 EB 34	MBT	2		Vickers	
01 EB 35	MBT	2	Feb 00	Vickers	Bovington Willich AVRE
01 EB 36	MBT	2	Nov 96	Vickers	Lulworth ranges
01 EB 37	MBT	2		Vickers	Smelted
01 EB 38	MBT	2		Vickers	
01 EB 39	MBT	2		Vickers	Smelted

01 EB 40	MBT	2		Vickers	Smelted
01 EB 41	MBT	2	May 98	Vickers	AVRE RE Wing Bovington
01 EB 42	MBT	2	Dec 00	Vickers	Now AVRE at Bovington
01 EB 43	MBT	2		Vickers	Smelted
01 EB 44	MBT	2		Vickers	Smelted
01 EB 45	MBT	2	Aug 97	Vickers	Bovington
01 EB 46	MBT	2	Nov 96	Vickers	Tank Museum
01 EB 47	MBT	2		Vickers	
01 EB 48	MBT	2	Oct 97	Vickers	Bordon
01 EB 49	MBT	2	Aug 97	Vickers	Tank Museum
01 EB 50	MBT	2		Vickers	Smelted
01 EB 51	MBT	2	Oct 98	Vickers	Warcop ranges
01 EB 52	MBT	2	Jan 98	Vickers	Ashchurch
01 EB 53	MBT	2	Mar 98	Vickers	Castlemartin ranges
01 EB 54	MBT	2		Vickers	
01 EB 55	MBT	2	Nov 96	Vickers	Lulworth ranges
01 EB 56	MBT	2	Mar 98	Vickers	Castlemartin ranges
01 EB 57	MBT	2		Vickers	
01 EB 58	MBT	2	Mar 98	Vickers	Castlemartin ranges
01 EB 59	MBT	2	Sep 00	Vickers	Saumur Tank Museum, France
01 EB 60	MBT	2		Vickers	
01 EB 61	MBT	2		Vickers	Smelted
01 EB 62	MBT	2	Feb 98	Vickers	Warminster
01 EB 63	MBT	2		Vickers	
01 EB 64	MBT	2		Vickers	
01 EB 65	MBT	2	Dec 99	Vickers	REME College, Arborfield
01 EB 66	MBT	2	Nov 97	Vickers	Withams dealer
01 EB 67	MBT	2		Vickers	
01 EB 68	MBT	2	Feb 98	Vickers	Warminster
01 EB 69	MBT	2		Vickers	Smelted
01 EB 70	MBT	2	Aug 97	Vickers	Duxford
01 EB 71	MBT	2		Vickers	
01 EB 72	MBT	2		Vickers	
01 EB 73	MBT	2		Vickers	Smelted
01 EB 74	MBT	2	Mar 98	Vickers	Castlemartin
01 EB 75	MBT	2		Vickers	Smelted
01 EB 76	MBT	2	Dec 00	Vickers	Lulworth ranges
01 EB 77	MBT	2		Vickers	
01 EB 78	MBT	2		Vickers	
01 EB 79	MBT	2	Jan 98	Vickers	Ashchurch
01 EB 80	MBT	2		Vickers	
01 EB 81	MBT	2	Mar 00	Vickers	Otterburn ranges
01 EB 82	MBT	2		Vickers	Smelted
01 EB 83	MBT	2		Vickers	
01 EB 84	MBT	2		Vickers	Smelted
01 EB 85	MBT	2		Vickers	Smelted
01 EB 86	MBT	2		Vickers	
01 EB 87	MBT	2	Jan 98	Vickers	Ashchurch
01 EB 88	MBT	2	Jul 95	Vickers	Smelted
01 EB 89	MBT	2		Vickers	Smelted
01 EB 90	MBT	2		Vickers	
01 EB 91	MBT	2	May 98	Vickers	Bovington
01 EB 92	MBT	2	Mar 99	Vickers	Ottawa War Museum, Canada
01 EB 93	MBT	2		Vickers	Smelted
01 EB 94	MBT	2	Nov 96	Vickers	Lulworth ranges
01 EB 95	MBT	2		Vickers	
01 EB 96	MBT	2		Vickers	
01 EB 97	MBT	2		Vickers	Smelted
01 EB 98	MBT	2		Vickers	
01 EB 99	MBT	2		Vickers	

02 EB 00	MBT	2		Vickers	Castlemartin
02 EB 01	MBT	2		Vickers	Smelted
02 EB 02	MBT	2		Vickers	Smelted
02 EB 03	MBT	2		Vickers	Smelted
02 EB 04	MBT	2		Vickers	
02 EB 05	MBT	2		Vickers	
02 EB 06	MBT	2	Dec 96	Vickers	Stourbridge
02 EB 07	MBT	2	Jan 00	Vickers	AVRE 32 Engineer Regiment
02 EB 08	MBT	2		Vickers	
02 EB 09	MBT	2	May 98	Vickers	Willich AVRE Bovington
02 EB 10	MBT	2	Jan 98	Vickers	Ashchurch
02 EB 11	MBT	2		Vickers	
02 EB 12	MBT	2	Dec 00	Vickers	Lulworth ranges
02 EB 13	MBT	2		Leeds	
02 EB 14	MBT	2	Feb 00	Leeds	Crane Shoeburyness
02 EB 15	MBT	2		Leeds	
02 EB 16	MBT	2		Leeds	
02 EB 17	MBT	2	Aug 98	Leeds	Bovington
02 EB 18	MBT	2		Leeds	
02 EB 19	MBT	2		Leeds	
02 EB 20	MBT	2	Oct 97	Leeds	Bordon
02 EB 21	MBT	2		Leeds	
02 EB 22	MBT	1		Leeds	
02 EB 23	MBT	1	Nov 96	Leeds	Lulworth ranges
02 EB 24	MBT	1	Mar 98	Leeds	Castlemartin ranges
02 EB 25	MBT	1		Leeds	
02 EB 26	MBT	1	Feb 98	Leeds	Thetford
02 EB 27	MBT	1		Leeds	
02 EB 28	MBT	1		Leeds	
02 EB 29	MBT	1	Aug 96	Leeds	CFE destroyed by explosion
02 EB 30	MBT	1	Feb 98	Leeds	Thetford
02 EB 31	MBT	1	Jun 00	Leeds	AVLB now. Demo Squadron
02 EB 32	MBT	1	Oct 97	Leeds	Bordon
02 EB 33	MBT	1	Dec 00	Leeds	Lulworth ranges
02 EB 34	MBT	1	Oct 97	Leeds	Bordon
02 EB 35	MBT	1	Feb 98	Leeds	Thetford
02 EB 36	MBT	1	Feb 98	Leeds	Thetford
02 EB 37	MBT	1		Leeds	
02 EB 38	MBT	1	Jan 96	Leeds	Gate Guard Ashchurch
02 EB 39	MBT	2		Leeds	
02 EB 40	MBT	2	Oct 98	Leeds	Warcop ranges
02 EB 41	MBT	2		Leeds	
02 EB 42	MBT	2	Oct 98	Leeds	Warcop
02 EB 43	MBT	2		Leeds	Smelted
02 EB 44	MBT	2	Nov 96	Leeds	Lulworth ranges
02 EB 45	MBT	2		Leeds	
02 EB 46	MBT	2	Mar 98	Leeds	Castlemartin
02 EB 47	MBT	2	Feb 98	Leeds	Warminster
02 EB 48	MBT	2		Leeds	
02 EB 49	MBT	2		Leeds	Feldom Moor
02 EB 50	MBT	2		Leeds	Smelted
02 EB 51	MBT	2		Leeds	
02 EB 52	MBT	2	Aug 99	Leeds	Lulworth ranges
02 EB 53	MBT	2		Leeds	
02 EB 54	MBT	2	Feb 98	Leeds	Warminster
02 EB 55	MBT	2		Leeds	Smelted
02 EB 56	MBT	2	Nov 99	Leeds	Private ownership
02 EB 57	MBT	2		Leeds	Otterburn
02 EB 58	MBT	2	Feb 95	Leeds	Otterburn
02 EB 59	MBT	2	Feb 98	Leeds	Lulworth

02 EB 60	MBT	2		Leeds	
02 EB 61	MBT	2		Leeds	Jacques Littlefield Collection USA
02 EB 62	MBT	2	Feb 98	Leeds	AVRE Ashchurch
02 EB 63	MBT	2	Jul 99	Leeds	ACF Hospitality Bristol
02 EB 64	MBT	2		Leeds	
02 EB 65	MBT	2	Aug 97	Leeds	Tank Museum
02 EB 66	MBT	2	Nov 97	Leeds	Withams dealer
02 EB 67	MBT	2	Dec 00	Leeds	Now AVRE at Bovington
02 EB 68	MBT	2	Dec 00	Leeds	Lulworth Ranges
02 EB 69	MBT	2		Leeds	
02 EB 70	MBT	2		Leeds	Smelted
02 EB 71	MBT	2		Leeds	
02 EB 72	MBT	2		Leeds	
02 EB 73	MBT	2		Leeds	
02 EB 74	MBT	2		Leeds	Smelted
02 EB 75	MBT	2		Leeds	Smelted
02 EB 76	MBT	2	Nov 96	Leeds	Lulworth ranges
02 EB 77	MBT	2		Leeds	Smelted
02 EB 78	MBT	2	Nov 96	Leeds	Lulworth ranges
02 EB 79	MBT	2		Leeds	
02 EB 80	MBT	2		Leeds	Willich AVRE
02 EB 81	MBT	2		Leeds	Smelted
02 EB 82	MBT	2		Leeds	Smelted
02 EB 83	MBT	2	Oct 96	Leeds	Highland Park
02 EB 84	MBT	2		Leeds	Smelted
02 EB 85	MBT	2		Leeds	Smelted
02 EB 86	MBT	2		Leeds	Smelted
02 EB 87	MBT	2	Nov 96	Leeds	Pilkington, Glasgow
02 EB 88	MBT	2	Mar 98	Leeds	Castlemartin ranges
02 EB 89	MBT	2	Dec 00	Leeds	Lulworth ranges
02 EB 90	MBT	2	Feb 98	Leeds	Warminster
02 EB 91	MBT	2	Mar 99	Leeds	Hard Target, BATUS
02 EB 92	MBT	2		Leeds	Smelted
02 EB 93	MBT	2		Leeds	Smelted
02 EB 94	MBT	2	Feb 98	Leeds	Warminster
02 EB 95	MBT	2		Leeds	Smelted
02 EB 96	MBT	2		Leeds	
02 EB 97	MBT	2	Mar 98	Leeds	Castlemartin ranges
02 EB 98	MBT	2	Feb 96	Leeds	Otterburn
02 EB 99	MBT	2		Leeds	Smelted
03 EB 00	MBT	2		Leeds	
03 EB 01	MBT	2	Aug 97	Leeds	Privately owned Manchester
03 EB 02	MBT	2		Leeds	Vickers AVRE conversion
03 EB 03	MBT	2		Leeds	Smelted
03 EB 04	MBT	2		Leeds	
03 EB 05	MBT	2	Feb 98	Leeds	Warminster
03 EB 06	MBT	2		Leeds	
03 EB 07	MBT	2		Leeds	
03 EB 08	MBT	2	Aug 99	Leeds	Privately owned
03 EB 09	MBT	2	Nov 97	Leeds	Withams dealer
03 EB 10	MBT	2		Leeds	
03 EB 11	MBT	2	Mar 99	Leeds	Hard target BATUS
03 EB 12	MBT	2	Feb 98	Leeds	Warminster
03 EB 13	MBT	2		Leeds	
03 EB 14	MBT	2		Leeds	Smelted
03 EB 15	MBT	2		Leeds	
03 EB 16	MBT	2		Leeds	Smelted
03 EB 17	MBT	2		Leeds	Smelted
03 EB 18	MBT	2	Feb 98	Leeds	Warminster
03 EB 19	MBT	2	Feb 98	Leeds	Warminster

03 EB 20	MBT	2	Aug 97	Leeds	Duxford
03 EB 21	MBT	2		Leeds	
03 EB 22	MBT	2		Leeds	
03 EB 23	MBT	2	Nov 96	Leeds	Lulworth ranges
03 EB 24	MBT	2	Apr 99	Leeds	Gate Guard BATUS
03 EB 25	MBT	2		Leeds	Smelted
03 EB 26	MBT	2		Leeds	Smelted
03 EB 27	MBT	2	August 00 Leeds		Lulworth ranges
03 EB 28	MBT	2	Jan 00	Leeds	Private owned
03 EB 29	MBT	2	Jul 97	Leeds	Bovington, AVRE conversion
03 EB 30	MBT	2	Jan 95	Leeds	Smelted
03 EB 31	MBT	2	May 91	Leeds	Catterick Marne Barracks
03 EB 32	MBT	2	Jan 00	Leeds	Castlemartin
03 EB 33	MBT	2		Leeds	Smelted
03 EB 34	MBT	2		Leeds	Smelted
03 EB 35	MBT	2	Apr 00	Leeds	Marconi/Chieftain 2000
03 EB 36	MBT	2		Leeds	Smelted
03 EB 37	MBT	2	Jan 98	Leeds	Ashchurch
03 EB 38	MBT	2		Leeds	
03 EB 39	MBT	2	Nov 99	Leeds	Private owned
03 EB 40	MBT	2		Leeds	
03 EB 41	MBT	2	July 87	Leeds	Mucklburgh collection
03 EB 42	MBT	2	Jan 98	Leeds	Ashchurch
03 EB 43	MBT	2		Leeds	
03 EB 44	MBT	2	Mar 96	Leeds	Defence NBC school
03 EB 45	MBT	2		Leeds	Smelted
03 EB 46	MBT	2	Oct 98	Leeds	Warcop
03 EB 47	MBT	2		Leeds	
03 EB 48	MBT	2		Leeds	
03 EB 49	MBT	2	Nov 96	Leeds	Lulworth ranges
03 EB 50	MBT	2		Leeds	Smelted
03 EB 51	MBT	2	Feb 00	Leeds	Privately cut up for scrap
03 EB 52	MBT	2		Leeds	Smelted
03 EB 53	MBT	2		Leeds	
03 EB 54	MBT	2		Leeds	
03 EB 55	MBT	2	Mar 99	Leeds	Hard target BATUS
03 EB 56	MBT	2	Feb 98	Leeds	Warminster
03 EB 57	MBT	2		Leeds	Smelted
03 EB 58	MBT	2		Leeds	
03 EB 59	MBT	2	Jan 00	Leeds	Castlemartin ranges
03 EB 60	MBT	2		Leeds	
03 EB 61	MBT	2	Mar 00	Leeds	Otterburn ranges
03 EB 62	MBT	2		Leeds	Smelted
03 EB 63	MBT	2	Jan 98	Leeds	Ashchurch
03 EB 64	MBT	2		Leeds	
03 EB 65	MBT	2	Jun 00	Leeds	Salisbury plain
03 EB 66	MBT	2		Leeds	
03 EB 67	MBT	2		Leeds	
03 EB 68	MBT	2	Nov 96	Leeds	Lower Lodge Horsham
03 EB 69	MBT	2	Oct 97	Leeds	Bordon
03 EB 70	MBT	2		Leeds	Smelted
03 EB 71	MBT	2		Leeds	
03 EB 72	MBT	2	Feb 98	Leeds	Thetford
03 EB 73	MBT	2		Leeds	Smelted
03 EB 74	MBT	2		Leeds	Smelted
03 EB 75	MBT	2	Dec 00	Leeds	Lulworth ranges
03 EB 76	MBT	2	Oct 96	Leeds	Lulworth. Ex author's
03 EB 77	MBT	2		Leeds	Smelted
03 EB 78	MBT	2		Leeds	Smelted
03 EB 79	MBT	2	Mar 99	Leeds	Bovington Heath

03 EB 80	MBT	2	Sep 00	Leeds	Five Star vehicles, USA
03 EB 81	MBT	2	Jan 98	Leeds	AVRE, Ashchurch
03 EB 82	MBT	2		Leeds	Smelted
03 EB 83	MBT	2	Aug 97	Leeds	Tank Museum
03 EB 84	MBT	2	Oct 98	Leeds	Warcop
03 EB 85	MBT	2		Leeds	
03 EB 86	MBT	2		Leeds	Smelted
03 EB 87	MBT	2		Leeds	Smelted
03 EB 88	MBT	2		Leeds	
03 EB 89	MBT	2		Leeds	
03 EB 90	MBT	2	Aug 99	Leeds	Bovington Heath
03 EB 91	MBT	2		Leeds	AVRE Willich, Bovington
03 EB 92	MBT	2		Leeds	
03 EB 93	MBT	2		Leeds	
03 EB 94	MBT	2	Oct 96	Leeds	Lulworth ranges
03 EB 95	MBT	2		Leeds	
03 EB 96	MBT	2		Leeds	
03 EB 97	MBT	2		Leeds	Smelted
03 EB 98	MBT	2		Leeds	Smelted
03 EB 99	MBT	2		Leeds	
04 EB 00	MBT	2	Feb 98	Leeds	Warminster
04 EB 01	MBT	2	Aug 99	Leeds	Lulworth ranges
04 EB 02	MBT	2		Leeds	
04 EB 03	MBT	2		Leeds	Smelted
04 EB 04	MBT	2		Leeds	Smelted
04 EB 05	MBT	2		Leeds	
04 EB 06	MBT	2		Leeds	
04 EB 07	MBT	2		Leeds	
04 EB 08	MBT	2		Leeds	Smelted
04 EB 09	MBT	2		Leeds	
04 EB 10	MBT	2	Oct 00	Leeds	AVRE gate guard ATDU
04 EB 11	MBT	2		Leeds	Smelted
04 EB 12	MBT	2		Leeds	
04 EB 13	MBT	2		Leeds	Smelted
04 EB 14	MBT	2		Leeds	
04 EB 15	MBT	2		Leeds	
04 EB 16	MBT	2		Leeds	
04 EB 17	MBT	2		Leeds	Smelted
04 EB 18	MBT	2		Leeds	Smelted
04 EB 19	MBT	2		Leeds	
04 EB 20	MBT	2	Dec 20	Leeds	A F Budge
04 EB 21	MBT	2	Jan 98	Leeds	RAC Centre plinth
04 EB 22	MBT	2	Jun 99	Leeds	Swynerton area prototype
04 EB 23	MBT	2		Leeds	Smelted
04 EB 24	MBT	2		Leeds	Smelted
04 EB 25	MBT	2		Leeds	Smelted
04 EB 26	MBT	2		Leeds	
04 EB 27	MBT	2		Leeds	
04 EB 28	MBT	2		Leeds	Smelted
04 EB 29	MBT	2	Feb 98	Leeds	Warminster
04 EB 30	MBT	2		Leeds	
04 EB 31	MBT	2	Jan 98	Leeds	Thetford
04 EB 32	MBT	2	Aug 98	Leeds	Anchor Surplus, Ripley
04 EB 33	MBT	2	Feb 96	Leeds	Otterburn
04 EB 34	MBT	2		Leeds	Smelted
04 EB 35	MBT	2		Leeds	
04 EB 36	MBT	2		Leeds	
04 EB 37	MBT	2		Leeds	
04 EB 38	MBT	2		Leeds	
04 EB 39	MBT	2	Sep 97	Leeds	Helston, Devon

04 EB 40	MBT	2	Mar 99	Leeds	Hard target, BATUS
04 EB 41	MBT	2		Leeds	
04 EB 42	MBT	2		Leeds	
04 EB 43	MBT	2	Aug 00	Leeds	Privately owned, Australia
04 EB 44	MBT	2	May 99	Leeds	Marne Barracks, Catterick
04 EB 45	MBT	2		Leeds	Smelted
04 EB 46	MBT	2	Mar 00	Leeds	Privately owned, Manchester
04 EB 47	MBT	2		Leeds	
04 EB 48	MBT	2		Leeds	Smelted
04 EB 49	MBT	2	Aug 99	Leeds	Lulworth ranges
04 EB 50	MBT	2		Leeds	
04 EB 51	MBT	2	Jan 00	Leeds	Castlemartin
04 EB 52	MBT	2		Leeds	
04 EB 53	MBT	2	Nov 96	Leeds	Privately owned, Stroud, UK
04 EB 54	MBT	2	Jan 98	Leeds	Ashchurch
04 EB 55	MBT	2		Leeds	Smelted
04 EB 56	MBT	2	Mar 98	Leeds	Castlemartin
04 EB 57	MBT	2		Leeds	
04 EB 58	MBT	2		Leeds	
04 EB 59	MBT	2		Leeds	
04 EB 60	MBT	2	Oct 97	Leeds	Bordon
04 EB 61	MBT	2		Leeds	
04 EB 62	MBT	2	Jul 96	Leeds	Tanks a Lot entertainment
04 EB 63	MBT	2		Leeds	Smelted
04 EB 64	MBT	2		Leeds	Smelted
04 EB 65	MBT	2	Jun 00	Leeds	Willich AVRE
04 EB 66	MBT	2		Leeds	Smelted
04 EB 67	MBT	2	Jun 00	Leeds	Willich AVRE
04 EB 68	MBT	2	Mar 00	Leeds	Otterburn
04 EB 69	MBT	2	Oct 96	Leeds	Warcop ranges
04 EB 70	MBT	2		Leeds	Smelted
04 EB 71	MBT	2		Leeds	Smelted
04 EB 72	MBT	2		Leeds	Smelted
04 EB 73	MBT	2		Leeds	Smelted
04 EB 74	MBT	2	Oct 96	Leeds	Highland Park
04 EB 75	MBT	2	Mar 99	Leeds	Hard target BATUS
04 EB 76	MBT	2		Leeds	Privately owned
04 EB 77	MBT	2	Oct 96	Leeds	Lulworth ranges
04 EB 78	MBT	2		Leeds	
04 EB 79	MBT	2	Oct 96	Leeds	Highland Park
04 EB 80	MBT	2		Leeds	Smelted
04 EB 81	MBT	2		Leeds	Smelted
04 EB 82	MBT	2		Leeds	
04 EB 83	MBT	2	Feb 99	Leeds	Bovington
04 EB 84	MBT	2		Leeds	
04 EB 85	MBT	2	May 98	Leeds	Now AVRE at Bovington
04 EB 86	MBT	2	Oct 96	Leeds	Highland Park
04 EB 87	MBT	2	Feb 96	Leeds	Otterburn
04 EB 88	MBT	2		Leeds	
04 EB 89	MBT	2	Sep 00	Leeds	Lulworth ranges
04 EB 90	MBT	2	Nov 96	Leeds	Lulworth ranges
04 EB 91	MBT	2	Mar-96	Leeds	Privately owned
04 EB 92	MBT	2		Leeds	Smelted
04 EB 93	MBT	2		Leeds	
04 EB 94	MBT	2	Jul 97	Leeds	Privately owned Manchester
04 EB 95	MBT	2	Feb 96	Leeds	Otterburn
04 EB 96	MBT	2		Leeds	
04 EB 97	MBT	2		Leeds	Smelted
04 EB 98	MBT	2	Aug 95	Leeds	Smelted
04 EB 99	MBT	2		Leeds	Smelted

05 EB 00	MBT	2		Leeds	
05 EB 01	MBT	2		Leeds	
05 EB 02	MBT	2	Aug 95	Leeds	Hard target BATUS
05 EB 03	MBT	2	Feb 98	Leeds	Warminster
05 EB 04	MBT	2	Feb 96	Leeds	Otterburn
05 EB 05	MBT	2		Leeds	
05 EB 06	MBT	2		Leeds	Smelted
05 EB 07	MBT	2		Leeds	Smelted
05 EB 08	MBT	2	Oct 98	Leeds	Warcop ranges
05 EB 09	MBT	2		Leeds	Smelted
05 EB 10	MBT	2		Leeds	Smelted
05 EB 11	MBT	2	Oct 96	Leeds	Highland Park
05 EB 12	MBT	2	Jan 00	Leeds	Juniper Leisure
05 EB 13	MBT	2		Leeds	
05 EB 14	MBT	2		Leeds	
05 EB 15	MBT	2		Leeds	
05 EB 16	MBT	2	Nov 97	Leeds	Withams dealers
05 EB 17	MBT	2		Leeds	Gate guard, Vickers
05 EB 18	MBT	2		Leeds	
05 EB 19	MBT	2		Leeds	
05 EB 20	MBT	2		Leeds	
05 EB 21	MBT	2		Leeds	
05 EB 22	MBT	2	Aug 99	Leeds	Bovington Heath training aid
05 EB 23	MBT	2	May 98	Leeds	Bovington
05 EB 24	MBT	2		Leeds	Smelted
05 EB 25	MBT	2		Leeds	
05 EB 26	MBT	2	Feb 98	Leeds	Warminster
05 EB 27	MBT	2		Leeds	Smelted
05 EB 28	MBT	2		Leeds	Smelted
05 EB 29	MBT	2		Leeds	
05 EB 30	MBT	2	Dec 00	Leeds	Now AVRE at Bovington
05 EB 31	MBT	2		Leeds	Smelted
05 EB 32	MBT	2		Leeds	
05 EB 33	MBT	2		Leeds	
05 EB 34	MBT	2		Leeds	
05 EB 35	MBT	2		Leeds	
05 EB 36	MBT	2		Leeds	
05 EB 37	MBT	2		Leeds	
05 EB 38	MBT	2	Feb 98	Leeds	Warminster
05 EB 39	MBT	2		Leeds	Smelted
05 EB 40	MBT	2		Leeds	
05 EB 41	MBT	2	Sep 97	Leeds	Pounds Yard, Portsmouth
05 EB 42	MBT	2	Aug 97	Leeds	Smelted
05 EB 43	MBT	2	Aug 97	Leeds	Willich AVRE at Duxford
05 EB 44	MBT	2	May 97	Leeds	Bovington
05 EB 45	MBT	2		Leeds	
05 EB 46	MBT	2		Leeds	Smelted
05 EB 47	MBT	2		Leeds	Smelted
05 EB 48	MBT	2	Dec 99	Leeds	Juniper Leisure Driving
05 EB 49	MBT	2		Leeds	Smelted
05 EB 50	MBT	2		Leeds	
05 EB 51	MBT	2		Leeds	
05 EB 52	MBT	2		Leeds	Smelted
05 EB 53	MBT	2	Nov 97	Leeds	Withams dealer
05 EB 54	MBT	2	Aug 97	Leeds	Llanbedr
05 EB 55	MBT	2		Leeds	
05 EB 56	MBT	2		Leeds	
05 EB 57	MBT	2	Jan 98	Leeds	Ashchurch
05 EB 58	MBT	2	Jan 98	Leeds	Ashchurch
05 EB 59	MBT	2	Mar 99	Leeds	

05 EB 60	MBT	2	Mar 99	Leeds	Bovington Heath
05 EB 61	MBT	2		Leeds	Smelted
05 EB 62	MBT	2		Leeds	Smelted
05 EB 63	MBT	2		Leeds	Smelted
05 EB 64	MBT	2	Nov 97	Leeds	Withams dealer
05 EB 65	MBT	2	Aug 00	Leeds	Gate guard ATDU Bovington
05 EB 66	MBT	2		Leeds	
05 EB 67	MBT	2	Mar 98	Leeds	Castlemartin
05 EB 68	MBT	2		Leeds	Smelted
05 EB 69	MBT	2	Jun 95	Leeds	Smelted
05 EB 70	MBT	2		Leeds	
05 EB 71	MBT	2	Jul 97	Leeds	Wild Track
05 EB 72	MBT	2		Leeds	Smelted
05 EB 73	MBT	2	Jul 95	Leeds	Smelted
05 EB 74	MBT	2		Leeds	Smelted
05 EB 75	MBT	2		Leeds	Smelted
05 EB 76	MBT	2	Nov 99	Leeds	Dead weight, Bulford
05 EB 77	MBT	2		Leeds	Smelted
05 EB 78	MBT	2	Jan 00	Leeds	Privately owned
05 EB 79	MBT	2	Nov 97	Leeds	Withams dealer
05 EB 80	MBT	2	Nov 99	Leeds	Dead weight, Bulford
05 EB 81	MBT	2		Leeds	
05 EB 82	MBT	2		Leeds	Smelted
05 EB 83	MBT	2	Feb 98	Leeds	Warminster
05 EB 84	MBT	2		Leeds	
05 EB 85	MBT	2		Leeds	Smelted
05 EB 86	MBT	2	Oct 97	Leeds	Bordon
05 EB 87	MBT	2	Mar 99	Leeds	Hard target BATUS
05 EB 88	MBT	2	Jan 00	Leeds	Castlemartin ranges
05 EB 89	MBT	2		Leeds	
05 EB 90	MBT	2	Jan 98	Leeds	Thetford
05 EB 91	MBT	2		Leeds	Smelted
05 EB 92	MBT	2	May 99	Leeds	Ashchurch
05 EB 93	MBT	2		Leeds	Smelted
05 FA 84	MBT	3	May 99	Leeds	Hard target BATUS
05 FA 85	MBT	3		Leeds	
05 FA 86	MBT	3		Leeds	
05 FA 87	MBT	3		Leeds	Smelted
05 FA 88	MBT	3		Leeds	
05 FA 89	MBT	3	Jun 95	Leeds	Smelted
05 FA 90	MBT	3		Leeds	Smelted
05 FA 91	MBT	3		Leeds	USA
05 FA 92	MBT	3	Nov 98	Leeds	Withams dealer
05 FA 93	MBT	3		Leeds	Smelted
05 FA 94	MBT	3		Leeds	
05 FA 95	MBT	3		Leeds	
05 FA 96	MBT	3		Leeds	Smelted
05 FA 97	MBT	3		Leeds	DERA
05 FA 98	MBT	3	Nov 98	Leeds	Withams dealer
05 FA 99	MBT	3	Aug 99	Leeds	ATR Winchester gate guard
06 FA 00	MBT	3		Leeds	Smelted
06 FA 01	MBT	3		Leeds	Smelted
06 FA 02	MBT	3		Leeds	
06 FA 03	MBT	3	May 98	Leeds	RCMS Shrivenham
06 FA 04	MBT	3		Leeds	Smelted
06 FA 05	MBT	3		Leeds	
06 FA 06	MBT	3		Leeds	Smelted
06 FA 07	MBT	3	Mar 99	Leeds	Bovington Heath training aid
06 FA 08	MBT	3		Leeds	
06 FA 09	MBT	3		Leeds	

06 FA 10	MBT	3	Jul 97	Leeds	Tank Museum
06 FA 11	MBT	3	Nov 96	Leeds	Lulworth ranges
06 FA 12	MBT	3		Leeds	Smelted
06 FA 13	MBT	3		Leeds	Smelted
06 FA 14	MBT	3		Leeds	Smelted
06 FA 15	MBT	3	Jul-97	Leeds	Privately owned, Manchester
06 FA 16	MBT	3		Leeds	
06 FA 17	MBT	3		Leeds	
06 FA 18	MBT	3		Leeds	
06 FA 19	MBT	3	Aug 95	Leeds	Smelted
06 FA 20	MBT	3		Leeds	Smelted
06 FA 21	MBT	3	Nov 97	Leeds	Withams dealer
06 FA 22	MBT	3		Leeds	
06 FA 23	MBT	3	Nov 96	Leeds	Lulworth ranges
06 FA 24	MBT	3		Leeds	Smelted
06 FA 25	MBT	3		Leeds	Smelted
06 FA 26	MBT	3		Leeds	
06 FA 27	MBT	3		Leeds	
06 FA 28	MBT	3	Feb 98	Leeds	Warminster
06 FA 29	MBT	3		Leeds	
06 FA 30	MBT	3	Nov 97	Leeds	Withams dealer
06 FA 31	MBT	3	Oct 00	Leeds	Puckapunyal, Australia
06 FA 32	MBT	3		Leeds	
06 FA 33	MBT	3	Nov 96	Leeds	Lulworth ranges
06 FA 34	MBT	3	Nov 96	Leeds	Lulworth ranges
06 FA 35	MBT	3		Leeds	
06 FA 36	MBT	3		Leeds	
06 FA 37	MBT	3	Jul 95	Leeds	Smelted
06 FA 38	MBT	3		Leeds	Smelted
06 FA 39	MBT	3	Jul 97	Leeds	Bovington
06 FA 40	MBT	3	Jan 98	Leeds	Smelted
06 FA 41	MBT	3		Leeds	Smelted
06 FA 42	MBT	3		Leeds	Smelted
06 FA 43	MBT	3	Nov 97	Leeds	Withams dealer
06 FA 44	MBT	3		Leeds	
06 FA 45	MBT	3	Nov 96	Leeds	Lulworth ranges
06 FA 46	MBT	3		Leeds	Smelted
06 FA 47	MBT	3	Feb 00	Leeds	Privately owned
06 FA 48	MBT	3		Leeds	
06 FA 49	MBT	3	Feb 98	Leeds	DERA
06 FA 50	MBT	3		Leeds	Smelted
06 FA 51	MBT	3	Feb 00	Leeds	AVRE Bovington
06 FA 52	MBT	3		Leeds	Smelted
06 FA 53	MBT	3		Leeds	
06 FA 54	MBT	3	Aug 98	Leeds	Bovington heath
06 FA 55	MBT	3		Leeds	Smelted
06 FA 56	MBT	3		Leeds	Smelted
06 FA 57	MBT	3		Leeds	Smelted
06 FA 58	MBT	3		Leeds	
06 FA 59	MBT	3		Leeds	Now AVRE
06 FA 60	MBT	3		Leeds	Smelted
06 FA 61	MBT	3		Leeds	Smelted
06 FA 62	MBT	3		Leeds	
06 FA 63	MBT	3		Leeds	Smelted
06 FA 64	MBT	3	Nov 96	Leeds	Lulworth ranges
06 FA 65	MBT	3		Leeds	
06 FA 66	MBT	3	Mar 98	Leeds	Castlemartin
06 FA 67	MBT	3		Leeds	Smelted
06 FA 68	MBT	3		Leeds	Smelted
06 FA 69	MBT	3		Leeds	

06 FA 70	MBT	3		Leeds	
06 FA 71	MBT	3	Feb 98	Leeds	Private owned
06 FA 72	MBT	3		Leeds	
06 FA 73	MBT	3	Jan 98	Leeds	Thetford
06 FA 74	MBT	3		Leeds	Smelted
06 FA 75	MBT	3	Oct 98	Leeds	Warcop ranges
06 FA 76	MBT	3		Leeds	Smelted
06 FA 77	MBT	3	Aug 97	Leeds	Privately owned, Manchester
06 FA 78	MBT	3	May 99	Leeds	Privately owned
06 FA 79	MBT	3	Nov 97	Leeds	Withams dealer
06 FA 80	MBT	3		Leeds	
06 FA 81	MBT	3		Leeds	
06 FA 82	MBT	3		Leeds	
06 FA 83	MBT	3		Leeds	
06 FA 84	MBT	3	Nov 97	Leeds	Withams dealer
06 FA 85	MBT	3	Nov 97	Leeds	Private deal
06 FA 86	MBT	3	Mar 00	Leeds	Otterburn ranges
06 FA 87	MBT	3	Dec 00	Leeds	Lulworth ranges
06 FA 88	MBT	3		Leeds	
06 FA 89	MBT	3	Feb 00	Leeds	Cut up for scrap
06 FA 90	MBT	3		Leeds	Smelted
06 FA 91	MBT	3	Nov 99	Leeds	Bulford
06 FA 92	MBT	3	Feb 01	Leeds	Sindorf Trading, Holland
06 FA 93	MBT	3		Leeds	
06 FA 94	MBT	3		Leeds	Smelted
06 FA 95	MBT	3		Leeds	
06 FA 96	MBT	3	June 00	Leeds	AVRE Demo Sqn
06 FA 97	MBT	3	Feb 00	Leeds	Cut up for scrap
06 FA 98	MBT	3		Leeds	Smelted
06 FA 99	MBT	3		Leeds	Smelted
07 FA 00	MBT	3	Mar 99	Leeds	Hard target BATUS
07 FA 01	MBT	3		Leeds	Smelted
07 FA 02	MBT	3	Feb 97	Leeds	Thetford
07 FA 03	MBT	3		Leeds	
07 FA 04	MBT	3		Leeds	Smelted
07 FA 05	MBT	3		Leeds	Smelted
07 FA 06	MBT	3		Leeds	Smelted
07 FA 07	MBT	3		Leeds	
07 FA 08	MBT	3		Leeds	Smelted
07 FA 09	MBT	3		Leeds	Jackson's sale
07 FA 10	MBT	3		Leeds	
07 FA 11	MBT	3		Leeds	
07 FA 12	MBT	3		Leeds	Smelted
07 FA 13	MBT	3		Leeds	Smelted
07 FA 14	MBT	3	Nov 97	Leeds	Withams dealer
07 FA 15	MBT	3		Leeds	Smelted
07 FA 16	MBT	3		Leeds	Smelted
07 FA 17	MBT	3	Sep 00	Leeds	Privately owned, USA
00 FB 01	AVLB			Leeds	
00 FB 02	AVLB			Leeds	
00 FB 03	AVLB			Leeds	
00 FB 04	AVLB			Leeds	
00 FC 04	MBT	3/3	Feb 96	Leeds	Otterburn
00 FC 05	MBT	3/3	Jun 00	Leeds	Salisbury plain
00 FC 06	MBT	3/3	May 98	Leeds	Lulworth ranges
00 FC 07	MBT	3/3		Leeds	Smelted
00 FC 08	MBT	3/3	Apr 96	Leeds	Hard target, BATUS
00 FC 09	MBT	3/3	Aug 99	Leeds	Lulworth ranges
00 FC 10	MBT			Leeds	
00 FC 11	MBT	3/3	Jan 98	Leeds	Lulworth ranges

00 FC 12	MBT	3/3		Leeds	Smelted
00 FC 13	MBT	3/3	Aug 95	Leeds	Smelted
00 FC 14	MBT	3/3	Mar 98	Leeds	Castlemartin
00 FC 15	MBT	3/3		Leeds	Smelted
00 FC 16	MBT	3/3		Leeds	
00 FC 17	MBT	3/3		Leeds	Smelted
00 FC 18	MBT	3/3		Leeds	Smelted
00 FC 19	MBT	3/3	Mar 98	Leeds	Castlemartin
00 FC 20	MBT	3/3	May 00	Leeds	M.A.D entertainment
00 FC 21	MBT	3/3		Leeds	Smelted
00 FC 22	MBT	3/3		Leeds	
00 FC 23	MBT	3/3		Leeds	
00 FC 24	MBT	3/3	May 98	Leeds	Lulworth ranges
00 FC 25	MBT	3/3		Leeds	
00 FC 26	MBT	3/3		Leeds	Smelted
00 FC 27	MBT	3/3	Jan 98	Leeds	Ashchurch
00 FC 28	MBT	3/3		Leeds	
00 FC 29	MBT	3/3	Mar 99	Leeds	Hard target BATUS
00 FC 30	MBT	3/3	Jun 97	Leeds	AVRE, Mrkonjic Grad, Bosnia
00 FC 31	MBT	3/3		Leeds	
00 FC 32	MBT	3/3		Leeds	
00 FC 33	MBT	3/3		Leeds	
00 FC 34	MBT	3/3		Leeds	
00 FC 35	MBT	3/3		Leeds	
00 FC 36	MBT	3/3		Leeds	
00 FC 37	MBT	3/3		Leeds	
00 FC 38	MBT	3/3		Leeds	
00 FC 39	MBT	3/3		Leeds	
00 FC 40	MBT	3/3		Leeds	
00 FC 41	MBT	3/3		Leeds	
00 FC 42	MBT	3/3		Leeds	
00 FC 43	MBT	3/3		Leeds	
00 FC 44	MBT	3/3		Leeds	
00 FC 45	MBT	3/3		Leeds	
00 FC 46	MBT	3/3		Leeds	
00 FC 47	MBT	3/3		Leeds	
00 FC 48	MBT	3/3		Leeds	
00 FC 49	MBT	3/3		Leeds	
00 FC 50	MBT	3/3		Leeds	
00 FC 51	MBT	3	Feb 98	Leeds	DERA
00 FC 52	MBT	3	Mar 93	Leeds	Unknown disposal
00 FC 53	MBT	3		Leeds	Smelted
00 FC 54	MBT	3		Leeds	Smelted
00 FC 55	MBT	3		Leeds	Smelted
00 FC 56	MBT	3		Leeds	Smelted
00 FC 57	MBT	3		Leeds	Smelted
00 FC 58	MBT	3		Leeds	
00 FC 59	MBT	3		Leeds	Smelted
00 FC 60	MBT	3	Feb 98	Leeds	Chequers Pub, Gravesend
00 FC 61	MBT	3		Leeds	
00 FC 62	MBT	3	Nov 96	Leeds	Otterburn
00 FC 63	MBT	3		Leeds	Smelted
00 FC 64	MBT	3		Leeds	
00 FC 65	MBT	3	Jan 98	Leeds	Ashchurch
00 FC 66	MBT	3		Leeds	Smelted
00 FC 67	MBT	3	Aug 99	Leeds	Lulworth ranges
00 FC 68	MBT	3	Nov 99	Leeds	FIBUA village Catterick
00 FD 01	MBT	3/3		Leeds	
00 FD 02	MBT	3/3		Leeds	Smelted
00 FD 03	MBT	3/3		Leeds	

00 FD 04	MBT	3/3	Jan 96	Leeds	Lulworth
00 FD 05	MBT	3/3	May 99	Leeds	Privately Owned
00 FD 06	MBT	3/3		Leeds	Smelted
00 FD 07	MBT	3/3	Nov 96	Leeds	Lower Lodge Horsham
00 FD 08	MBT	3/3		Leeds	Smelted
00 FD 09	MBT	3/3		Leeds	
00 FD 10	MBT	3/3	Jan 96	Leeds	Withams dealer
00 FD 11	MBT	3/3	Oct 98	Leeds	Warcop ranges
00 FD 12	MBT	3/3	Nov-96	Leeds	Lulworth ranges
00 FD 13	MBT	3/3		Leeds	Smelted
00 FD 14	MBT	3/3		Leeds	Smelted
00 FD 15	MBT	3/3	Jan 98	Leeds	Ashchurch
00 FD 16	MBT	3/3	Nov 96	Leeds	Lulworth ranges
00 FD 17	MBT	3/3	Mar 98	Leeds	Castlemartin
00 FD 18	MBT	3/3	Jul 95	Leeds	Smelted
00 FD 19	MBT	3/3		Leeds	Smelted
00 FD 20	MBT	3/3	Jan 00	Leeds	Castlemartin ranges
00 FD 21	MBT	3/3		Leeds	Smelted
00 FD 22	MBT	3/3	May 98	Leeds	Lulworth ranges
00 FD 23	MBT	3/3		Leeds	
00 FD 24	MBT	3/3		Leeds	Smelted
00 FD 25	MBT	3/3	Mar 99	Leeds	Smelted
00 FD 26	MBT	3/3		Leeds	
00 FD 27	MBT	3/3	Nov 96	Leeds	Private dealer
00 FD 28	MBT	3/3		Leeds	
00 FD 54	MBT	5		Leeds	Smelted
00 FD 55	MBT	5	Nov 96	Leeds	Otterburn
00 FD 56	MBT	5	Mar 98	Leeds	Pembroke
00 FD 57	MBT	5		Leeds	
00 FD 58	MBT	5		Leeds	AVRE conversion, smelted
00 FD 59	MBT	5		Leeds	Smelted
00 FD 60	MBT	5		Leeds	Smelted
00 FD 61	MBT	5	Feb 98	Leeds	Warminster
00 FD 62	MBT	5		Leeds	
00 FD 63	MBT	5		Leeds	Smelted
00 FD 64	MBT	5	May 99	Leeds	Marne Barracks, Catterick
00 FD 65	MBT	5		Leeds	
00 FD 66	MBT	5	Dec 00	Leeds	Lulworth ranges
00 FD 67	MBT	5	May 99	Leeds	Feldom Moor, Catterick
00 FD 68	MBT	5		Leeds	Smelted
00 FD 69	MBT	5	Aug 97	Leeds	Tank Museum
00 FD 70	MBT	5		Leeds	Smelted
00 FD 71	MBT	5	Oct-98	Leeds	Warcop ranges
00 FD 72	MBT	5		Leeds	Smelted
00 FD 73	MBT	5		Leeds	Smelted
00 FD 74	MBT	5		Leeds	Smelted
00 FD 75	MBT	5		Leeds	
00 FD 76	MBT	5	Feb 00	Leeds	AVRE at BATUS
00 FD 77	MBT	5	Apr 00	Leeds	Gate guard, Bulford
00 FD 78	MBT	5		Leeds	
00 FD 79	MBT	5	Nov 96	Leeds	Lulworth ranges
00 FD 80	MBT	5		Leeds	
00 FD 81	MBT	5		Leeds	
00 FD 82	MBT	5		Leeds	Gate guard, Vickers
00 FD 83	MBT	5		Leeds	
00 FD 84	MBT	5		Leeds	Smelted
00 FD 85	MBT	5		Leeds	
00 FD 86	MBT	5		Leeds	
00 FD 87	MBT	5		Leeds	Smelted
00 FD 88	MBT	5		Leeds	

00 FD 89	MBT	5	Aug 99	Leeds	Lulworth ranges gate guard
00 FD 90	MBT	5	Jan 00	Leeds	Castlemartin
00 FD 91	MBT	5		Leeds	Smelted
00 FD 92	MBT	5	Oct 98	Leeds	Warcop ranges
00 FD 93	MBT	5		Leeds	
00 FD 94	MBT	5		Leeds	
00 FD 95	MBT	5		Leeds	
00 FD 96	MBT	5		Leeds	Smelted
00 FD 97	MBT	5	Jan 00	Leeds	Castlemartin
00 FD 98	MBT	5	Mar 99	Leeds	Hard target BATUS
00 FD 99	MBT	5		Leeds	
01 FD 00	MBT	3(S)		Leeds	
01 FD 01	MBT	3(S)		Leeds	
01 FD 02	MBT	3(S)		Leeds	Smelted
01 FD 03	MBT	3(S)		Leeds	
01 FD 04	MBT	3(S)		Leeds	
01 FD 05	MBT	3(S)	Oct 99	Leeds	Plinth in Byker, Newcastle
01 FD 06	MBT	3(S)		Leeds	
01 FD 07	MBT	3(S)		Leeds	
01 FD 08	MBT	3(S)	Feb 00	Leeds	Bovington
01 FD 09	MBT	3(S)	Mar 98	Leeds	Castlemartin
01 FD 10	MBT	3(S)		Leeds	Smelted
01 FD 11	MBT	3(S)	Jan 98	Leeds	Ashchurch
01 FD 12	MBT	3(S)		Leeds	
01 FD 13	MBT	3(S)	Feb 98	Leeds	Warminster
01 FD 14	MBT	3(S)	Jun 95	Leeds	Smelted
01 FD 15	MBT	3(S)	Mar 99	Leeds	Hard target BATUS
01 FD 16	MBT	3(S)		Leeds	AVRE conversion
01 FD 17	MBT	3(S)	Apr 95	Leeds	Smelted
01 FD 18	MBT	3(S)		Leeds	
01 FD 19	MBT	3(S)	Jul 95	Leeds	Smelted
01 FD 20	MBT	3(S)	Feb 98	Leeds	Warminster
01 FD 21	MBT	3(S)	Oct 98	Leeds	Warcop ranges
01 FD 22	MBT	3(S)	Oct 98	Leeds	Warcop ranges
01 FD 23	MBT	3(S)		Leeds	
01 FD 24	MBT	3(S)		Leeds	
01 FD 25	MBT	3(S)		Leeds	
01 FD 26	MBT	3(S)		Leeds	
01 FD 27	MBT	3(S)		Leeds	
01 FD 28	MBT	3(S)	Jan 98	Leeds	Catterick
01 FD 29	MBT	3(S)	May 95	Leeds	Smelted
01 FD 30	MBT	3(S)	Dec 00	Leeds	Now AVRE at Bovington
01 FD 31	MBT	3(S)		Leeds	Smelted
01 FD 32	MBT	3(S)		Leeds	Smelted
01 FD 33	MBT	3(S)		Leeds	Smelted
01 FD 34	MBT	3(S)		Leeds	
01 FD 35	MBT	3(S)		Leeds	Smelted
01 FD 36	MBT	3(S)	Jun 95	Leeds	Smelted
01 FD 37	MBT	3(S)	Jan 98	Leeds	Thornicome, Dorset
01 FD 38	MBT	3(S)	Jun 00	Leeds	AVRE Demo Squadron
01 FD 39	MBT	3(S)	Jan 98	Leeds	Thetford
01 FD 40	MBT	3(G)	Apr 98	Leeds	Bordon
01 FD 41	MBT	3(G)		Leeds	Smelted
01 FD 42	MBT	3(G)		Leeds	Smelted
01 FD 43	MBT	3(G)		Leeds	Smelted
01 FD 44	MBT	3(G)		Leeds	
01 FD 45	MBT	3(G)	Nov 96	Leeds	Lulworth ranges
01 FD 46	AVLB			Leeds	
01 FD 47	AVLB			Leeds	
01 FD 48	AVLB			Leeds	

01 FD 49	AVLB			Leeds	
01 FD 50	AVLB			Leeds	
01 FD 51	AVLB			Leeds	
01 FD 52	AVLB			Leeds	
01 FD 53	AVLB		Mar 98	Leeds	Castlemartin
01 FD 54	AVLB			Leeds	
01 FD 55	AVLB		Jun 97	Leeds	Mrkonjic Grad Bosnia
01 FD 56	AVLB			Leeds	
01 FD 57	AVLB		Jun 97	Leeds	Mrkonjic Grad Bosnia
01 FD 58	AVLB			Leeds	
01 FD 59	AVLB			Leeds	
01 FD 60	AVLB			Leeds	
01 FD 61	AVLB			Leeds	
01 FD 62	AVLB		Sep 95	Leeds	Smelted
01 FD 63	AVLB		Jan 00	Leeds	32 Engineer Regiment
01 FD 64	AVLB			Leeds	
01 FD 65	AVLB			Leeds	
01 FD 66	AVLB		Jun 00	Leeds	Demo Squadron
01 FD 67	AVLB			Leeds	
01 FD 68	AVLB			Leeds	
01 FD 69	AVLB			Leeds	
01 FD 70	AVLB			Leeds	
01 FD 71	AVLB			Leeds	
01 FD 72	AVLB		Dec 00	Leeds	Bovington
01 FD 73	AVLB		May 98	Leeds	Bovington
01 FD 74	AVLB			Leeds	
01 FD 75	AVLB			Leeds	
01 FD 76	AVLB			Leeds	Converted to AVRE
01 FD 77	AVLB			Leeds	
01 FD 78	AVLB			Leeds	
01 FD 79	AVLB		Feb 00	Leeds	Bovington
01 FD 80	AVLB			Leeds	
01 FD 81	AVLB			Leeds	
01 FD 82	AVLB		Jun 97	Leeds	Mrkonjic Grad, Bosnia
08 FD 51	MBT	5		Leeds	Smelted
08 FD 52	MBT	5	Mar 99	Leeds	Hard target BATUS
08 FD 53	MBT	5		Leeds	Smelted
08 FD 54	MBT	5		Leeds	
08 FD 55	MBT	5	Sep 97	Leeds	Helston, Devon
08 FD 56	MBT	5		Leeds	Smelted
11 FD 32	MBT	5		Leeds	Smelted
11 FD 33	MBT	5	Aug 99	Leeds	Lulworth hard standing
11 FD 34	MBT	5		Leeds	
11 FD 35	MBT	5	Feb 98	Leeds	Warminster
11 FD 36	MBT	5	Feb 01	Leeds	Gate Guard Sennelager
11 FD 37	MBT	5		Leeds	
11 FD 38	MBT	5	Nov 97	Leeds	Withams dealer
11 FD 39	MBT	5	May 99	Leeds	Marne Barracks, Catterick
11 FD 40	MBT	5	Feb 98	Leeds	Thetford
11 FD 41	MBT	5		Leeds	Smelted
11 FD 42	MBT	5		Leeds	
11 FD 43	MBT	5		Leeds	Smelted
11 FD 44	MBT	5		Leeds	Smelted
11 FD 45	MBT	5		Leeds	Smelted
11 FD 46	MBT	5		Leeds	Smelted
11 FD 47	MBT	5		Leeds	
11 FD 48	MBT	5	Apr 95	Leeds	Smelted
11 FD 49	MBT	5	Jan 98	Leeds	Ashchurch
11 FD 50	MBT	5	Jan 98	Leeds	Ashchurch
11 FD 51	MBT	5	Nov 97	Leeds	Withams dealer

11 FD 52	MBT	5	Jun 00	Leeds	Salisbury Plain
11 FD 53	MBT	5		Leeds	Smelted
11 FD 54	MBT	5		Leeds	Smelted
11 FD 55	MBT	5	Mar 99	Leeds	Hard target, BATUS
11 FD 56	MBT	5	May 91	Leeds	Sweden
11 FD 57	MBT	5		Leeds	
11 FD 58	MBT	5	Aug 97	Leeds	Tank Museum
11 FD 59	MBT	5		Leeds	Smelted
11 FD 60	MBT	5		Leeds	Smelted
11 FD 61	MBT	5		Leeds	
11 FD 62	MBT	5		Leeds	Smelted
11 FD 63	MBT	5	Nov 96	Leeds	Lulworth ranges
11 FD 64	MBT	5		Leeds	Smelted
11 FD 65	MBT	5	Oct 99	Leeds	Adventure Activities, Warwick
11 FD 66	MBT	5	Dec 00	Leeds	Lulworth ranges
11 FD 67	MBT	5		Leeds	
11 FD 68	MBT	5	Jun 00	Leeds	Salisbury plain
11 FD 69	MBT	5		Leeds	Smelted
11 FD 70	MBT	5		Leeds	Smelted
11 FD 71	MBT	5		Leeds	Smelted
11 FD 72	MBT	5		Leeds	Smelted
11 FD 73	MBT	5	Jun 00	Leeds	Salisbury plain
11 FD 74	MBT	5	Mar 99	Leeds	Calgary War Museum, Canada
11 FD 75	MBT	5		Leeds	
11 FD 76	MBT	5	Jun 97	Leeds	Mrkonjic Grad AVRE
06 FF 78	ARV		Jun 97	Leeds	Mrkonjic Grad, Bosnia
06 FF 80	ARV			Vickers	
06 FF 81	ARV			Vickers	
06 FF 82	ARV			Vickers	
06 FF 83	ARV			Vickers	
06 FF 84	ARV			Vickers	
06 FF 85	ARV			Vickers	
06 FF 86	ARV			Vickers	
06 FF 87	ARV			Vickers	
06 FF 88	ARV			Vickers	
06 FF 89	ARV			Vickers	
06 FF 90	ARV			Vickers	
06 FF 91	ARV			Vickers	
06 FF 92	ARV			Vickers	
06 FF 93	ARV			Vickers	
06 FF 94	ARV			Vickers	
06 FF 95	ARV			Vickers	
06 FF 96	ARV			Vickers	
06 FF 97	ARV			Vickers	
06 FF 98	ARV			Vickers	
06 FF 99	ARV			Vickers	
07 FF 00	ARV			Vickers	
07 FF 01	ARV			Vickers	
07 FF 02	ARV			Vickers	
07 FF 03	ARV			Vickers	
07 FF 04	ARV			Vickers	
07 FF 05	ARV			Vickers	Jacques Littlefield Collection
07 FF 06	ARV			Vickers	
07 FF 07	ARV		Jan 98	Vickers	Ashchurch
07 FF 08	ARV			Vickers	
07 FF 09	ARV		May 98	Vickers	Bordon
07 FF 10	ARV			Vickers	
07 FF 11	ARV			Vickers	
07 FF 12	ARV			Vickers	
07 FF 13	ARV		Jan 98	Vickers	Ashchurch

07 FF 14	ARV		Vickers	
07 FF 15	ARV		Vickers	
07 FF 16	ARV		Vickers	
07 FF 17	ARV		Vickers	
07 FF 18	ARV		Vickers	
07 FF 19	ARV		Vickers	
07 FF 20	ARV	Jan 98	Vickers	Ashchurch
07 FF 21	ARV		Vickers	
07 FF 22	ARV		Vickers	
07 FF 23	ARV		Vickers	
07 FF 24	ARV		Vickers	
07 FF 25	ARV	Jan 98	Vickers	Ashchurch
07 FF 26	ARV		Vickers	
07 FF 27	ARV		Vickers	
07 FF 28	ARV	Jan 98	Vickers	Ashchurch
07 FF 29	ARV		Vickers	
07 FF 30	ARV		Vickers	
07 FF 31	ARV		Vickers	
07 FF 32	ARV		Vickers	
07 FF 33	ARV	Jan 98	Vickers	Ashchurch
07 FF 34	ARV		Vickers	
07 FF 35	ARV	Jan 98	Vickers	Ashchurch
07 FF 36	ARV		Vickers	
07 FF 37	ARV	Jan 98	Vickers	Ashchurch
07 FF 38	ARV		Vickers	
07 FF 39	ARV	Jan 98	Vickers	Ashchurch
07 FF 40	ARV		Vickers	
07 FF 41	ARV		Vickers	
07 FF 42	ARV		Vickers	
07 FF 43	ARV		Vickers	
07 FF 44	ARV		Vickers	
07 FF 45	ARV	Jan 98	Vickers	Ashchurch
07 FF 46	ARV	Jan 98	Vickers	Ashchurch
07 FF 47	ARV		Vickers	
07 FF 48	ARV		Vickers	
07 FF 49	ARV		Vickers	
07 FF 50	ARV		Vickers	
07 FF 51	ARV		Vickers	
07 FF 52	ARV		Vickers	
07 FF 92	ARV	Jan 98	Vickers	Ashchurch
00 GC 01	ARV		Vickers	
00 GC 02	ARV		Vickers	
00 GC 03	ARV		Vickers	
00 GC 04	ARV		Vickers	
00 GC 05	ARV		Vickers	
00 GC 06	ARV		Vickers	
00 GC 07	ARV		Vickers	
00 GC 08	ARV		Vickers	
00 GC 09	ARV		Vickers	
00 GC 10	ARV		Vickers	
00 GC 11	ARV		Vickers	
00 HB 81	ARV	Apr 98	Vickers	Arborfield REME museum
00 HB 82	ARV	Jul 95	Vickers	Plinth 3 Field Workshop
00 HB 83	ARV		Vickers	

Appendix II:
Ammunition Details

As we have seen, Chieftain carried various types of ammunition: 7.62 for its machine guns, and various types of main armament round for the 120mm. The following drawings give the reader an insight as to how the rounds were constructed, and what they looked like.

The UK uses two types of tank-killing round: HESH, that works on the chemical principle to defeat armour, while armour-piercing rounds depend on kinetic energy to achieve their purpose. HESH will defeat armour at longer ranges, as it does not need the speed of AP to penetrate. When HESH hits the target it collapses and forms a cowpat on the armour; the base fuse then sets off the explosive, sending shock waves through the armour. These then cause a scab to fracture on the inside, which then flies around cutting a swathe of damage through men and equipment.

Armour-penetrating rounds defeat armour by their speed and the density of the penetrator core: as they penetrate, they collapse and turn into a molten mass, and again, this causes lethal damage once it bursts into the vehicle.

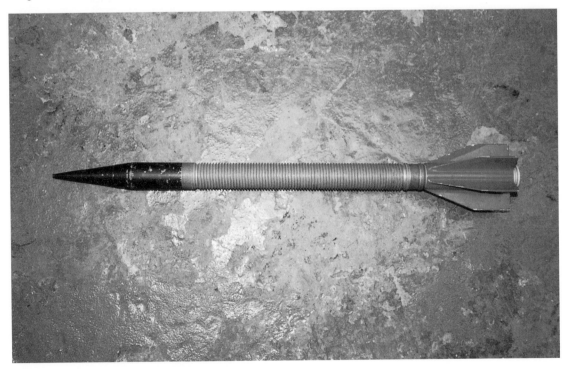

The actual core of a 120mm APFSDS. It looks much like an overgrown dart.
(Author via RCMS Shrivenham)

DS/T round.

120mm APFSDS round stowed in the turret.
(Author via RCMS Shrivenham)

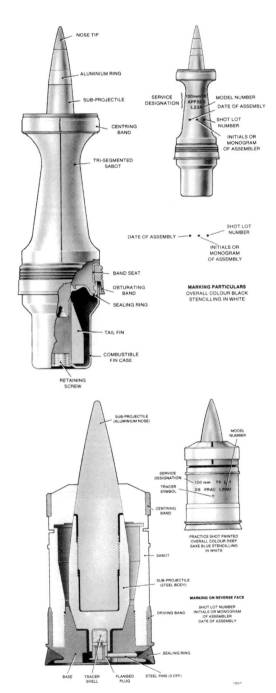

This is the practice round for APDS. In construction it is the same as APDS, except that a solid steel core now replaces the tungsten core. The round is coloured deep Saxe blue with white stencilling and weighs 5.9kg.

Left: *This is the current anti-armour round of Chieftain. It destroys armour by the kinetic energy imparted to it on firing. The round consists of a tungsten dart often called a long rod penetrator. This is supported in the barrel by three segments known as 'sabot'. These are required as the dart is very narrow; the sabot takes up the width making it 120mm. On firing, the sabot fall away and leave the dart to travel to the target at speeds in the area of 1500mps. On hitting the target the dart punches its way through the armour, throwing out hot fragments of tungsten and armour into the target. The round weighs 8kg and is coloured black overall, with white stencil markings. Later versions of the round have the tungsten core replaced with Depleted Uranium.*

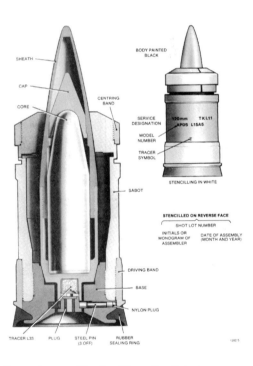

Above: *Armour Piercing Discarding Sabot was the main anti-armour round for many years. It works in a similar manner to APFS-DS, the main difference being in its size and muzzle velocity. It also depends on being spun by the rifling to stabilize it in flight, whereas APFSDS uses its fins. The round weighs 10.4kg, and again is overall black with white stencilling.*

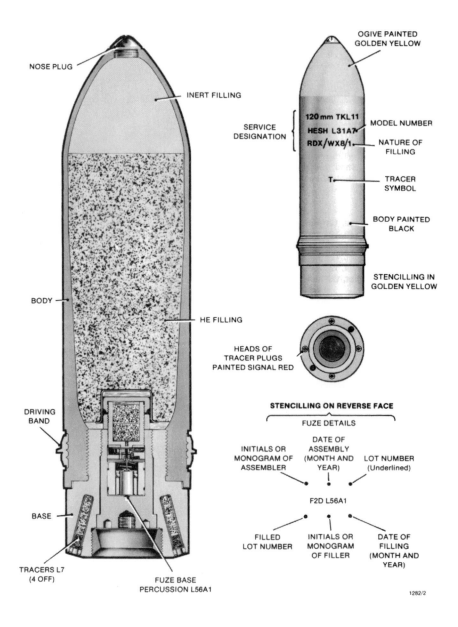

NOSE PLUG

INERT FILLING

OGIVE PAINTED
GOLDEN YELLOW

SERVICE
DESIGNATION

120 mm TKL11   MODEL NUMBER

HESH L31A7

RDX/WX8/1   NATURE OF
FILLING

T   TRACER
SYMBOL

BODY PAINTED
BLACK

BODY

HE FILLING

STENCILLING IN
GOLDEN YELLOW

HEADS OF
TRACER PLUGS
PAINTED SIGNAL RED

DRIVING
BAND

STENCILLING ON REVERSE FACE

FUZE DETAILS

INITIALS OR
MONOGRAM OF
ASSEMBLER

DATE OF
ASSEMBLY
(MONTH AND
YEAR)

LOT NUMBER
(Underlined)

F2D L56A1

BASE

FILLED
LOT NUMBER

INITIALS OR
MONOGRAM
OF FILLER

DATE OF
FILLING
(MONTH AND
YEAR)

TRACERS L7
(4 OFF)

FUZE BASE
PERCUSSION L56A1

1282/2

120mm Tk HESH, L37A7, stands for 'High Explosive Squash Head'. It is a dual purpose round, in that it can be used against armour or soft targets. If required, it can also be used out to the extreme range of the 120mm. The round depends on chemical energy, that is an explosion, to defeat armour rather than the kinetic energy of armour piercing rounds. When used against armour it firstly hits the target then will collapse forming a 'cow pat' on the armour. This allows a fuse in the base to detonate the explosive, which in turn sends shock waves through the armour. This will cause 'scabs' of armour to break off on the inside of the target and be hurled around at high velocity, destroying crew and equipment. The round weighs 17.1 kg and is coloured black with a yellow nose and yellow stencilling on the case.

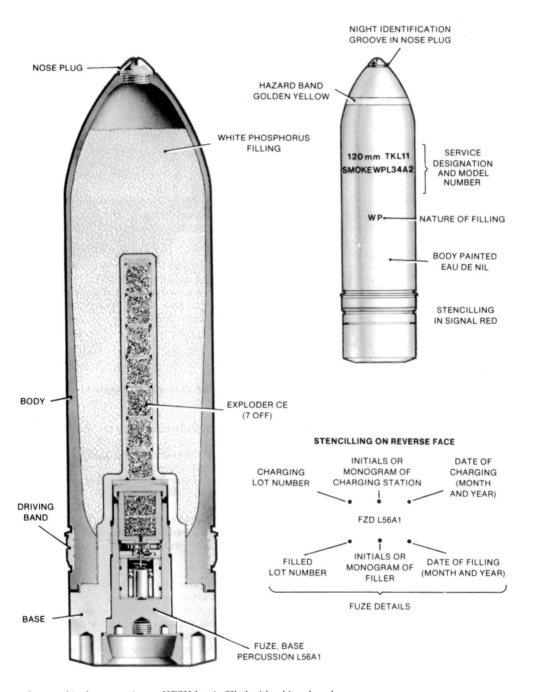

NIGHT IDENTIFICATION
GROOVE IN NOSE PLUG

NOSE PLUG

HAZARD BAND
GOLDEN YELLOW

WHITE PHOSPHORUS
FILLING

120 mm TKL11
SMOKE WPL34A2

SERVICE
DESIGNATION
AND MODEL
NUMBER

W P — NATURE OF FILLING

BODY PAINTED
EAU DE NIL

BODY

EXPLODER CE
(7 OFF)

STENCILLING
IN SIGNAL RED

STENCILLING ON REVERSE FACE

CHARGING
LOT NUMBER

INITIALS OR
MONOGRAM OF
CHARGING STATION

DATE OF
CHARGING
(MONTH
AND YEAR)

FZD L56A1

DRIVING
BAND

FILLED
LOT NUMBER

INITIALS OR
MONOGRAM OF
FILLER

DATE OF FILLING
(MONTH AND YEAR)

FUZE DETAILS

BASE

FUZE, BASE
PERCUSSION L56A1

*The smoke round is the same size as HESH but is filled with white phosphorus.
On hitting the ground the case breaks open, allowing the phosphorus to come in
contact with the air causing clouds of white smoke. The round weighs 17.1kg
and is coloured eau-de-nil green overall.*

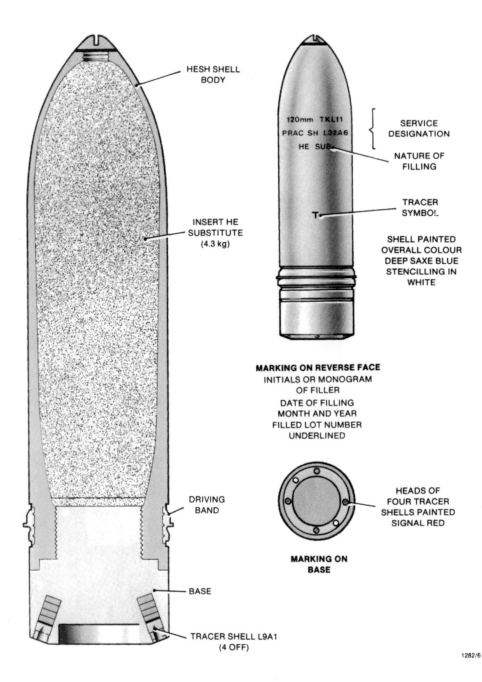

HESH SHELL BODY

INSERT HE SUBSTITUTE (4.3 kg)

DRIVING BAND

BASE

TRACER SHELL L9A1 (4 OFF)

120mm TKL11
PRAC SH L32A6
HE SUB.

SERVICE DESIGNATION

NATURE OF FILLING

TRACER SYMBOL

SHELL PAINTED OVERALL COLOUR DEEP SAXE BLUE STENCILLING IN WHITE

MARKING ON REVERSE FACE
INITIALS OR MONOGRAM OF FILLER
DATE OF FILLING
MONTH AND YEAR
FILLED LOT NUMBER UNDERLINED

HEADS OF FOUR TRACER SHELLS PAINTED SIGNAL RED

MARKING ON BASE

1282/6

This is the practice round for HESH, is of the same size, and weighs 17.1kg. The casing is filled with concrete and tracer is fitted to the base, as in HESH. This provides a cheap practice round that has similar ballistic properties to the service round. The round is overall deep Saxe blue, with the base in grey plastic and white stencilling on the body.

Glossary of Terms

AFV	Armoured fighting vehicle
AP	Armour-piercing :type of tank ammunition to defeat armour
APDS	Armour-piercing discarding sabot: small calibre, solid core carried in a fly-off carrier (sabot)
APFSDS	Armour-piercing fin stabalized discarding sabot: the latest version, like a big dart
ARDE	Armament research and development establishmen
ARRV	Armoured repair and recovery vehicle
ARV	Armoured recovery vehicle
AVLB	Armoured vehicle-launched bridge
AVRE	Armoured vehicle Royal Engineers
BAT	Battalion anti-tank gun, towed gun basis for the weapon on project Prodigal
BAOR	British Army of the Rhine
C42	Type of VHF radio found in vehicles in the early 1970s
Carden-Lloyd	Type of light, two-man tank popular between the wars
Clansman	Current series of radios
Co-axial	Mounted on the same axis as the main weapon
CUBS	Crew user binoculars IR binoculars worn on a steel helmet; not popular
DRAC	Director Royal Armoured Corp
FACE	Field artillery computer equipment
FNA	Firing needle assembly
FV 4211	The aluminium Chieftain used to show off the Chobham armour layout that would be used on Challenger 1
FV214	Conqueror
FV300	Projected series of light armoured vehicles never built
FVGCE	Fighting vehicle gun control equipment
FVRDE	Fighting vehicle research development establishment
HEAT	High explosive anti-tank
HESH	High explosive squash head
HVAP	High velocity armour-piercing
JS3	Type of Russian heavy tank
Khalid	Variation of Chieftain combining Chieftain front and Challenger power pack
L11A1-5	Designation of the 120mm gun
Larkspur	Type of radio system before Clansman
M103	American heavy tank armed with 120mm gun, same generation as Conqueror
Malkara	Australian manufactured guided missile from the early 1960s
Mils	Military unit of measure for a circle 6,400 mils to a circle
MRS	Muzzle reference system
MV	Muzzle velocity
NBC	Nuclear biological chemical warfare
RAC	Royal Armoured Corps
RMG	Ranging machine gun
RTR	Royal Tank Regiment
Sheridan	M551 American light tank armed with 152mm gun/launcher
Simfics	Weapons-effect simulator laser fitted in the end of the barrel
Simfire	Earlier version of Simfics laser fitted on barrel
Sno-Cat	Articulated tracked vehicle for use in snowy conditions
T10	Russian heavy tank armed with 122mm gun
TLS	Tank laser sight
TN12	Chieftain gearbox designation
TOGS	Thermal optical gunnery system
WO	War Office

Index